Quicken® 2012

FOR

DUMMIES®

Quicken® 2012

FOR

DUMMIES®

by Stephen L. Nelson, MBA, CPA

WILEY

John Wiley & Sons, Inc.

Quicken® 2012 For Dummies®

Published by
John Wiley & Sons, Inc.
111 River Street
Hoboken, NJ 07030-5774

www.wiley.com

Copyright © 2012 by John Wiley & Sons, Inc., Hoboken, New Jersey

Published by John Wiley & Sons, Inc., Hoboken, New Jersey

Published simultaneously in Canada

For general information on our other products and services, please contact our Customer Care Department within the U.S. at 877-762-2974, outside the U.S. at 317-572-3993, or fax 317-572-4002.

For technical support, please visit www.wiley.com/techsupport.

Wiley also publishes its books in a variety of electronic formats and by print-on-demand. Not all content that is available in standard print versions of this book may appear or be packaged in all book formats. If you have purchased a version of this book that did not include media that is referenced by or accompanies a standard print version, you may request this media by visiting http://booksupport.wiley.com. For more information about Wiley products, visit us at www.wiley.com.

Library of Congress Control Number: 2011942769

ISBN 978-1-118-09121-0 (pbk); ISBN 978-1-118-22353-6 (ebk); ISBN 978-1-118-23588-1 (ebk); ISBN 978-1-118-24144-8 (ebk)

Manufactured in the United States of America

10 9 8 7 6 5 4 3 2 1

WILEY

About the Author

Stephen L. Nelson is a CPA in Redmond, Washington. Nelson has an undergraduate degree in accounting, a Master of Business Administration degree in finance, and a Master of Science degree in taxation. He's spent three decades helping individuals, real estate investors, and businesses manage their finances — usually, in part, by better use of computer systems such as Quicken.

As corny as it sounds, Steve truly enjoys writing books that make using personal computers easier and more fun. In fact, a substantiated rumor that appeared first in *The Wall Street Journal* says Steve has written more than 150 computer books.

Steve is the best-selling author on the Quicken product. In fact, John Wiley & Sons, Inc., recently tallied up Steve's *Quicken For Dummies* sales — and darned if the publisher hasn't printed more than one million copies!

Author's Acknowledgments

I want to acknowledge the help of two groups. First, a huge thanks to the wonderful folks at Intuit who helped me by providing the beta software and other friendly assistance for this and past editions of this book, especially including Roger Kimble, Dale Knievel, Laura Messerschmitt, Aaron Patzer, Kjirsten Petersen, and Jayme Ringer.

Another big thank-you to the editorial folks at John Wiley & Sons, Inc., including Kevin Kirschner (project editor), Debbye Butler (copy editor), and Bob Woerner (executive editor). Thanks also to David Ringstrom for his technical assistance and superb attention to detail. Finally, thanks, too, to the composition staff.

Publisher's Acknowledgments

We're proud of this book; please send us your comments through our online registration form located at www.dummies.com/register/.

Some of the people who helped bring this book to market include the following:

Acquisitions, Editorial, and Vertical Websites

Project Editor: Kevin Kirschner

Executive Editor: Bob Woerner

Copy Editor: Debbye Butler

Technical Editor: David H. Ringstrom

Media Project Supervisor: Laura Moss-Hollister

Editorial Assistant: Amanda Graham

Sr. Editorial Assistant: Cherie Case

Cartoons: Rich Tennant (www.the5thwave.com)

Composition Services

Project Coordinator: Patrick Redmond

Layout and Graphics: Carl Byers, Corrie Socolovitch

Proofreaders: Rebecca Denoncour, Penny L. Stuart

Indexer: Joan K. Griffitts

Publishing and Editorial for Technology Dummies

> **Richard Swadley,** Vice President and Executive Group Publisher

> **Andy Cummings,** Vice President and Publisher

> **Mary Bednarek,** Executive Acquisitions Director

> **Mary C. Corder,** Editorial Director

Publishing for Consumer Dummies

> **Kathleen Nebenhaus,** Vice President and Executive Publisher

Composition Services

> **Debbie Stailey,** Director of Composition Services

Contents at a Glance

Table of Contents

Introduction

· ·

You aren't a dummy, of course. But here's the deal: You don't have to be some sort of technogeek or financial wizard to manage your financial affairs on a PC. You have other things to do, places to go, and people to meet. And that's where *Quicken 2012 For Dummies* comes in.

In the pages that follow, I give you the straight scoop on how to use Quicken 2012 for Windows, without a lot of extra baggage, goofy tangential information, or misguided advice.

About This Book

This book isn't meant to be read from cover to cover like some Stieg Larsson page turner. Rather, it's organized into tiny, no-sweat descriptions of how to do the things you need to do. If you're the sort of person who just doesn't feel right not reading a book from cover to cover, you can, of course, go ahead and read this thing from front to back.

I can recommend this approach, however, only for people who have already checked the TV listings. There may, after all, be an *NCIS* rerun on.

How to Use This Book

This comment dates me, but I'm not ashamed to say that I always enjoyed reading those encyclopedias my parents bought for my siblings and me. I could flip open, say, the *E* volume, look up *elephants,* and then learn just about everything I needed to know about elephants for a fifth-grade report: where elephants live, how much they weigh, and why they eat so much.

You won't read anything about elephants here, but you can use this book in the same way. If you want to learn about something, look through the Table of Contents or Index and find the topic — printing checks, for example. Then flip to the correct chapter or page and read as much as you need or enjoy. No muss. No fuss.

If you want to find out about anything else, you can, of course, just repeat the process.

Conventions Used in This Book

To make the best use of your time and energy, you should know about the following conventions I use in this book.

When I want you to type something, such as **Hydraulics screamed as the pilot lowered his landing gear**, I put it in bold letters.

By the way, with Quicken, you don't have to worry about the case of the stuff you type (except for passwords, which are case sensitive). If I tell you to type **Hillary**, you can type **HILLARY**. Or you can follow e. e. cummings's lead and type **hillary**.

Whenever I describe a message or information that you see on the screen, I present it as follows:

```
Surprise! This is a message on-screen.
```

What You Can Safely Ignore

Sometimes I provide step-by-step descriptions of tasks. I feel very bad that I have to do this. So to make things easier for you, I highlight the tasks with bold text. That way, you'll know exactly what you're supposed to do. I also often provide a more detailed explanation in regular text. You can skip the regular text that accompanies the step-by-step descriptions if you already understand the process.

Here's an example that shows what I mean:

1. **Press Enter.**

   Find the key that's labeled Enter. Extend your index finger so that it rests ever so gently on the Enter key. In one sure, fluid motion, press the Enter key by using your index finger. Then release the key.

Okay, that's kind of an extreme example. I never go into that much detail. But you get the idea. If you know how to press Enter, you can just do that and not read further. If you need help — say, with the finger depression part or something — just read the nitty-gritty details.

Can you skip anything else? Let me see now. . . . You can skip the paragraphs with the Technical Stuff icons next to them. See the "Special Icons" section, later in this Introduction, for an example of the Technical Stuff icon. The information I stick in those paragraphs is really only for those of you who like that technical kind of stuff.

What You Should Not Ignore (Unless You're a Masochist)

Don't skip the Warnings. They're the text flagged with the picture of the 19th-century bomb. They describe some things you really shouldn't do.

Out of respect for you, I'm not going to put such stuff in these paragraphs as "Don't smoke." I figure that you're an adult. You can make your own lifestyle decisions.

So I'll reserve the Warnings for more urgent and immediate dangers — things akin to "Don't smoke while you're filling your car with gasoline."

Three Foolish Assumptions

I assume just three things:

- ✔ You have a PC with Microsoft Windows XP, Windows Vista, or Windows 7.
- ✔ You know how to turn it on.
- ✔ You want to use some flavor of Quicken 2012.

The Flavors of Quicken

Okay. I lied in the preceding section. I'm going to assume one more thing: You own or somehow have access to a copy of Quicken.

You may be interested to know that Quicken comes in several versions. It doesn't really matter which one of the several versions you have. Each version works in basically the same way, and this book applies to them all. But because each version has a few unique features, you may find that your screen doesn't look exactly like the screens shown in this book. You may, for example, have a few buttons that you don't see in the figures I show you. Don't worry if this happens. It probably means that you're working with a different version than I am.

Just to let you know, I used the super-duper, includes-everything version to write this book. You can tell this because the menu bar, which appears in some of the figures, shows both a Rental Property menu and a Business menu. If you have a different version, your menu bar will not show these menus. Your title bar (if you compare) will also show a different name.

The upshot here? Don't freak out if your version of Quicken 2012 looks a wee bit different from the figures shown in this book.

How This Book Is Organized

This book is organized into six mostly coherent parts.

Part I: Zen, Quicken, and the Big Picture

Part I covers some up-front stuff you need to take care of. I promise I won't waste your time here. I just want to make sure that you get off on the right foot.

Part II: The Absolute Basics

This second part of the book explains the core knowledge you need to know in order to keep a personal or business checkbook with Quicken: using the checkbook, printing, reporting on your finances, using online banking, balancing your bank accounts, and using the Quicken calculators.

Some of this stuff isn't very exciting compared to _The Colbert Report_ — which really is a good show, isn't it? — so I work hard to make things fun for you.

Part III: Home Finances

Part III talks about the sorts of things you may want to do with Quicken if you're using it at home: credit cards, loans, mutual funds, stocks, and bonds. You get the idea. If you don't ever get this far — hey, that's cool.

If you do get this far, you'll find that Quicken provides some tools that eliminate not only the drudgery of keeping a checkbook, but also the drudgery of most other financial burdens.

While I'm on the subject, I also want to categorically deny that Part III contains any secret messages if you read it backward.

Part IV: Very Serious Business

The "Very Serious Business" part helps people who use Quicken in a business or for real estate investing.

If you're pulling your hair out because you're using Quicken in a business, postpone the hair pulling — at least for the time being. Read Part IV first. It tells you about measuring profits, preparing payroll for any employees, tracking the amounts that customers owe you, and other wildly exciting stuff.

Part V: The Part of Tens

By tradition, a *For Dummies* book includes "The Part of Tens." It provides a collection of ten-something lists: ten answers to frequently asked questions about Quicken, ten ways not to become a millionaire, and ten tips for trouble-shooting Quicken when you encounter a problem.

Part VI: Appendixes

It's an unwritten rule that computer books have appendixes, so I include two. Appendix A gives you a quick-and-dirty overview of Windows for those new to the world of Windows. Appendix B is a glossary of key business, financial, and computer terms.

Special Icons

Like many computer books, this book uses *icons,* or little pictures, to flag things that don't quite fit into the flow of things. *For Dummies* books use a standard set of icons that flag little digressions, such as the following.

This icon points out nerdy technical material that you may want to skip (or read, if you're feeling particularly bright).

Here's a shortcut to make your life easier.

This icon is just a friendly reminder to do something.

And this icon is a friendly reminder *not* to do something . . . or else.

Where to Next?

If you're just getting started, flip the page and start reading the first chapter.

If you have a special problem or question, use the Table of Contents or the Index to find out where that topic is covered and then turn to that page.

Part I
Zen, Quicken, and the Big Picture

The 5th Wave   By Rich Tennant

"I bought a software program that should help us monitor and control our spending habits, and while I was there, I picked up a few new games, a couple of screen savers, 4 new mousepads, this nifty pullout keyboard cradle..."

In this part . . .

When you go to a movie theater, some prerequisites are necessary for the show to be truly enjoyable. And I'm not referring to the presence of Angelina Jolie or Daniel Craig on the screen. Purchasing a bucket of popcorn is essential, for example. One should think strategically both about seating and about soda size. And one may even have items of a, well, personal nature to take care of — such as visiting the little boys' or girls' room.

I mention all this stuff for one simple reason: To make getting started with Quicken as easy and fun as possible, you have to complete some prerequisites, too. And this first part of *Quicken 2012 For Dummies* talks about these sorts of things.

Chapter 1

Setting Up Shop

· ·

In This Chapter

▶ Installing and setting up Quicken

▶ Setting up your bank (or other) accounts if you're a first-time user

▶ Providing a Quicken overview

▶ Solving setup problems

· ·

*I*f you've never used Quicken, begin here. This chapter tells you how to install Quicken (if you haven't already) and how to start the program for the first time. You also find out how you go about setting up Quicken accounts to track banking activities — specifically, the money that goes into and out of a checking or savings account.

If you've already begun to use Quicken, don't waste any time reading this chapter unless you want the review. You already know the stuff it covers.

By the way, if you have Windows, I assume that you know a little bit about it. No, you don't have to be some sort of expert. Shoot, you don't even have to be all that proficient. You do need to know how to start Windows applications (such as Quicken). It also helps immensely if you know how to choose commands on menus and how to enter stuff in windows and dialog boxes. If you don't know how to do these kinds of things, flip to Appendix A. It provides a quick-and-dirty overview of how you work in Windows. Read the stuff in the appendix, or at least skim it, and then come back to this chapter.

When I say Windows, I mean a recent version of Windows — something Microsoft is either currently selling or has sold in the last few years. Quicken 2012 won't run on Windows versions earlier than Windows XP, so if you want to run the latest version, I'm afraid it's time to upgrade. By the way, for the computer I used to write this book, I used Windows 7.

Installing and Starting Quicken

You install Quicken the same way that you install any program in Windows. If you already know how to install programs, you don't need any help from me. Stop reading here, do the installation thing, start your newly installed Quicken program, and then start reading the next section, "Finishing Setup If You've Used Quicken Before."

If you need help installing Quicken, here are the step-by-step instructions. Installing Quicken from a CD is as easy as one, two, three, four:

1. **Insert the CD into the CD-ROM drive.**

   In a short amount of time, Quicken should display the Quicken 2012 install wizard window. I'm not going to show this window in a figure. There's really nothing in the window to talk about. The window just reads `Welcome to Quicken 2012!`.

   Note: If nothing happens when you put the CD into the CD-ROM drive, don't panic! First, try removing the CD and then putting it in again. If Windows still doesn't recognize the CD, you need to *tell* Windows that it should install your Quicken program. In many versions of Windows (but not necessarily with your version), you do this with the Windows Control Panel by using the Programs tool. To do this, refer to your Windows user guide or a good book about your version of Windows (such as Andy Rathbone's *Windows 7 For Dummies,* published by John Wiley & Sons, Inc.).

2. **Click Next.**

   Quicken then displays a window that asks you a couple of questions:

   - Whether you accept the Quicken license agreement.
   - Whether you're okay if Quicken sends anonymous usage statistics to Intuit.

   You can answer the install wizard's questions by checking the boxes in front of the questions.

3. **Click Next.**

   Quicken displays the next window of the install wizard, which asks where you want to install Quicken. You should accept the installation's program suggestion. (The installation program suggests a Quicken subfolder in your Program Files folder.)

4. **Click Next.**

   Quicken displays yet another window of the install wizard that indicates the wizard needs to install the Quicken software and may need to update the software, too. Assuming you're okay with all this — and you should be — click the Install button.

   Quicken installs itself. This process takes a few minutes. Along the way, you may see other screenfuls of messages, including marketing information about the features new to Quicken and some progress reports on the installation itself.

   After the installation is complete, Quicken displays an `installation complete` message.

5. **Click Done.**

   Congratulations. You're done.

After installing the Quicken software, the installation program starts the Quicken program to finish the setup process.

Finishing Setup If You've Used Quicken Before

If you've used a previous version of Quicken, the Quicken program might show option buttons to indicate what you want to do next: Open the found data file. (Alternatively, you can indicate that you want to open some other data file.) You're done. You're ready to begin Quicken-ing.

The Quicken setup process can usually tell whether you've used Quicken before. The setup process knows where the Quicken installation program usually puts the Quicken program and data files, and the installation program will look there. If you've used Quicken before but Quicken can't see this, two possibilities exist: The first possibility is that you put the Quicken data file someplace weird. (If that's the case, hopefully, you remember the weird place you hid the Quicken data file. But if not, see the section, "The mysterious case of the missing Quicken data files," at the end of this chapter.) The second possibility is that you didn't do anything with the Quicken data file but that the data file has somehow gone missing. (If that's the case, hopefully you backed up the Quicken data file to a CD or to some other disc from which you can restore the data file.)

Finishing Setup If You've Not Used Quicken Before

To finish up the setup when you've not used Quicken before, the program displays a friendly welcome message (not shown), which asks you to indicate whether you're a new Quicken user (or someone who wants to start over from scratch as if you're a new user) or if you're already a Quicken user and need to open a file from a previous version of Quicken.

You indicate your Quicken status by selecting the appropriate option button and then clicking the big, blue Get Started button. What happens next depends on which button you click.

Already a Quicken user?

If you've used Quicken before and select the I Am Already A Quicken User option, Quicken then displays another Get Started With Quicken 2012 window that asks whether you want to open a Quicken file located on this computer, restore a Quicken data file you've backed up to CD or disc, or start over and create a new data file.

If you indicate that you want to open another Quicken data file located on the computer, Quicken displays a dialog box that asks where that file is. If you indicate that you want to grab a backup copy of the Quicken file, Quicken displays a dialog box that asks where that file is. Presumably, if either of these situations is your case, you'll know where the data file or backup copy of the data file is.

Are you new to Quicken?

If you indicate that you're a new Quicken user, Quicken automatically sets up a data file for you (you don't need to worry about it). Next, Quicken prompts you to register. (You might as well do this. The registration takes only a few minutes. All you do, in a nutshell, is provide your name and address, a bit of information about how you use Quicken, and your e-mail address.)

After the data file is set up, Quicken starts the home page (see Figure 1-1). The Setup Center walks you through the steps for setting up Quicken. (You can find out much more on this process in the next section.)

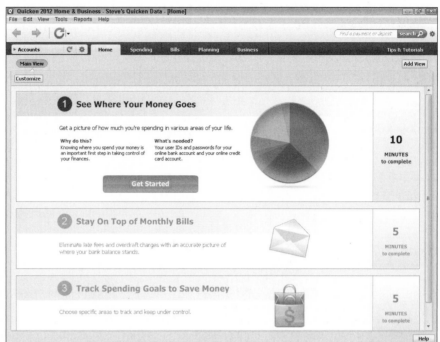

Figure 1-1:
The Quicken
home page.

Describing Your Banking

If you haven't used Quicken before or are starting from scratch, the first time
you start Quicken 2012, the program shows a home page that includes a big
Get Started button in (roughly) the middle of the screen.

Clicking the Get Started button allows you to provide information about
your primary checking account and its current balance. Figure 1-2 shows the
window that collects the first part of this information, but just so you don't
get confused, here are the precise steps you take:

1. **Identify the financial institution — usually a bank — by typing your
   institution's name in the text box provided.**

   As you type, Quicken displays a list of financial institutions that match
   what you've typed so far. The more you type, the shorter the list of possible matching institutions.

2. **Tell Quicken whether you want to download transactions directly
   from your bank or enter transactions manually.**

Figure 1-2:
The first
Add Your
Primary
Checking
Account
window.

If your bank provides Internet access to your bank account — and many banks do — Quicken knows. And as a result, Quicken attempts to not-so-subtly push you into just grabbing data from the bank's website. I'm going to suggest, however, that you maintain your account manually. You have plenty of time later to find out how online banking works. (Online banking is really cool, though. See Chapter 6 for more information.)

That said, however, if you see your bank listed and you want to use online banking, select the bank and click Next. When you click the Next button, Quicken displays another version of the Add Your Primary Checking Account window, which asks for the username and password required to access your bank account electronically. To download transactions and account balance information directly from your bank's website, you will need to provide this information. After you provide this information, click the Connect button to test the username and password information.

If you don't want to use online banking quite yet and are happy to start slow and go manually at the start, click the Advanced Setup hyperlink at the bottom of the first Add Your Primary Checking Account window. Quicken won't quite believe you're bold enough to ignore its strong advice to go digital and so will display another Add Your Primary Checking Account window that provides option buttons you can use to indicate you want to download transactions or that you want to enter transactions manually (see Figure 1-3). Select the I Want To Enter My Transactions Manually button.

Figure 1-3:
The second
Add Your
Primary
Checking
Account
window
attempts to
force you
to do online
banking.

Note: Quicken may not get into this online banking stuff if Quicken can tell that your bank doesn't support online banking.

3. Tell Quicken the name you want to use for the checking account.

You do so by typing a name in the Account Name/Nickname text box, shown in Figure 1-4. Furthermore, if given the choice, click one of the option buttons that may appear below the Account Name/Nickname text box to indicate whether you're using the bank account primarily for business finances, personal finances, and so on. By the way, as far as the account name goes, you can be as general or as specific as you want. But brevity is a virtue here, so be concise: Quicken uses your account name to label stuff within the Quicken window and on Quicken reports. If you use a long account name, the name may not always fit on reports and screens.

4. Enter the ending bank statement date by referring to your bank statement.

After you provide Quicken with a name and general description of the account's transactions, click Next, and Quicken displays another account setup dialog box (shown in Figure 1-5) that asks about the account's ending statement date and ending statement balance. Enter the date of your last bank statement into the Statement Ending Date text box. This date, by the way, is forward from which you will start using Quicken. Enter the date in *MM/DD/YYYY* or *MM/DD/YY* fashion.

"Geez, Steve," you're now saying to yourself, "what's *MM/DD/YYYY* fashion?" Okay. Here's an example: If your bank statement is dated August 30, 2012, type **8/30/2012**, or you can type **083012**.

Figure 1-4:
The third
Add Your
Primary
Checking
Account
window.

Figure 1-5:
The fourth
Adding Your
Primary
Checking
Account
window.

5. **Enter the ending bank statement balance by referring to your latest bank statement.**

This balance is whatever appears on your bank statement. This balance is also the amount of money in your account on the date you begin your financial record keeping. If you have $4.16 in your checking account, type **4.16** in the Statement Ending Balance text box.

6. **After you type the bank statement balance, click the Next button to continue moving through the account setup.**

   Ultimately, you'll see a window that provides buttons you can click to start using Quicken and to add additional bank accounts and even credit card accounts.

   If you have several other bank accounts that you want to set up within Quicken, repeat the preceding steps for each account. Just click the button that refers to adding another bank account.

Slogging through More Setup Stuff

Okay, from my perspective, after you've described your bank account(s), you're ready to start using Quicken. With Quicken, the key thing you want to do is track your bank account or accounts so you can monitor and measure your income and your outgo. And so that you know how much money you have in an account.

The folks at Intuit, however, allow you to provide the Quicken program with a lot more information about your financial affairs. Specifically, the Intuit gang let you describe in detail your income sources and your regular expenditures.

To tell Quicken all about your income and outgo, click the Get Started button in the Stay On Top Of Monthly Bills area of the home page. When you do, Quicken displays the first Stay On Top Of Monthly Bills window, shown in Figure 1-6. To describe a recurring bill (like your rent check, car loan payment, and so on), you click the Add A Bill button. Then, when Quicken displays the Add Bill Reminder dialog box (not shown), you describe the bill in detail, including who gets paid, when they should be paid, why they're paid, and so forth. (I'm not going to describe the Add Bill Reminder dialog box here because I talk about it in detail in Chapter 12 when the subject of loan payments comes up.)

If you click the Next button shown in the bottom-right corner of the Stay On Top Of Monthly Bills window, Quicken displays a second version of the Stay On Top Of Monthly Bills window, shown in Figure 1-7. The second version of the Stay On Top Of Monthly Bills window provides an Add Income Reminder button.

To provide information about your income to Quicken, click the Add Income Reminder button. Quicken displays dialog boxes that ask for the gory details.

The best way to get started

Quicken wants you to use your last bank statement to set up the bank account you track. This way, your financial records synchronize with the bank's records when you start using Quicken.

But I want to suggest something slightly different to you. Go back farther than just to the beginning of the preceding month (which is what you do when you use your last bank statement). Go back to the beginning of the year, and use the last bank statement of the preceding year — even if it's now several months after the beginning of the year. Now, I'm not trying to waste your time. Let me point out two big

advantages to having a complete year's data in Quicken: Tracking and tallying your tax deductions will be a snap, and planning your finances will be easier. When you enter the activity, be sure to enter any outstanding checks or deposits from the prior period with their correct dates also. That way, they are there to check off when you do your first reconciliation.

Going back to the beginning of the year isn't as hard as you may think. Quicken provides a bunch of tools to help you enter several months' worth of data in a very short time, as you can see in this chapter and in the two or three that follow.

Steve's Overview

You don't need to know much about the mechanics of the Quicken *interface* — the way its window looks and works — to begin working with Quicken, especially in any chapters in this book in which I cover the basics. I provide plenty of detailed instructions, but I have a couple of quick comments now.

Starting Quicken for the second time

The second time you start Quicken — and every subsequent time — things work pretty much the same way as the first time. Double-click the Quicken icon on your desktop. Or, if you like doing things the hard way, click Start and then choose Quicken 2012.

Using the Accounts bar

Along the left edge of the program window, just beneath the boldface word Accounts, Quicken lists the accounts you've set up. In other words, if you set up a single checking account, the Accounts bar shows just that single checking account. If you set up 13 bank accounts because that's just the sort of person you are, the Accounts bar shows the 13 checking and savings accounts.

You can display the transactions you've entered for an account shown in the Accounts bar by clicking the account name. (I talk more about this in Chapter 4.)

You can collapse the Accounts bar by clicking the minus (–) symbol that appears in front of the word Accounts. If you've previously collapsed the Accounts bar, you can expand the bar by clicking the plus (+) symbol that appears in front of the word Accounts.

Navigating with tabs

Quicken arranges all its features — whistles, bells, or whatever else you want to call them — using navigation tabs that appear near the top edge of the window. For example, if you look closely at Figure 1-1, you will see tabs labeled Home, Spending, Bills, Planning, and Business.

If you're still confused, click the buttons and bits of text in the area of the Quicken window that I'm talking about. You'll clearly see how things work.

If you click the Home or Bills tab and you haven't yet set up enough of Quicken to use the features provided by the tab, you encounter a blue Get Started button. If you click the Get Started button, Quicken steps you through setting up the tabs features.

Solving Tricky Setup Problems

I want to quickly go over a handful of annoying setup problems new Quicken users may encounter. If you have Quicken set up and are ready to roll, skip this stuff.

Did somebody say Macintosh?

You can use the existing old Quicken files if you're working with a new version of Quicken. In fact, if the Quicken installation program can find a version of old Quicken files on your computer, it gives you the option of just skipping all the Quicken Express Setup stuff. In this case, you just begin using your existing files. (I mention this point earlier in this chapter, in fact.)

If you've been using Quicken for Macintosh, however, you have to export your data from the Macintosh before you can read it in the Windows version. And I can think of about a million things more fun to do than exporting Quicken data from a Mac to Windows. See the section in Chapter 17 on importing data from an old accounting system for a brief discussion on the procedure and some suggestions for better ways to spend your time.

The mysterious case of the missing Quicken data files

If Quicken doesn't find the old files, you need to open the specific files. But if you have this problem, you should be able to solve it yourself. What has happened, if you find yourself in this boat, is that you've moved or messed around with the Quicken files with some other program, such as Windows. If you did that, presumably you had a reason. And more to the point, you should know where you put the files.

Migrating from Microsoft Money

Suppose that you're moving from Microsoft Money to Quicken. The question of the hour is this: Can you reuse your old or existing Money files in Quicken? The answer is, "Yes, sort of."

First of all, the Quicken File menu includes an Import command that lets you import files from Microsoft Money 2007 or 2008. So far, so good.

Further, if you've got an older version of Microsoft Money you want to convert data from, you can download a program called Data Converter from the Quicken support website. Data Converter converts Microsoft Money data files from Microsoft Money 2003 and later versions to the Quicken 2004, 2005, 2006, 2007, and 2008 file format. Quicken 2012 should easily then convert one of these old-format Quicken files to the Quicken 2012 file format. So, theoretically, you can move old Microsoft Money data files to Quicken.

Practically, however, moving financial information from Quicken to Money or vice versa doesn't seem to work all that well. Transactions seem to get lost. Account balances get messed up. People ruin their lives. Well, maybe that last comment is a slight exaggeration. But, no kidding: Migrating is problematic. If you do want to move from one program to another, I suggest making sure that you have a really good reason for doing so and that you allow yourself enough time to track down and correct any errors. The Data Converter is available from `http://quicken.intuit.com/support/` — use the search term *Microsoft Money* after you select your Quicken version.

Chapter 2

Introduction to the Big Picture

· ·

In This Chapter

▶ Distilling Quicken to its very essence

▶ Setting up additional bank accounts

▶ Adding, removing, and modifying categories

▶ Understanding tags

· ·

*B*efore you spend a bunch of time on Quicken, you have to understand the big picture. You need to know what Quicken can do. You need to know what you want to do. And, as a practical matter, you need to tell Quicken what you want it to do.

Boiling Quicken Down to Its Essence

When you boil Quicken down to its essence, it does six things:

✔ **It lets you track your tax deductions.**

This feature makes preparing your personal or business tax return easier for you or your poor accountant, Cratchit.

✔ **It lets you monitor your income and outgo either on-screen or by using printed reports.**

Usually, this stuff is great fodder for discussions about the family finances. And, if you're running a business or investing in real estate rental properties, this income and expense information becomes more than just great conversation fodder — the information helps you better manage your business.

✔ **It lets you print checks (and sometimes other forms, too).**

This device is mostly a timesaver, but it can also be useful for people who are neat freaks.

✔ **It lets you track the things you own (such as bank accounts, investments, and real estate) and the debts you owe (such as home mortgage principal, car loan balances, and credit card balances).**

These things are really important to know.

✔ **It helps you make better personal financial planning decisions about such matters as retirement, your children's future college costs, and your savings and investments.**

I think this stuff is really neat.

✔ **It gives you the opportunity to pay bills electronically and, in some cases, even do all your banking electronically.**

This stuff is pretty neat, too. No, let me amend that. Online bill paying and banking are really neat. I do have some minor (very minor) reservations that I discuss in Chapter 6, which deals with online banking in depth.

Tracking tax deductions

To track your tax deductions, make a list of the deductions you want to track. To do so, pull out last year's tax return. Note which lines you filled in. (Perhaps mortgage interest, property taxes, state income taxes, and charitable contributions?) This method works because there's a darn good chance that the tax deductions you claimed last year will also be the tax deductions you'll claim in the future.

I cover the Quicken categories, which you use to track your tax deductions, a little later in this chapter.

Monitoring spending

At our house, we (my wife, Sue, and I, your humble author) use Quicken to monitor our spending on the mundane little necessities of life: groceries, clothing, dog food, cable television, and, well . . . you get the picture. To keep track of how much we spend on various items, we also use the Quicken categories.

If you want to monitor a particular spending category, decide up front what the category should be before you begin recording your data.

Your list of spending categories, by the way, shouldn't be an exhaustive list of superfine pigeonholes, such as *Friday-night Mexican food, Fast food for lunch,* and so on. To track your spending on eating out, one category named something like *Meals* or *Grub* usually is easiest.

In fact, I'm going to go out on a limb. You can probably start with a dozen categories, more or less:

- ✔ Car
- ✔ Clothing
- ✔ Entertainment and vacation
- ✔ Groceries
- ✔ Household expenses (besides food)
- ✔ Insurance
- ✔ Medical and dental
- ✔ Rent (or mortgage payments)
- ✔ Taxes
- ✔ Utilities (electric, water, cable television)
- ✔ Work expenses

If you want to, and over time, you can expand this list. Heck, you can create dozens and dozens of categories. My experience, though, is that you'll probably use only a handful of categories.

Printing checks (and other forms)

You can use Quicken to print checks. This little trick provides a couple of benefits: It's really fast if you have several checks to print, and your printed checks look very neat and darn professional.

To print checks, you need to do just two things. First, look through the check supply information that comes with Quicken, and pick a check form that suits your style. Then order the form. (The check forms that come with *remittance advices* — or check stubs — work well for businesses.)

Preprinted check forms aren't cheap. If you're using Quicken at home with personal-style checks (such as those that go in your wallet), using computer checks may not be cost effective. Even if you're using Quicken for a business, and you're used to buying those outrageously expensive business-style checks, you'll still find computer checks a bit more expensive.

I'm pretty much a cheapskate, so I don't use printed checks at home (although I do use them in my business). I should admit, however, that I also don't write very many checks.

By the way, I've "checked" around. Although you can order Quicken check forms from other sources (such as your local office supplies store), they're about the same price from Intuit (the maker of Quicken). If you want to order from Intuit, you can refer to the catalog that came in the Quicken packaging. You can also visit www.quicken.com.

One other comment here about printing checks: If you're going to pay bills electronically, you don't need to print checks with Quicken. Oh, sure, you can print checks if you want. But you won't want to. Paying a bill electronically is easier and cheaper than paying a bill with a Quicken-printed check.

A general comment about printing other forms: If you run a business, and the business needs to produce invoices, you can use Quicken Home & Business and Quicken Rental Property Manager (two business-y flavors of Quicken) to produce invoice forms, too. (Both of these features can be added by choosing a command from the Help menu.)

Tracking bank accounts, credit cards, and other stuff

You must decide which bank accounts and credit cards you want to track. In most cases, you want to track each bank account you use and any credit card on which you carry a balance.

You may also want to track other assets and liabilities. *Assets* are just things you own: investments, cars, a house, and so on. *Liabilities* are things you owe: margin loans from your broker, car loans, a mortgage, and so on.

Shoot, I suppose that you could even track the things your neighbor owns — or perhaps just those things you especially covet. I'm not sure that this is a very good idea, though. (Maybe a healthier approach is to track just those things that you've borrowed from your neighbor.)

Planning your personal finances

Your computer's computational horsepower makes it the ideal tool for doing complicated calculations. So maybe you're not surprised that Quicken comes with five powerful calculators that let you make smarter borrowing choices, better mortgage-refinancing decisions, more accurate savings and investment calculations, and extremely helpful retirement and college savings calculations.

I believe that these financial planning tools are the most valuable features that Quicken offers. I'm just sorry that I have to wait until Chapter 10 to talk about them.

Banking online

If you want, you can tell Quicken that it should do the work of paying some person or merchant electronically. In other words, at the same time that you describe some check to Quicken — you do so by entering stuff in a window — you can say to Quicken, "I not only want you to record this check for me, but I also want you to pay it for me."

If your bank supports online banking, you may also be able to move money between your accounts and get up-to-date statements electronically. Ask your bank for details about this service if you're interested.

To perform this sort of online banking, you need to have an Internet connection, and you need to do a little bit of paperwork. But the Quicken online banking features can save you scads of time. And the features are easy to use. Basically, all you do is use Quicken in the usual way — which is what I talk about in the chapters that follow — and then click a couple of extra buttons.

Setting Up Additional Accounts

When you first began working with Quicken — and this may have only been a few minutes ago or several years ago — you were prompted to set up an account. And you probably set up at least a checking account because this is probably your most active bank account. If you want to track any additional accounts — for example, a savings account — you must set them up, too.

Setting up another banking account

To set up an additional checking, savings, or money market account, you give the account a name and then its balance as of a set date. Here's how:

1. **Click the Add An Account button.**

   Quicken displays the Add Account window, shown in Figure 2-1.

Figure 2-1:
The Add
Account
window.

The Add An Account button is located near the bottom of the Accounts bar, which appears along the left edge of the Quicken program window. You can collapse and expand the Accounts bar by clicking the small arrow button just left of the Accounts label. If the arrow button points down, clicking the button collapses the Accounts bar. If the button points right, clicking the button expands the previously collapsed Accounts bar.

 2. **Click either the Checking or Savings button and then click Next.**

When you click Next, Quicken displays a version of the Add Account window, shown in Figure 2-2, which asks for the bank name.

Figure 2-2:
The first Add
Account
window
used for
a bank
account.

3. (Optional) Identify the financial institution and then click Next.

To identify the bank and (simultaneously) set up the account for online banking, enter the bank's name in the Enter The Name Of Your Bank text box. As you type the bank name, Quicken creates a list of banks that match what you're typing. When you see your bank listed, select its name. Quicken then asks you to enter the bank's online sign-on information for the account. (This information probably includes a username and password or equivalent information.) If you want to enable online access to the bank account information, provide the requested information and then click the Connect button. Alternatively, if you don't want to identify your bank, you can click the Advanced Setup link (near the bottom of the window) to display a second Add Account window (not shown) that asks whether you want to connect to your bank automatically so you can download transactions or want to enter transactions manually.

4. Indicate whether you want to download transactions or manually enter transactions, and then click Next.

When Quicken asks whether you want to download account activity and balance information directly from your bank or enter the information manually, indicate that you just enter transactions manually. (Quicken asks the "manual versus online" questions if you select a financial institution that allows for online banking.)

5. Name the account, and then click Next.

When Quicken displays the first Add Savings Account dialog box (see Figure 2-3), move the cursor to the Account Name/Nickname text box and type a name in that box. Click Next after you do this. You're almost done.

Figure 2-3:
The Add Savings Account dialog box.

6. Enter the account balance date.

When Quicken displays the Statement Ending Date and Statement Ending Balance dialog box shown in Figure 2-4, enter the date that you're going to start keeping records for the bank account with Quicken. (Quicken wants you to start your record keeping for an account on a bank statement date because on a bank statement date, you have a really good balance from the bank.) Move the cursor to the Statement Ending Date text box and type the month number, a slash, the day number, a slash, and the year number. If you start on August 30, 2011, for example, type **08/30/2011**. Or, if this is way too complicated for you, click the button at the end of the Statement Ending Date text box so that Quicken displays a pop-up calendar. Then click the date. Use the << and >> buttons to move back and forth a month at a time.

Figure 2-4:
The
Statement
Date and
Balance
dialog box.

Note: If you want to keep your transaction records for tax purposes, of course, it makes sense to track whatever accounts you can from the first of the year, assuming that you have all the necessary statements or your own records of all the transactions.

7. Click inside the Statement Ending Balance text box and enter the bank account balance.

Use the number keys to enter the balance. The folks at Intuit, by the way, really want you to use the balance from your bank statement. If you have terrible financial records — for example, you haven't reconciled your account since the first George Bush left the White House — this idea is probably good advice. If you have neat, accurate financial records, go ahead and use your check register balance.

If you do use the bank statement balance as your starting balance, be sure to enter all the transactions that cleared or will clear after the bank statement balance date. (This should make sense, right? If a check or deposit isn't reflected in the bank statement figure, you must enter it with its correct date into Quicken.)

8. Click Next and then the Finish button.

Quicken re-displays the Home tab.

Hey, Quicken, I want to use that account!

In Quicken, you work with one account at a time. The logic is simple: You record income and expenses for a particular account — a specific checking account, savings account, and so on. That makes sense, right?

Here's the next thing you want to know about using these accounts: In general, you work with an individual account by using the register window, as shown in Figure 2-5. I talk about using the register window a lot more in the chapters that follow, but in a nutshell, you enter account transactions in the register. Entering transactions in a register is the basic, Quicken record-keeping task.

Figure 2-5: The register window.

Here's another thing you need to know about working with a particular Quicken account. You use the Accounts bar, which appears along the left edge in the Quicken program window (refer to Figure 2-5), to tell Quicken which account you want to work with in a register window.

To use the Quicken Accounts bar, you click its hyperlinks. In other words, select the account you want by clicking the account name. Quicken displays the register window for that account.

You can collapse and expand the Accounts bar by clicking the small button marked with a plus symbol or a minus symbol that's just left of Accounts. If the button shows a minus symbol, clicking the button collapses the Accounts bar. If the button shows a plus symbol, clicking the button expands a previously collapsed Accounts bar.

Whipping Your Category Lists into Shape

Quicken supplies categories to, well, categorize your spending. For example, you would probably use the Rent category to categorize all the checks you write to pay rent.

The predefined categories list may be just what you want. Then again, it may not. Table 2-1 shows the all-inclusive category list.

Your category list may vary somewhat from the one shown in Table 2-1. Quicken may customize your starting category list based on the version of Quicken you install. For example, if you install the version of Quicken that supports tracking rental property, the category list may include rental property income and expense categories.

Take a minute to look through the category list. If you find categories you don't need, cross them off the list in the book. You can delete them from Quicken in a minute or so. If you need categories you don't see, add them at the bottom of the list. You can add them in about two minutes or so.

✔ To track a certain income or spending item for income tax purposes — wages, property taxes, and so on — you need a Quicken category.

✔ To track a certain income or spending item because you're just interested in knowing how much you spend on it (for example, renting DVDs), you need a Quicken category.

✔ To budget by categories (because you need a category for any income or spending item that you want to budget), you need a Quicken category.

Table 2-1	The Category List
Categories	*Descriptions*
Income Categories	
Div Income	Dividends earned from stocks you own
Interest Inc	Interest income on bank accounts, and so on
Net Salary	Your net-of-taxes income from a job
Net Salary Spouse	Your spouse's net-of-taxes income from a job
Other Inc	Income that doesn't fit into another category
Expense Categories	
Auto & Transport	The big "catchall" category for auto and transportation expenses
Auto Insurance	Car insurance premiums
Auto Payment	Car loan or lease payments
Car Wash	Car washes and (maybe) detailing?
Gas & Fuel	Gas, diesel, biodiesel, and so on
Parking	Parking and hopefully no parking tickets
Public Transportation	Bus, subway, elevated and commuter trains, and rickshaws (in some areas)
Registration	Vehicle registration fees
Service & Parts	Services and repairs expenses
Tolls	Toll charges
Bills & Utilities	The big general category for regular bills and utilities expenses
Credit Card Payment	Amounts paid on your credit card when you're not tracking this stuff in granular detail
Home Phone	Land line phone
Internet	Internet service provider
Mobile Phone	Cell phone (and text messaging?)
Television	Cable television
Utilities	Water, sewer, electricity, and gas
Cash & ATM	Pocket spending via ATM and mad money
Deposit to Savings	Not a real spending category, but a shortcut for people who don't want to set up a savings account
Education	The general category for education

(continued)

Table 2-1 *(continued)*

Categories	Descriptions
Expense Categories	
Books & Supplies	Books and other school supplies
Student Loan	Student loan payments
Tuition	Tuition and lab fees
Entertainment	Catchall "parent" category for entertainment spending
Amusement	Hey, whatever spins your propeller
Arts	Catchall "subcategory" for stuff that follows
Movies & DVDs	Movie rentals and purchases as well as cinema tickets
Music	Music CDs, music downloads, street musician payments
Newspaper & Magazines	Periodical subscriptions
Fees & Charges	Catchall "parent" category for bank, credit card, and similar fees
ATM Fee	Cash machine charges
Bank Fee	Bank fees, penalties, and service charges
Late Fee	Late fees charged by vendors
Service Fee	Miscellaneous service charges
Trade Commissions	Broker commissions
Financial	Catchall "parent" category for financial services and products
Financial Advisor	Investment advisor fees
Life Insurance	Life insurance premiums
Food & Dining	Another "catchall" parent category
Alcohol & Bars	Yeah, I wanted to talk to you about this
Coffee Shops	Caffeine expenditures
Fast Food	What you should eat less of
Groceries	What you should eat more of
Restaurants	Restaurant charges, including gratuities
Gifts & Donations	The giving "parent" category
Charity	Gifts to nonprofit, religious, and similar organizations
Gift	Usually for gifts to family members and friends

Categories	*Descriptions*
Expense Categories	
Health & Fitness	The parent category for all your medical and fitness related expenses
Dentist	Dentistry expenses
Doctor	Physician's fees
Eyecare	Optometrist fees, eyeglasses, contacts, and similar items
Gym	Fitness club and gym expenses and fees
Pharmacy	Prescriptions and over-the-counter expenses
Sports	Sporting expenses and similar activities
Home	Household expenses "parent" category
Furnishings	Furniture and accessories
HOA Dues	Homeowners association dues
Home Improvement	Home repairs and improvements
Home Insurance	Homeowners & Renters insurance
Home Services	Home cleaning and maintenance services
Home Supplies	Home cleaning and maintenance supplies
Lawn & Garden	Landscaping-type expenses
Mortgage & Rent	Mortgage principal payments (for people not tracking mortgage loan balances) and rent payments
Mortgage Interest	Interest component of a home mortgage payment
Interest Exp	Interest expense on personal lines of credit and other non-mortgage debts
IRA Contribution	Individual retirement account contribution
Kids	Catchall "parent" category for Kids-related subcategories
Allowance	Kids' allowance money
Baby Supplies	Diapers, and so forth
Babysitter & Daycare	Costs of childcare
Kids Activities	Little League, dance classes, Karate summer camp, and so forth
Toys	Toys, games, computer games
Misc.	Stuff you can't categorize someplace else
Not Sure	Stuff you can't categorize someplace else and yet oddly feel uncomfortable putting into the Misc. category

(continued)

Table 2-1 (continued)

Categories	Descriptions
Expense Categories	
Personal Care	The catchall "parent" category for the personal care subcategories
Hair	Haircuts, colorings, extensions, weaves, and other what-have-you's
Laundry	Dry cleaning and other laundry services
Spa & Massage	Spa treatments, massage therapy
Pets	The catchall "parent" category for pet-related expenses
Pet Food & Supplies	What you feed Rover and Twinkle the cat
Pet Grooming	Dog shampoos, cat shampoos, nail clippings
Vet	Veterinarian bills
Shopping	The catchall "shopping" category
Books	My personal weakness
Clothing	Work and casual clothing, including shoes
Electronics & Software	Electronics (including computer) gear and software
Hobbies	Hobby and craft expenses and activity costs
Sporting Goods	Sporting and recreational equipment
Tax	Personal tax expenses "parent" category
Property	Real estate and personal property taxes
Travel	Personal travel expenses
Air Travel	Airplane tickets
Hotel	Hotel and other lodging charges
Rental Car & Taxi	Rental cars, taxis, and similar costs (including airport transfers)
Vacation	Personal and family vacation expenses

Subcategories . . . yikes, what are they?

You surely didn't buy Quicken so that you could spend all day Saturday sitting at your computer instead of taking the kids to the zoo. I realize this and want to make Quicken easier for you to use. To do so, I figure I should tell you which Quicken features you can ignore if you're feeling a bit overwhelmed. Subcategories are among those things I think that you can ignore.

"Subcategories?" you ask. "Yikes! What are they?"

Subcategories are categories within categories. If you look at the Auto & Transport expense category in Table 2-1, for example, you'll notice a bunch of categories that follow the category and are slightly indented: Auto Insurance, Auto payment, Car Wash, Gas & Fuel, Parking, Public Transportation, Registration, Service & Parts, and Tolls.

When you use subcategories, you can subcategorize a transaction that pays, for example, auto and transportation expenses; you can further break down this category into subcategories such as insurance, fuel, service, and so on. If you want to see a list of the ways you've spent your money, Quicken summarizes your spending both by category and, within a category, by subcategory. On a Quicken report, then, you might see this level of detail:

Category	*Expense*
Auto & Transport	
Auto insurance	900
Gas & Fuel	100
Service & Parts	<u>700</u>
Total taxes	1,700

No doubt about it: Subcategories are useful tools. But they make working with Quicken a little more complicated and a little more difficult. As a practical matter, you usually don't need them as you start off. If later on you want to track a spending category in fine, granular detail, you can go ape on the subcategory thing then, okay? For these reasons, I'm not going to get into subcategories here.

If you get excited about the topic of subcategories later — after you have the hang of Quicken — you can peruse the Quicken documentation for more information.

If you *do* want to use the Quicken subcategories, don't delete the subcategories shown in Table 2-1. If you *don't* want to use the subcategories, go ahead and delete them. (I tell you how to remove categories in "Removing categories you loathe" later in this chapter.)

Category groups . . . double yikes!

Category groups, which were known as *supercategories* in a previous version of Quicken, combine categories into sets that you can use in reports and in your budgeting. Sure, they're sort of cool, but you don't need to worry about them if you're just starting with Quicken.

If you're dying to know more about category groups, you can refer to the Quicken online Help. Quicken Help works like Help in other Windows programs. If you don't know Windows all that well — or at least not well enough to comfortably use Help — see Appendix A.

Four tips on categorization

I have just four tips for categorizing:

- ✔ **Cross off any category you won't use.**

  If you don't pay state income taxes in the state you live in, for example, get rid of the state tax category. Extra, unneeded categories just clutter your list. I think it's great if you can get down to just a handful of categories.

- ✔ **Don't be afraid to lump together similar spending categories.**

  Take your utilities expense, for example. If you pay water, natural gas, electricity, and sewer, why not use a single Utilities category? If you pay different utility companies for your water, natural gas, electricity, and sewer, you can still see what you spend on just electricity, for example, even with a single catchall category for utilities.

- ✔ **Be sure to categorize anything that may be a tax deduction.**

  Categorize alimony, educational, medical, and dental expenses; state and local income taxes; real estate taxes; personal property taxes; home mortgage interest and points; investment interest; charitable contributions; casualty and theft losses; moving expenses; unreimbursed employee expenses; and all those vague, miscellaneous deductions. (By the way, the foregoing is a pretty complete list of itemized deductions in the United States at the time this book was written.)

- ✔ **Don't sweat this category stuff too much.**

  In spite of the preceding three tips, don't let these category lists or the work of customizing them scare you. If you want to spend a few minutes cleaning up the list, hey, that's great. If not, or if you're starting to get anxious, just skip ahead to Chapter 3.

Ch-ch-changing a category list

You should now be ready to fix any category list problems. Basically, you need to do three things: add categories, remove categories, and change category names and descriptions.

Adding individual categories you'd love to use

Adding individual categories is a snap. Here's all you have to do:

1. Choose Tools⊳Category List on the menu bar.

Quicken displays the Category List window (shown in Figure 2-6). This window lists the categories available and the accounts you've set up. Careful readers may notice that the categories shown in Figure 2-6 include those shown in Table 2-1.

Figure 2-6:
The
Category
List window.

2. Click the New button in the Category List window.

The New button, by the way, is the third button on the lower left. Quicken dutifully displays the Set Up Category dialog box (shown in Figure 2-7). You probably aren't surprised that you use this puppy to describe the new category.

Figure 2-7:
The Set Up
Category
dialog box.

3. **Enter a short name for the category.**

   Move the cursor to the Name text box and type a name. Although you can use up to 15 characters, use as short of a name as possible to clearly identify the category. Why? Because you use this category name every time you want to tag a transaction to fall into the category.

4. **Enter a description for the category.**

   Move the cursor to the Description text box and then describe the category. Quicken uses the category description on reports that show the category. If you don't add a description, Quicken just uses the category name. You don't need a description, obviously, if your category name is, well, adequately descriptive.

5. **(Optional) Identify the category group.**

   If you disregarded my earlier suggestion to *not* worry about category groups, click the Options button at the bottom of the Category List window and choose Assign Category Group from the menu that Quicken displays. When Quicken displays the Assign Category Groups dialog box, click the Add Custom Groups button to create a new category group. Then, with the Assign Category Groups dialog box still displayed, select the category you want to group from the Find The Category You'd Like to Re-assign list box (shown on the left half of the dialog box) and then the category group you want to use from the Assign It To A Custom Category Group list box (shown on the right half of the dialog box). Click Done when you're, well, done.

6. **Indicate whether the category is an income category or an expense category.**

Select the appropriate Income, Expense, or Subcategory Of option button — just select the appropriate option button with your furry little friend, the mouse. If you've totally blown off my admonition not to use subcategories just yet, use the dialog box's drop-down list to indicate into which income or expense category a new subcategory falls.

7. **Indicate whether the category tracks an amount you will use on an input line on next year's tax return.**

   By *line,* I mean the actual tax form line — such as the line on the U.S. 1040 form that tracks alimony.

   If a category does track a tax deduction, click on the Tax Reporting tab of the Set Up Category dialog box, move the cursor to the Tax-Related check box, and then *select the check box* if the category is tax-related or *deselect the check box* if the category isn't tax-related. Just to clear up any confusion, vacationing in Hawaii probably isn't a tax deduction — even if your neighbor promises that it is. Then identify the form and line by opening the Tax Line Item drop-down list box and selecting one of its entries.

8. **Click OK.**

   Quicken adds the new category in the Category List window (refer to Figure 2-6) and then redisplays the window. Now that you understand the stuff in the Category List window, note that it shows the category name, its type, notations concerning the category's tax-reporting status, and, golly darn, even its description and group. (The tax information about on which tax return line a category gets reported appears only if the Show Tax Line Item choice under the option button is selected.)

Adding categories from a situational list

Quicken keeps lists of categories that are standard for people in certain situations, including Quicken users who are married, homeowners, real estate investors, and business owners.

To use these situational lists as a source of new categories, follow these steps:

1. **Choose Tools⇨Category List on the menu bar.**

   Quicken displays the Category List window (refer to Figure 2-6).

2. **Click the Options button and then choose the Manage Categories command from the menu.**

   Quicken displays the Manage Categories dialog box. This window lists the categories that may be useful in certain situations.

3. **Select one of the situational lists.**

   Open the Available Categories drop-down list box — you can do this simply by clicking the box — and select the situational list of categories you want to display: standard, married, homeowner, business, children, investment, or rents and royalties. Quicken displays the categories from the situational list selected.

4. **Select the categories you want to add.**

   Click the categories in the Categories list that you want to add. Quicken marks the categories you select with a check. You can, by the way, mark all the categories shown in the situational list by clicking the Mark All button. You can unmark all the "marked" categories by clicking the Clear All button.

5. **Add the selected categories.**

   After you mark the categories you want to add, click the Add button. Quicken adds the categories to the Categories To Add list. To complete the addition of the categories, click Add.

Removing categories you loathe

Removing categories takes only a couple of keystrokes. With the Category List window displayed, follow these steps:

1. **Click the category you want to remove and then choose the Delete button that appears.**

   If no transactions are in the category, Quicken displays a message that asks you to confirm your decision. You can't remove any categories you're using for some old transaction. Accordingly, you may need to first re-categorize transactions that use a category you want to nuke.

2. **If you want to remove the selected category, click OK.**

   Otherwise, press the Esc key or click the Cancel button.

Changing category names and descriptions

You can change a category name, its type, its description, and its tax-related setting if you later discover you made some mistake, such as misspelling a word in a description.

To do so, follow these steps:

1. **Display the Category List window (refer to Figure 2-6).**

2. **Use the arrow keys or click with your mouse to select the category you want to change, and then click the Edit button.**

Quicken displays a dialog box that has text boxes and option buttons describing the selected category's information: its name, description, type, and tax-related settings.

3. **Make the changes you want by replacing text box contents or changing option button settings. Click OK to save your changes and return to the Category List window.**

Merging categories

A quick, related point: If you select a category and then click the Merge button — the button appears to the right of the category information — Quicken displays a Merge Category dialog box, which you use to re-categorize transactions in the selected category. The dialog box provides a drop-down list box you use to select the new category you want to use. The dialog box also provides a check box you can select if you want to delete the category after moving transactions out of it. Note that you may need to maximize the Category List window to see the Merge button or scroll the window to the right using the scroll bar at the bottom of the window.

Want to Play Tag?

Using categories isn't the only way that you can summarize your financial records. Quicken provides a second tool, called *tags,* which lets you summarize transactions in addition to the way you summarize transactions with categories. (In previous versions of Quicken, tags were known by another name: *classes.*)

Now, typically, tags are not something you need to worry about — especially if you're just using Quicken to regain control over your personal finances. However, tags can be very useful if you're using Quicken in a business or if you're investing in rental real estate.

For these reasons, I want to quickly describe how you set up tags.

To set up a tag (or several tags), take these steps:

1. **Display the Tag List window.**

   To do this, choose Tools⇨Tag List.

2. **Click the New button in the Tag List window.**

   Quicken displays the New Tag dialog box (shown in Figure 2-8).

3. Enter a short name for the tag.

Move the cursor to the Name text box and type a name. Use as short of a name as possible to clearly identify the tag. You use this tag name every time you want to tag a transaction. (If you're using tags to identify real estate rental properties — which is probably their most common use — you might want to use the street name as the tag: *Winston* as the tag for the duplex on Winston Street, *Roosevelt* as the tag for the cottage on Roosevelt Avenue, and so on.)

The reason real estate investors tag transactions is this: By tagging each income or deduction transaction with, for example, the property name, Quicken easily produces a profit and loss statement for each property using the categories and tags to slice and dice the data.

4. Enter a description for the tag.

Move the cursor to the Description text box and then describe the tag. Quicken uses the tag description on reports that show the tag. If you don't add a description, Quicken just uses the tag name. You don't need a description, obviously, if your tag name is, well, adequately descriptive.

The technical editor, David (who's also a CPA), wants me to tell you that you should just ignore the Copy Number box. He's probably right. But, if you're just dying to know what this box does, click the Tell Me More link.

5. Click OK.

Quicken adds the new tag in the Tag List window and then redisplays the window. And that is that.

Chapter 3

Maximum Fun, Maximum Profits

. . . .

In This Chapter

▶ Deciding whether you need a budget

▶ Discovering tips for personal and business budgets

▶ Setting up and reviewing a budget

. . . .

I don't think that a budget amounts to financial handcuffs, and neither should you. A budget is really a plan that outlines the way you need to spend your money to achieve the maximum amount of fun or the way a business needs to spend its money to make the most profit.

Should You Even Bother with a Budget?

A *budget*, as you probably know, is a list of the ways you earn and spend your money. If you create a good, workable category list with Quicken (see Chapter 2), you're halfway to a good, solid budget. (In fact, the only step left is to specify how much you earn in each income category and how much you spend in each expense category.)

Does everybody need a budget? No, of course not. Maybe, at your house, you're already having a bunch of fun with your money. Maybe, in your business, you make money so effortlessly that you really don't plan your income and outgo.

For the rest of us, though, a budget improves our chances of getting to wherever it is we want to go financially. In fact, I'll stop calling it a budget. The word has such negative connotations. I know — I'll call it a *Secret Plan.*

Serious Advice about Your Secret Plan

Before I walk you through the mechanics of outlining your Secret Plan (your budget), I want to give you a few tips.

Your personal Secret Plan

You can do four things to make your Secret Plan more likely to work:

✔ **Plan your income and expenses as a family.**

With this sort of planning, two heads are invariably better than one. What's more, though I don't really want to get into marriage counseling here, a family's budget — oops, I mean *Secret Plan* — needs to reflect the priorities and feelings of everyone who has to live within the plan. Don't use a Secret Plan as a way to minimize what your spouse spends on clothing or on long-distance telephone charges talking to relatives in the old country. You need to resolve issues regarding your clothing and long-distance charges before you finalize your Secret Plan.

✔ **Include some cushion in your plan.**

In other words, don't budget to spend every last dollar. If you plan from the start to spend every dollar you make, you undoubtedly have to fight the mother of all financial battles: paying for unexpected expenses when you don't have any money. (You know the sorts of things I mean — car repairs, medical expenses, or that cocktail dress or tuxedo you absolutely *must* have for a special party.)

✔ **Regularly compare your actual income and outgo to your planned income and outgo.**

This part of your plan is probably the most important and also the part that Quicken helps you with the most. As long as you use Quicken to record what you receive and spend, you can print reports showing what you planned and what actually occurred.

✔ **Make adjustments as necessary.**

When you have problems with your Secret Plan — and you will — you'll know that your plan isn't working. You can then make adjustments, for example, by spending a little less calling the old country.

TIP

A Secret Plan for your business

The tips for personal Secret Plans also apply to businesses, but I have a special tip for small businesses using Quicken. (I'm going to write very quietly now so that no one else hears....)

Go to the library, ask for the RMA (Risk Management Association) survey, and look up the ways that other businesses like yours spend money. If your library doesn't have the RMA survey, see whether it has the Dun & Bradstreet survey or Troy's Almanac of Business and Industrial Financial Ratios survey.

These surveys are really cool:

- ✔ The **RMA** surveys bank-lending officers, creates a summary of the information these bankers receive from their customers, and publishes the results.

- ✔ **Dun & Bradstreet** collects and summarizes its proprietary financial information.

- ✔ **Troy** (who's actually a business PhD) collects Internal Revenue Service data and publishes the same sort of financial results.

In the preceding surveys, you can get really useful information about what businesses like yours spend, make, and own. For example, you can look up what percentage of sales the average tavern spends on beer and peanuts, the average profit your CPA makes, and the profit a car dealer makes on the average car sale. (Isn't that all kind of interesting stuff?)

By the way, the surveys will not actually have a line on the taverns page labeled *beer and peanuts*. It'll be called *cost of goods sold* or some similarly vague accounting term.

Two things that really goof up Secret Plans

Because I'm talking about you-know-what, let me touch on a couple of things that really goof up your financial plans: windfalls and monster changes.

The problem with windfalls

Your boss smiles, calls you into his office, and then gives you the good news. You're getting a $5,000 bonus! "It's about time," you think. Outside, of course, you maintain your dignity. You act grateful but not gushy. Then you call your husband.

Here's what happens next. Bob (that's your husband's name) gets excited, congratulates you, and tells you he'll pick up a bottle of wine on the way home to celebrate.

On your drive home, you mull over the possibilities and conclude that you can use the $5,000 as a big down payment for that new family minivan you've been looking at. (With the trade-in and the $5,000, your payments will be a manageable $300 per month.)

On his way home, Bob stops to look at those golf clubs he's been coveting, charges $800 on his credit card, and then, feeling slightly guilty, buys you the $600 set. (Pretend that you're just starting to play golf.)

You may laugh at this scenario, but suppose that it really happened. Furthermore, pretend that you really do buy the minivan. At this point, you spent $6,400 on a van and golf clubs, and you've signed up for what you're guessing will be another $300-per-month payment.

This turn of events doesn't sound all that bad now, does it?

Here's the problem: When you get your check, it's not going to be $5,000. You're probably going to pay roughly $400 in Social Security and Medicare taxes, and maybe around $1,500 in federal and state income taxes. Other money may be taken out, too, for forced savings plans — such as a 401(k) plan — or for charitable giving. After all is said and done, you get maybe half the bonus in cash — say $2,500.

Now you see the problem. You have $2,500 in cold hard cash, but with Bob's help, you've already spent $6,400 and signed up for $300-per-month minivan payments.

In a nutshell, you face two big problems with windfalls:

- ✔ You never get the entire windfall, yet spending as if you will is quite easy.

- ✔ Windfalls, by their very nature, tend to get used for big purchases (often as down payments) that ratchet up your living expenses: boats, new houses, cars, and so forth.

Regarding windfalls, my advice to you is simple:

- ✔ Don't spend a windfall until you actually hold the check in your hot little hand. (You're even better off to wait, say, six months. That way, Bob can really think about whether he needs those new golf clubs.)

- ✔ Don't spend a windfall on something that increases your monthly living expenses without first redoing your budget.

The problem with monster income changes

If your income changes radically, planning a budget becomes really hard. Suppose that your income more than doubles. One day you're cruising along making $70,000, and the next day you're suddenly making $170,000. (Congratulations, by the way.) I'll tell you what you'll discover, however, should you find yourself in this position: You'll find that $170,000 a year isn't as much money as you may think. (By the way, this business about monster income changes is true no matter what your income level. Like, if you're cruising along making $500,000 and see your income rocket to $1,000,000, everything I'm saying here still applies.)

Go ahead. Laugh. But for one thing — if your income doubles, your income taxes almost certainly more than quadruple.

One of the great myths about income taxes is that the rich don't pay very much or that they pay the same percentage. But that's not actually true. If you make $70,000 per year and you have an average family, you might pay about $2,000 in federal income taxes. If you make $170,000 a year, though, you pay about $20,000 per year. So, if your salary slightly more than doubles from $70,000 to $170,000 (perhaps your spouse gets a really good job), your income taxes increase almost tenfold, going from $2,000 to $20,000. I don't bring this fact up to get you agitated about whether it's right or fair that you should pay a bunch of any extra income you make in taxes. I bring it up so that you can better plan for any monster income changes you experience.

Another thing — and I know it sounds crazy — is that you'll find it hard to spend an extra $100,000 wisely when you've been making a lot less. And if you start making some big purchases, such as houses and cars and speed-boats, you'll not only burn through a great deal of cash, but you'll also ratchet up your monthly living expenses.

Monster income changes that go the other way are even more difficult. If you've been making, say, $170,000 a year and then see your salary drop to a darn respectable $70,000, it's going to hurt, too. And probably more than you think. That old living-expense ratcheting effect comes into play here. Presumably, if you've been making $170,000 a year, you've been spending it — or most of it.

But other reasons contribute — at least initially — to making a monster salary drop very difficult. You've probably chosen friends (nice people, such as the Joneses), clothing stores, and hobbies that are in line with your income.

Another thing about a monster salary drop is sort of subtle. You probably denominate your purchases in amounts related to your income. Make $70,000, and you think in terms of $10 purchases. But make $170,000 a year, and you think in terms of $20 purchases. This observation all makes perfect sense. But if your income drops from $170,000 down to $70,000, you'll probably still find yourself thinking of those old $20 purchases.

So what to do? If you experience a monster income change, redo your Secret Plan. And be particularly careful and thoughtful.

Setting Up a Secret Plan

Okay, now you're ready to set up your budget — er, I mean, Secret Plan.

Introducing the Budgets window

To get to the window in which you enter your budget, click the Planning tab and click the Budgets button. This causes Quicken to display the Budgets window — though the window won't show any budgeting information because you won't yet have created any budgets.

If you click the Get Started button, which appears in the middle of the Budgets window if you haven't created a budget, Quicken displays the Create A New Budget dialog box (see Figure 3-1). You now can begin the process of creating a budget. With the sort of kindness you often don't expect from strangers, Quicken even suggests a name for your budget and enters it into the Budget Name text box. The name will be something really clever like "Budget 1" or "Budget 2," but you can replace Quicken's idea of clever.

Figure 3-1:
The Create
A New
Budget
dialog box.

Automatic budgets are easy but rough

You can click the Automatic Budget button in the Create A New Budget dialog box if you want Quicken to create a starting budget using any existing financial data. This rough-hewn approach, obviously, doesn't work unless you've already been using Quicken and so have some existing financial data. But if you do click Automatic Budget and then OK, Quicken looks through your transactions for the selected time period (month, quarter, or year) and creates a budget for the five largest spending categories.

When Quicken finishes with these tasks, it displays the budgeted information in the Budgets window, setting the budgeted amount for each of the big five spending categories to whatever the actual spending equals (see Figure 3-2).

Figure 3-2:
The Budgets
window
with
automatically
created
budget
amounts.

To change an automatically budgeted amount, click the category you want
to budget and then the Edit hyperlink. (The Edit hyperlink doesn't appear
until you point to or click on the category.) Quicken then displays the Edit a
Budget Category dialog box (see Figure 3-3), which lets you set the budgeted
amount for the spending category to some other amount.

Figure 3-3:
The Edit
a Budget
Category
window.

If you want to automatically budget more than just your top five spending
categories, click the Add Category hyperlink, shown in the bottom-left corner
of the Budgets window (refer to Figure 3-2). When Quicken displays the
Add Budget Category dialog box (not shown), select the category you want

to budget, click Next, and then provide the budgeted amount and interval (monthly, daily, weekly, and so on). When you click Done, Quicken returns you to the Budgets window.

Advanced budgets are more work but more accurate

You click the Advanced Budget button in the Create A New Budget dialog box (refer to Figure 3-1), when you want use Quicken's advanced budget feature. When you do this, Quicken displays the Advanced Budget Setup window (see Figure 3-4), listing any income or expense categories you've already used.

You can add a category to the Advanced Budget Setup window by clicking the Add More Categories link (see upper-left corner of window) and then choosing the categories you want to budget from the Select Categories To Budget dialog box (see Figure 3-5).

To budget an amount for a category shown in the Advanced Budget Setup window, click the income or expense category and then, when Quicken opens a text box for the category, enter the budgeted amount into the Your Budget column. You can use the Period column's text box to specify the budgeting interval: Monthly, Daily, Weekly, and so on.

If you want set specific amounts for each budgeting interval, select Specific from the Amount column and then enter the interval-specific budget amount for each month, day, week, or whatever into the text boxes that Quicken opens (see Figure 3-6).

Figure 3-4:
The
Advanced
Budget
Setup
window.

Figure 3-5:
The Select
Categories
To Budget
dialog box.

Figure 3-6:
The
Advanced
Budget
Setup
window
budgeting
a specific
amount.

As you enter amounts, Quicken updates any subtotals and grand totals that use those amounts. Note, too, that Quicken displays a little calculator icon when you've selected a text box that accepts a value. Click the Calculator icon to display a pop-up calculator to make computations on the fly. When you finish with the Advanced Budget Setup window, click Done to return to the Budgets window.

Reviewing the options

If you click the Budget Actions button (which appears in the upper-right corner of the Budgets window), Quicken displays a menu with seven commands useful for working with your budgets:

- ✔ **Advanced Budget:** Displays the Advanced Budget Setup window (refer to Figure 3-3) so you can fine-tune individual budget amounts in the current budget.

- ✔ **Edit Budget Name:** Displays a text box you can use to change the name of the budget.

- ✔ **Use historical values for past months:** This command is a switch that tells Quicken to use actual historical values for past months' budgeted amounts. If the "historical values" switch is on, Quicken marks the command with a check.

- ✔ **Budget Reports:** Displays a submenu that lists the two Quicken reports that summarize budgeting information: Budget Report and Monthly Budget Report. These reports are also available on the Reports menu, as discussed in Chapter 7.

- ✔ **Delete This Budget:** Deletes the currently displayed budget.

- ✔ **Duplicate This Budget:** Creates a copy of the currently displayed budget and then prompts you to give the copy a name.

- ✔ **Create New Budget:** Displays the Create A New Budget dialog box (refer to Figure 3-1) so you can begin the process of creating yet another budget either automatically or using the Advanced Budget Setup window.

Reviewing your budget

After you complete your budget, you'll want to review your handiwork, of course. And you perform your review using the Budgets window (refer to Figure 3-2). If you've created several budgets, by the way, you need to use the first unlabeled drop-down list box in the top-left corner of the Budgets window to select the budget you want to review. You can use the second unlabeled drop-down list box in the top-left corner to select a budgeting interval (such as Monthly) and the third unlabeled list box to select the specific period (August 2012, for example).

If a careful review of your budget shows things have become, well, rather a mess, click the Budget Actions button and choose the Delete This Budget command. You can then start your work over.

What to do after you enter your budget

After you create your Secret Plan, you don't have to do anything special to save your work. When you create a budget, Quicken automatically saves your work for you.

I talk more about using the budget in later chapters (Chapter 7, for example). If you want to print a *hard copy* (computerese for *paper*) of the budget, choose Reports➪Spending➪Budget. If you have a printing question, go to Chapter 5.

You're not going to use the Secret Plan for a while. But don't worry; in Chapter 7, I explain how to print reports, including a report that compares your actual spending with, uh, your budget.

Part II
The Absolute Basics

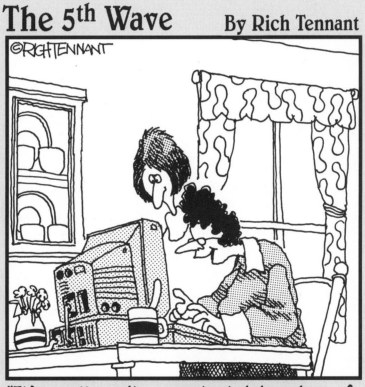

The 5th Wave   By Rich Tennant

"It's really quite an entertaining piece of software. There's roller coaster action, suspense and drama, where skill and strategy are matched against winning and losing. And I thought managing our budget would be dull."

In this part . . .

Okay, you're ready for the show to start (which is good). This part covers all the nitty-gritty details of using Quicken to keep your personal and business financial records. Whether you're just starting to use the Quicken program or you've just come from Part I, you'll find the stuff covered here dang important — dare I say, essential — to using Quicken in even the most basic way.

Chapter 4

Checkbook on a Computer

. . . .

In This Chapter

▶ Recording checks, deposits, and transfers

▶ Splitting categories

▶ Deleting and voiding your transactions

▶ Understanding the register phenomenon

▶ Discovering Quicken's calculators and calendars

▶ Attaching an image, a flag, or a note to a transaction

. . . .

This is it. The big time. You're finally going to do those everyday Quicken things: entering checks, deposits, and transfers. Along the way, you also use some of the neat tools that Quicken provides for making these tasks easier, more precise, and faster.

Getting Started

Okay. I'm going to start at the very beginning.

As you start working with Quicken, you probably want to work from the Spending tab (shown in Figure 4-1). Basically, it looks and works (sort of) like a web page that provides clickable hyperlinks to some of the most popular banking and bookkeeping features of Quicken and supplies interesting tidbits of financial trivia. But initially, before you start entering data, the tab looks pretty sparse. (This is how Figure 4-1 looks.)

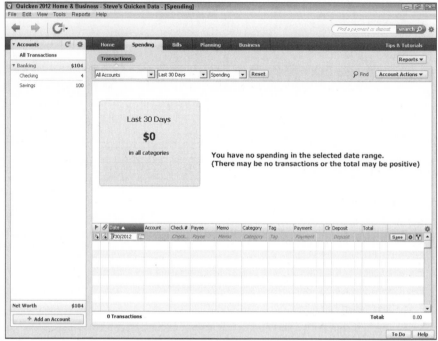

Figure 4-1:
The
Spending
tab, or
window.

Finding Your Checkbook

To enter checkbook transactions, look for the bank account you want to work with listed in the Accounts bar. When you see the bank account, you can click it to display that account's transactions in a register (shown in Figure 4-2).

Figure 4-2 shows the account name — Checking — highlighted in the Accounts bar and in the Quicken program window title bar.

The starting balance you specified as part of setting up the account is the first amount that Quicken lists. In Figure 4-2, for example, the starting balance is $4.16. Bummer.

Interested in online banking and bill payment?

If you want to know more about how Online Bill Payment and online banking work, read Chapter 6. For now, just pay attention to how the Quicken register works. Everything you read about in this chapter will help you more easily use the Quicken Online Account Access feature.

Figure 4-2:
The account
transactions
showing in
a register
window.

Recording Checks

First things first: You can enter checks by using the Spending tab and its
register window (refer to Figure 4-2) or the Write And Print Checks window,
which I describe in Chapter 5.

You use the Spending tab's register window for the checks that you don't
want to print or pay electronically with Quicken; you use the Write And Print
Checks window to enter the checks that you do want to print or pay electronically with Quicken. (This rule isn't etched in stone, but it does make things
easier, so it's the rule that I follow.)

Entering a check in the register

Entering a check in the register is a simple matter of describing to whom you
wrote the check and how much you paid. Suppose, for example, that you
paid $25.50 to the cable television company for your monthly cable service.
Here's how you enter this check.

1. **Enter the check date.**

   Move the cursor to the Date field in the next empty row of the register (if it isn't already there) and type the date by using the *MM/DD* format. To enter August 31, 2012, for example, type **8/31**. You usually don't have to type the year because Quicken retrieves the current year number from the little clock inside your computer.

   You can adjust the date in a Date field by using the + and – keys on your keyboard. The + key adds one day to the current date; the – key subtracts one day from the current date.

2. **Enter the check number.**

   Move the cursor (or tab) to the Check Number field and type the check number. Alternatively, move the cursor to the Check Number field and then, when Quicken displays a list box of entries (such as ATM, Deposit, EFT, Next Check Number, Print Check, Send Online Payment, and Transfer Funds), select Next Check Number if you want. Quicken then fills in the number with its guess as to the new check number — one more than the preceding check number you entered. If this guess is right, you can just leave it in place. If it isn't right, type over what Quicken guessed with the correct number or use the + or – key to increase or decrease the check number.

3. **Enter the payee.**

   Move the cursor to the Payee field. Type the name of the person or business you're paying. If the cable company's name is Movies Galore, for example, type **Movies Galore**. (In the future, you can probably select payee names in the Payee list box.)

4. **Enter the check amount.**

   Move the cursor to the Payment field and type the check amount — **25.50** in this example. You don't have to type the dollar sign, but you do need to type the period to indicate the decimal place and cents.

5. **Enter the category.**

   Move the cursor to the Category field. Quicken displays a drop-down list box of category names from your category list. You can select one of these categories by using the arrow keys or the mouse. Or, if you're the independent type, just type the name yourself. For example, if you use the standard Quicken categories list, you may categorize a payment to your cable company as Bills & Utilities: Television. The first part of this entry, Bills & Utilities, is the category. The second part, Television, is the subcategory.

   If you go with the typing approach and you're not a superfast typist, Quicken can probably guess which category you're entering before you enter it. When you start typing **Bi**, for example, Quicken fills in the rest of the category name — *lls & Utilities* for you (*Bi + lls & Utilities = Bills & Utilities*). This feature is called *QuickFill,* and I talk about it in more detail in the section, "Working with a kooky (and clever) little thing named QuickFill" later in this chapter.

6. **(Optional) Tag that transaction.**

If, after reading about tags in Chapter 2, you decided to use tags, you can also enter a tag in the Tag field. Just to make this a bit clearer, suppose that you're using tags to segregate expenses by house because you actually own two homes: your principal residence and a cabin in the mountains. If you've set up two tags — *principal* and *cabin* — you record utilities expenses for your principal residence by entering **utilities** into the Category field and **principal** into the Tag field. You record utilities expenses for your cabin by entering **utilities** into the Category field and **cabin** into the Tag field.

7. **(Optional) Enter a memo description.**

If you're using the Two-Line Display mode, move the cursor to the Memo field and describe the specific reason that you're paying the check. You may identify the cable payment as the June payment, for example. If you're using Quicken for a business, use this field to identify the paid invoice — usually by entering the invoice number you're paying. You don't have to enter anything in this field, by the way.

8. **Click the Enter button.**

Click the Enter button that appears in the transaction's row of the register. This option tells Quicken that you want to record the transaction into your register. Quicken beeps in acknowledgment, calculates the new account balance, and moves the cursor to the next slot, or row, in the register.

TIP

A neat little trick

You can expand and edit the list box of Check Number entries that Quicken displays. If you want to add some new entry to the Check Number drop-down list box, for example, do the following:

1. **Click the Edit List button, which appears at the bottom of the Check Number drop-down list.**

Quicken displays the Edit Num List dialog box.

2. **Click the New button and then complete the dialog box that Quicken displays.**

You can also remove any new Num entries you add by using the Edit Num List dialog box.

I won't spend anymore time describing how this works, so if you want to figure it all out, just experiment. You can't hurt anything.

Figure 4-3 shows the cable television check recorded into the register. You can't see it in this black-and-white figure, but the –21.34 in the Balance field is in red after the $25.50 check is recorded. This red number indicates that you've overdrawn your account. I don't need to tell you what that means: overdraft charges.

Changing a check you've entered

What if you need to change a check that you've already entered? Suppose that you make a terrible mistake, such as recording a $52.50 check as $25.20. Can you fix it? Sure. Just use the arrow keys or click the mouse to highlight the check transaction that you want to change. Use the Tab and Shift+Tab keys to move the cursor to the field you want to change. (You can also select the field by clicking in it with the mouse.) Then make your fix. Click the Enter button when you finish or press Enter on the keyboard.

Figure 4-3:
The Quicken register after recording the check to Movies Galore.

Packing more checks into the register

Normally, Quicken displays a single row of information about each check that you enter. It also displays a single row of information about each of the other types of transactions you enter. The single-row approach is often pretty illegible, unfortunately. If you want to show more transaction information, click the Account Actions button (which appears near the top-right corner of the register), and then choose the Two-Line Display command on the menu that Quicken displays. After you do, Quicken displays all the register information in a double-line format (shown in Figure 4-4). To return to the single-line format, click the Account Actions button and choose the Two-Line Display again.

Sorting transactions

If you click the Account Actions button, you notice that it also displays a bunch of other commands, in addition to the Two-Line Display command I talk about in the preceding paragraph. Most of these commands I talk about elsewhere in this book, but let me mention one set of the commands here. If you choose the Sorting Options command, Quicken displays a submenu of commands that begin with *By*. These commands all work the same basic way. They let you reorganize the transactions shown in the register in some new way: by date, amount, check number, and so on.

Figure 4-4:
How the register looks with the Two-Line Display format.

Memorized payees

Quicken provides another feature — memorized payees — which is almost irrelevant to day-to-day Quicken use now that the QuickFill feature exists. But because you may hear about this tool, I briefly describe how it works.

A *memorized payee* is one that you've stored or that Quicken has stored in a special list. (To store the transaction, you select it in the register and choose Edit⇨Transaction⇨Memorize Payee.)

To later use or abuse a memorized transaction, choose Tools⇨Memorized Payee List to display

a list of previously memorized payees. When Quicken displays the list, select the payee you want to reuse and click Use.

A memorized payees list is a handy tool. But if you're feeling a little overwhelmed, don't spin your wheels trying to get up to speed on this feature. QuickFill almost always does the job for you because — get this — it automatically grabs memorized payees from the list.

Don't worry. I'm not going to waste your precious time telling you things such as that the By Date command sorts transactions by their dates or that the By Category command sorts transactions by category.

If you point to the column heading for the Payee field, the Payment field, or the Cleared Status field (labeled with Clr), Quicken displays a pop-up command that you can use to re-sort the transactions in the register. These options are self-explanatory. The one that appears when you point to the Payee field is Sort By Payee. And the one that appears when you point to the Cleared Status field is Sort By Cleared. You get the picture.

Working with a kooky (and clever) little thing named QuickFill

Here's kind of a funny quirk about Quicken: If Quicken can guess what you're typing in a field, it fills in the rest of the field for you. Earlier in this chapter, I mention how this QuickFill feature works when you type category names. But it gets even better than that.

The second time you use a payee name, for example, Quicken knows that it's the second time. Quicken also figures that, "Hey, some stuff from the last Movies Galore transaction will probably be the same for this transaction."

When you type the first few letters of the payee name, Quicken supplies a payee name for you. After you press the Tab key to accept the name, Quicken uses the last transaction's information to fill in all the current transaction's fields.

This feature is a real timesaver. Suppose that you did write a $25.50 check to Movies Galore for your June cable television bill. When you type **Movies Galore** to record July's cable television check, the amount will probably be the same. The complete payee name will certainly be the same, and the category will also be the same. So Quicken fills in all these fields, too.

QuickFill doesn't do everything for you, however. You still need to make sure that the date and check number are correct. If Quicken QuickFills a field with the wrong information, just replace the wrong information with the right information.

Recording Deposits

Recording a deposit works almost the same way as recording a check. The only difference is that you enter the deposit amount in the Deposit field rather than enter the check amount in the Payment field.

Entering a deposit into the register

Suppose that you receive $100 as a birthday gift from your elderly Aunt Enid and deposit it into your checking account. Here's how you record this deposit in the register:

1. **Enter the deposit date.**

   Move the cursor to the Date field of the next empty row of the register (if it isn't already there) and type the date. Use the *MM/DD* format. You enter August 31, 2012, for example, as **8/31**. As with check dates, you have to enter the year only if the current year number, which Quicken retrieves from the little clock inside your computer, is wrong.

   You can adjust the date in a Date field in Quicken by using the + and – keys. The + key adds one day to the current date; the – key subtracts one day from the current date.

2. **Type the code DEP (for *deposit*) in the Check Number field.**

   Are you the meticulous type? Then go ahead and move the cursor to the Check Number field. Open the Num drop-down list box and select Deposit.

3. **Type the name of the person from whom you received the deposit.**

   In this case, move the cursor to the Payee field and type **Aunt Enid**. (I don't mean to sound presumptuous, but, well, the next time Aunt Enid sends you birthday money, you can select her name in the Payee drop-down list box.)

4. **Enter the deposit amount.**

   Move the cursor to the Deposit field and type **100**. Don't type the dollar sign — or any other punctuation. (If Aunt Enid sweats money and sometimes passes out $1,000 gifts, for example, you record the deposit as **1000** — not 1,000 or $1,000.)

5. **(Optional) Enter a memo description.**

   Move the cursor to the Memo field and describe something, such as the reason for the deposit. Aunt Enid's money may be described as **birthday gift**. If you're a business depositing a customer's check, use this entry to identify the invoice the customer is paying.

6. **Enter the category.**

   You know how this works by now. Move the cursor to the Category field. Open the Category drop-down list box, if necessary, and select the appropriate category. Alternatively, if you like living on the edge, try typing the category name. You might describe Aunt Enid's check as **Other Inc**.

   To add a category, type a name in the Category field and move to another field. When Quicken doesn't recognize the category name, it asks you whether you want to add the category. Click Yes, and Quicken displays the Set Up Category dialog box. See Chapter 2 if you have questions about how this works.

7. **(Optional) Enter a tag.**

   If you're tagging transactions because categories don't provide you enough detail about transactions, enter a tag into the Tag box. If you don't know what tags are and want to learn, refer to Chapter 2's discussion, "Want to Play Tag?"

8. **Click the Save button.**

   This command tells Quicken that you want to record the transaction in your register. Quicken beeps in protest but then adds the transaction.

Figure 4-5 shows the Checking register (in the Two-Line Display format) after you enter Aunt Enid's thoughtful gift. Your account is no longer overdrawn — so you have that going for you. Maybe before you go any further, you should call Aunt Enid to thank her.

Figure 4-5:
A Checking register as you record your first deposit.

See the ending balance given at the bottom in the register window? The Ending Balance shows the account balance after every register transaction. If you enter future-dated transactions, the register window shows both a *current balance* — the balance as of the current date — and an *ending balance,* which is the balance after all the transactions.

Quicken also includes a Paycheck Setup Wizard that you can use to describe the taxes withheld from your paycheck and categorize the deductions from your paycheck. That much said, you probably don't need to keep track of these amounts unless, for some reason, you want precise estimates of the income taxes you pay. Remember that your employer already does this accounting. Also remember that you must use the employer's data, which appears on your W-2 form — and not your Quicken data — when you prepare your U.S. taxes. If you do decide to use the Paycheck Wizard, click Options, Add Reminder, Income Reminder, and then when Quicken displays the Add Income Reminder dialog box, click the Paycheck Setup Wizard link (which appears along the bottom of the dialog box). Quicken displays the Set Up Paycheck dialog box, which collects information about your payroll check and any deductions.

Changing a deposit you've already entered

Big surprise here — changing a deposit works just like changing a check. First, use the arrow keys or click with the mouse to select the deposit. Use the Tab and Shift+Tab keys to move the cursor to the field you want to change. Tab moves the cursor to the next field. Shift+Tab moves the cursor to the preceding field. (You can also select the field by clicking in it with the mouse.) Then make your fix and click the Save button.

Recording Account Transfers

Account transfers occur when you move money from one account, such as your savings account, to another account, such as your checking account. But jeepers, why am I telling you this? If you have one of those combined savings and checking accounts, you probably do this sort of thing all the time.

Oh, now I remember why I brought this up — Quicken makes quick work of account transfers as long as you already have *both* accounts set up.

If you don't have the second account set up, you need to do that first. If you don't know how, flip to Chapter 2.

Entering an account transfer

Buckle up. I speed through the steps for recording an account transfer. For the most part, you record an account transfer the same way you record a check or deposit.

Suppose that you want to record the transfer of $50 from your checking account to your savings account. Maybe you want to set aside a little money — *little,* presumably, being a key adjective — to purchase a gift for your generous Aunt Enid.

Say that you're working with your checking account and want to record a transfer to your account. Here's what you need to do:

1. **Enter the transfer date.**

   Move the cursor to the Date field. Then type the date that you move the money from one account to another.

2. **Flag the transaction as a transfer.**

   Move the cursor to the Check Number field. Open the drop-down list box and select the Transfer entry. Quicken abbreviates *transfer* as TXFR.

3. **(Optional) Enter a description of the transaction.**

   You don't have to do this, but you might want to use the Payee field to describe the transfer — for example, **Birthday**. You know how this works by now, don't you? You just move the cursor to the field. Then you pound away at the keyboard. Bang. Bang. Bang.

4. **Enter the transfer amount.**

   You enter amounts that you transfer out of an account in the Payment field, and you enter amounts that you transfer into an account in the Deposit field. So move the cursor to the right field (*right* as in *right and wrong,* not *right and left*) and then enter the transfer amount.

5. **(Optional) Enter a memo description.**

   Enter more information about the transaction (if you need to) in the Memo field. Perhaps a gift idea for Aunt Enid?

6. **Indicate the other account.**

   Move the cursor to the Category field, which has a modified name of Xfer Acct (standing for *Transfer Account*). When Quicken drops down a list box of accounts, select the other account. In Figure 4-6, I show the transfer as going to an account named Savings. I set up this account secretly, while you weren't watching. But note that the steps for setting up a second bank account parallel those for setting up a checking account. See Chapter 2 for more information.

7. **Click the Save button.**

   This command tells Quicken that you want to record the transfer transaction into your register.

Figure 4-6 shows the Checking register after you transfer money from your checking account to your savings account so that you'll have money to purchase something nice for Aunt Enid's next birthday — maybe that new Justin Beiber CD.

Take a look at the Category field. Notice that Quicken uses brackets — [ ] — to identify the Category field entry as an account and not as an income or expense category.

Working with the other half of the transfer

Here's the cool thing about transfer transactions: Quicken automatically records the other half of the transfer for you. Figure 4-6 shows the $50 reduction in the checking account because of the transfer. Quicken uses this information to record a $50 increase in the savings account. Automatically. Biddabam. Biddaboom.

Figure 4-6:
The
Checking
register
after you
enter the
transfer
transaction.

To see the other half of a transfer transaction, right-click the transfer transaction and choose the Go To Matching Transfer command on the shortcut menu. Quicken displays the other account in a new register window, shown in Figure 4-7.

Changing a transfer you've already entered

Predictably, this activity works just like changing a check or a deposit:

1. **Select the transfer by using the arrow keys or by clicking the mouse.**

2. **Use the Tab and Shift+Tab keys to move the cursor to the field that you want to change.**

3. **Make your fix, click the Save button, and then go to lunch.**

Figure 4-7:
The other
half of the
transfer
transaction.

Splitting Transactions

Here's a sort of Quicken riddle for you: Suppose that you have a check that pays more than one kind of expense. You trot down to the grocery store, for example, and pick up $10 worth of junk food and junk beverages (which you should categorize as a Groceries expense) and $10 worth of 10W-40 motor oil (which you should categorize as an Auto expense). How do you categorize a transaction like this? Well, I'll tell you. You use a *split category*.

Here's how a split category works: When you're ready to categorize the check, you click the Split button, and Quicken displays the Split Transaction window, shown in Figure 4-8. The Split button shows two arrows that look like a warning sign for a fork in the road.

Steps for splitting a check

Being a clever sort, you probably already know how the Split Transaction window works. I go through the steps anyway. Suppose that you want to categorize a $20 check that includes $10 for groceries and $10 for motor oil.

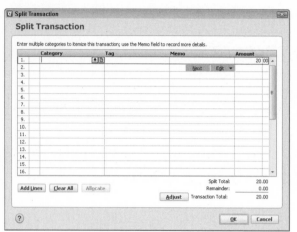

Figure 4-8:
The Split
Transaction
window.

To categorize a check in the Split Transaction window, do the following:

1. **Enter the first category name in the first Category field.**

   Move the cursor to the Category field (if it isn't already there). Activate the drop-down list box by pressing Alt+Down arrow or by clicking the down arrow and then selecting the category name.

   (Despite what a dietitian may say, you can call the soda and candy Groceries.)

2. **(Optional) Tag the first categorized portion of the check.**

   If you're using tags to further classify your spending, move the cursor to the first Tag field and then type the tag. If you have no idea what I'm talking about here, either just forget I said anything, or see the final paragraphs of Chapter 2.

3. **Enter a memo description for the first categorized portion of the check.**

   Move the cursor to the first Memo field and then type whatever you want. (Maybe a description of the food you bought. Er, then again, maybe if you're buying real junk, you should just leave this blank.)

4. **Enter the amount spent for the first category.**

   Move the cursor to the first Amount field and then type, well, the amount. If the first category is what you're calling Groceries and you spent $10 on this, you type **10**.

5. **Repeat Steps 1–4 for each spending category.**

If you spent another $10 on motor oil, for example, move the cursor to the second Category field and enter the category and, optionally, the subcategory you use to summarize auto maintenance expenses. In Figure 4-9, for example, I use the category-subcategory combination Auto & Transport:Service & Parts. Optionally, tag the transaction. Optionally (again), move the cursor to the second Memo field and enter a memo description of the expenditure, such as **motor oil**. Move the cursor to the second Amount field and enter the amount of the expenditure, such as **10**.

Figure 4-9 shows a Split Transaction window that is complete. A split transaction can have up to 30 pieces. Use the scroll bar or PgUp and PgDn keys to scroll through the list of split amounts.

Figure 4-9:
The completed Split Transaction window.

6. **Verify that the Split Transaction window shows no uncategorized spending.**

If you find extra spending — this shows up as the Remainder amount — either add the category you need or delete the split transaction line that's uncategorized. To delete a split transaction line, move the cursor to one of the fields in the line and choose Edit⇨Delete. You can also click the Adjust button to get rid of the Remainder amount — but in this case, Quicken adjusts the amount originally entered into the register so that it agrees with the details you've supplied in the Split Transaction window.

If you want to insert a new line, move the selection cursor to the line above where you want to make your insertion and choose Edit⇨Insert. If you're fed up and want to start over from scratch, choose Edit⇨Clear All (which causes Quicken to erase all the split transaction lines).

7. Click OK.

After you complete the Split Transaction window — that is, after you completely and correctly categorize all the little pieces of the transaction — click OK. Quicken closes the Split Transaction window. If you didn't enter an amount in the Payment column of the register before opening the Split Transaction window, Quicken displays a dialog box that asks whether the transaction is a payment or a deposit. You select an option button to make your choice known.

To let you know that the transaction is one that you've split, the Category field shows `--Split--` when you select the split transaction to show that you've split a transaction among categories or tags. Take a peek at Figure 4-10 to see for yourself.

8. Click the Enter button.

This command tells Quicken that you want to record the transaction in your register.

Figure 4-10:
The Checking register. Can you find the boxes labeled with *Split?*

Splitting hairs

Quicken assumes that any transaction amount you enter in the register should agree with the total of the individual split transaction amounts entered in the Split Transaction window.

If you're not sure what the split transaction amount's total is, your best bet is to NOT — I repeat, *NOT* — enter the amount on the Transactions tab. Instead, enter the individual split transaction amounts in the Split Transaction window. When you leave the Split Transaction window, Quicken totals your individual split amounts, and then prompts you to see whether the total is a payment or a deposit. Then it plugs this total into either the Payment or the Deposit field.

If you've already entered either a payment amount or a deposit amount, but you're not sure that the split transaction amounts agree with what you entered, you can tell Quicken to adjust the Payment or Deposit amount on the Transactions tab to whatever the individual split transaction amounts total. To do so, click the Split Transaction window's Adjust button. Quicken then adds the split transaction lines and plugs the total into the register. (This approach may best be called, "I don't care if it's a round hole; I want to pound this square peg into it.")

By the way, Quicken shows any difference between the amount shown on the Transactions tab and the individual split transaction amounts. It shows this difference as the last split transaction line, so you can tell whether the individual splits agree with the payment or deposit amount shown in the register.

Editing and deleting split categories

You can delete or change any individual line of a split category. To do so, first select the transaction (to display the Split Transaction window) and then click the check mark button, which appears in the register's Category field after you record the transaction. After Quicken dutifully displays the Split Transaction window, you can edit a field by selecting it and then typing over its contents. You can delete any line of the split transaction by choosing Edit⇨Delete. (If you want to delete all the lines of the split transaction so that you can start over, choose Clear All instead.)

If you want to unsplit the transaction so that you can assign it to a single category, you need to use a little trick. Click the X button that appears in the register's Category field after you record the transaction.

Steps for splitting deposits and transfers

Wondering whether you can split deposits and transfers? Well, you can. The steps for doing so work just like the steps for splitting categories for a check transaction. The basic trick — if you can call it a trick — is to use the Split Transaction window to list all the category names and amounts.

Sort of a voiding bug . . .

When you mark a transaction as void — you do this by selecting a transaction and choosing Edit⇨Transaction⇨Void Transaction(s) — Quicken does three things: It sticks VOID in the start of the Payee field, it marks the transaction as cleared, and it erases the amount in the Payment or Deposit field. So far, so good. But if you later fill in the Payment or Deposit field and don't pay attention to the warning from Quicken that you're editing a reconciled transaction, Quicken uses the payment or deposit amount that you enter to adjust the account balance — even though Quicken still shows the transaction as void. I keep thinking the folks at Intuit will fix this, but they haven't — at least not yet. The bottom line is that you need to make sure that you don't edit transactions after you void them. Otherwise, you can all too easily foul up your account balance — perhaps even overdraw your account. I won't tell you about how I happened to learn this. . . .

One other point I should make here is that you can mix and match categories and transfers in the Split Transaction window. Some of the splits, for example, can be categories, and some can be transfer accounts. This type of transaction is common in a business setting. (See Chapter 15 for more information.)

Deleting and Voiding Transactions

You can delete and void register transactions by using the More Actions button's Delete and Void Transaction(s) commands. If you've looked at the Edit button — it appears just beneath the selected transaction when you're entering data — you've probably already guessed as much. The More Actions button looks like a compass. Or Something.

Using either command is a snap: Just highlight the transaction you want to delete or void by using the arrow keys or by clicking the mouse. Then click the More Actions button and choose the command. And that's that.

Use the Void Transaction(s) command any time you void a check. Quicken leaves voided transactions in the register but marks them as void and erases the Payment or Deposit amount. So by using the Void Transaction(s) command, you keep a record of voided, or canceled, transactions.

Use the Delete command if you want to remove the transaction from your register.

The Big Register Phenomenon

If you start entering a bunch of checks, deposits, and transfers into your registers, you'll soon find yourself with registers that contain hundreds and even thousands of transactions. You can still work with one of these big registers by using the tools and techniques I talk about in the preceding paragraphs. Nevertheless, let me give you some more help for dealing with . . . (drumroll, please) . . . the big register phenomenon.

Moving through a big register

You can use the PgUp and PgDn keys to page up and down through your register a screenful of transactions at a time. Some people call this *scrolling*. You can call it whatever you want.

You can press Ctrl+Home to move to the first transaction in a register and Ctrl+End to move to the last transaction in a register.

You can also use the vertical scroll bar along the right edge of the Transactions tab. Click either above or below the square scroll bar marker to page back and forth through the register. Or, if you have no qualms about dragging the mouse around, you can drag the scroll bar marker up and down the scroll bar. If you drag the scroll bar marker to scroll through the register, Quicken displays a pop-up box that shows the transaction date you've scrolled to.

Finding that darn transaction

Want to find a specific check, deposit, or transfer? No problem. The Find command provides a handy way for doing just that. Here's what you do:

1. **Choose Edit⇨Find or press Ctrl+F.**

   Quicken, with restrained but obvious enthusiasm, displays the Quicken Find dialog box (shown in Figure 4-11). You use this dialog box to describe the transaction you want to find in as much detail as possible.

Figure 4-11:
The Quicken Find dialog box.

2. **Specify which pieces, or fields, of the register transaction you want Quicken to search.**

   Click the down arrow to the right of the first Find box; then in the drop-down list, select the field that Quicken should look at during the search: Amount, Cleared Status (the Clr field), Memo, Date, Check Number Category, Tag, or Payee. Or get truly crazy and pick the Any Fields list entry so that Quicken looks both high and low.

3. **Tell Quicken whether you're using a shotgun or a rifle.**

   You need to specify how closely the text or value you're searching for must match the data stored in the register. To do so, open the second Find box and select the appropriate matching rule:

   - *Contains:* Select this rule if the field or fields you're searching just need to use a piece of text. If you enter **Aunt** into the Find text box and use this matching rule to search Payee fields, Quicken finds transactions that use the following payee names: *Aunt Enid, Aunt Enid and Uncle Joob, Uncle Harry and Aunt Edna,* and — well, you get the idea.

   - *Exact:* Select this rule if the field you're searching needs to exactly match your Find text box entry. If you enter the Find text box entry as **Aunt**, for example, and you're searching Payee fields, Quicken looks for transactions where the Payee field shows *Aunt* — and nothing more and nothing less.

   - *Starts With:* Select this rule if the field you're searching for just needs to start with what you entered in the Find text box. For example, if you enter **Aunt** in the Find text box, and you're searching the Payee fields, Quicken looks for transactions where the Payee field starts with the word *Aunt* — such as *Aunt Enid* or *Aunt Enid and Uncle Joob.* (Uncle Joob and Aunt Enid wouldn't cut the mustard in this case, though.)

   - *Ends With:* Select this rule if the field you're searching for just needs to end with what you entered in the Find text box.

   - *Greater:* Select this rule if the field you're searching for needs to hold a value that exceeds the number you entered in the Find text box. This makes sense, right? Like you're looking for checks you wrote for more than $100?

   - *Greater Or Equal:* Select this rule if the field you're searching for needs to hold a value that either exceeds or equals the number you entered in the Find text box.

   - *Less:* Select this rule if the field you're searching for needs to hold a value that is less than the number you entered in the Find text box.

   - *Less Or Equal:* Select this rule if the field you're searching for needs to hold a value that is less than or equal to the number you entered in the Find text box.

4. **Enter the piece of text or number that identifies the transaction you want to locate.**

   Move the cursor to the third Find text box. Then type the text or number you want to find. By the way, the case of the text doesn't matter. If you type **aunt**, for example, Quicken finds *AUNT* or *Aunt*.

5. **Tell Quicken whether you want it to search forward or backward from the selected transaction.**

   Select the Search Backwards check box if you want to look backward starting from the selected transaction.

6. **Let the search begin.**

   You click either the Find or the Find All button to begin the search. If you click Find, Quicken looks through the register, and if it can find a transaction like you describe, it highlights the transaction.

   If you click Find All, Quicken looks through the register and builds a list of all the transactions that are like the one you describe. Then it displays the list in an expanded version of the Search Results window (shown in Figure 4-12). To edit a found transaction, select the transaction and click the Edit Transaction(s) button.

Figure 4-12:
The Search
Results
window
with a trans-
action that
matches
the search
criteria.

Quicken supplies another command that is similar to Find. The Edit menu Find/Replace command lets you both locate and modify transactions that look like the one you describe. (To use the Find/Replace command, choose Edit⇨Find & Replace⇨Find/Replace.) For example, you may want to locate transactions showing Aunt Enid as the payee so that you can replace *Aunt* with *Great Aunt.* The Find/Replace command works in a similar fashion to the Find command except that you need to describe what you want to modify in the found transactions. After you complete the initial dialog box that Quicken displays when you choose the command, Quicken displays a window list-ing the transactions it has found. (This window looks like the one shown in Figure 4-13.) You mark — by clicking — the transactions you want to modify, describe the replacement information, and then click the Replace button.

Figure 4-13:
The Find
And
Replace
dialog box.

You can use the Find/Replace command to find and replace categories, which is kind of a handy trick. For example, you may want to recategorize all your cable television payments as the Entertainment category (where earlier, you placed them in the Utilities category). To recategorize, use the Find And Replace command to search the Quicken register for the transactions you want to recategorize. Mark the transactions you're sure you want to recatego-rize. Then, click the arrow button next to the With box so that Quicken dis-plays a list of categories (see Figure 4-14) and select the category.

Figure 4-14:
The pop-up
categories
box you can
use to
recategorize.

Pop-Up Calendars and Calculators

Can I tell you just a couple more things? (If not, skip this section. If so, read on.) Quicken provides a pop-up calendar anytime you move the selection cursor to a Date field. To get to the calendar, click the button that appears at the right end of the Date field. Quicken displays a calendar for the current month (shown in Figure 4-15). All you have to do is select the day you want as the date. (If you want to see a calendar for a different month, click the << and >> buttons.)

Quicken also provides a pop-up calculator anytime you move the selection cursor to an Amount field (see Figure 4-16). To get to the calculator, click the button that appears at the right end of the Amount field.

Quicken displays a calculator like the one shown in Figure 4-16 when you choose the Tools⇨Calculator command. This baby works like a regular hand-held calculator. You just type the math you want to perform. Quicken displays the calculation result in the Amount field.

Figure 4-15:
The pop-up calendar.

Figure 4-16:
The pop-up
calculator.

Do the calculator keys make sense? Table 4-1 shows how they work.

Table 4-1   A Handyman's Guide to the Quicken Calculator Keys

Key Name	Operation
/ (slash)	Division
X	Multiplication
− (minus)	Subtraction
+ (plus)	Addition
. (period)	Indicates the decimal point
%	Indicates that the number you just typed is a percentage and should be converted to a decimal value
= (equal sign)	Calculates the amount and removes the pop-up calculator
<-	Removes, or clears, the last digit you entered
CE	Clears the last number entered into the calculator
C	Clears the Amount field
MC	Clears the calculator's memory
MR	Enters the number stored in the calculator's memory
MS	Stores the displayed value in the calculator's memory

If you type a number in the Amount field and then type any one of the math operand keys (+, –, /, *), Quicken pops open the calculator to continue the calculation. You don't have to click the calculator button first.

Attaching Flags, Notes, and Images

Quicken provides a couple of handy though easy to miss buttons inside the register window just beneath the date field: a Flag button and an Attach button. If you wouldn't mind, take a minute and see if you can find these babies. The Flag button shows a little flag. The Attach button shows a picture of a paper clip.

The Flag button, if clicked, displays the Transaction Notes and Flags dialog box which lets you append a note to a transaction, tell Quicken you want to flag the transaction in your register (by making the flag display in a different color) and, just possibly, command Quicken to display an alert message about the transaction on some specified future date.

When you click the Attach button, Quicken displays the Transaction Attachments dialog box, which you can use to attach an image of the check or some document to the transaction. You can attach images from a variety of sources, including files, scanned images, or the Clipboard.

Chapter 5

Printing 101

● ●

In This Chapter

▶ Printing a check

▶ Recovering from a mistake after you've printed the check

▶ Printing a register

● ●

I bet you can't guess what this chapter describes. Gee, you guessed it — how to print checks and reports.

Printing Checks

Printing checks in Quicken is, well, quick. All you basically need to do is enter the information you want to print on the check form and the number you want Quicken to use to identify the check. Sounds simple enough, doesn't it? It is, as you can read in the steps that follow.

To enter the information on a check form, follow these steps:

1. **Display the Write Checks window.**

   You can display the Write Checks window in a bunch of different ways. For example, you can choose the Tools⇨Write and Print Checks command. And when the Spending tab displays an account register, you can also click the Account Actions button and choose the Write Checks command. You can also use the command shortcut, Ctrl+W. Figure 5-1 shows the Write Checks: Checking window.

2. **Select the account on which you want to write the check.**

   This step is very important! To select the account you want to use, open the Write Checks From drop-down list in the top of the window. (You can do this by clicking the arrow button that's just to the right of the box.) When Quicken displays the list of accounts, choose the one you want to use.

Figure 5-1:
The Write
Checks:
Checking
window.

3. **Enter the check date.**

   First, use the mouse or Tab key to move the cursor to the Date field. Then, type the date that you're going to print the check (probably today's date). Remember to type the date in a *MM/DD/YYYY* format — enter August 31, 2012, as **8/31/2012**. You don't need to enter the year if the year number that Quicken retrieves from your computer's internal system clock is correct. You can adjust the date by a day by using + and – from the numeric keypad. You can also click the button at the end of the Date field to display your friend, the pop-up calendar.

4. **Enter the name of the person or business you're paying.**

   Move the cursor to the Pay To The Order Of field and type away. For example, to write a check to me, type **Steve Nelson**. (Feel free to do so, by the way. If you send me a check, I'll even cash it as a sort of public service.) If you've written a check to the payee before, when you start to type the name, Quicken recognizes it and fills in the rest for you.

5. **Enter the amount of the check.**

   Move the cursor to the $ text box and type the amount. (If you're sending a check to me, be sure to make the amount nominal — for sure, not more than $10 or $20. . . .) When you press the Tab key, the cursor moves down to the next field, and Quicken writes the amount in words on the line under the payee name and before the word Dollars.

6. **Enter the payee's address.**

If you plan to mail the check in a window envelope, move the cursor to the Address field. (You can do this by clicking in the field.) Then enter the name and address of the person or business you're paying.

TIP

Here's a little address entry trick: You can copy the payee name from the Pay To The Order Of text box to the first line of the Address field. Click the mouse in or select the first line of the address field. Then press the ' (apostrophe) key. Now fill in the rest of the address block, including the street number and name, city, state, and ZIP code. After you enter this, Quicken memorizes these address details for the next time you use this payee.

7. (Optional) Enter a memo description of the check.

Move the cursor to the Memo field and enter a description (such as an account number or an invoice number) of why you're sending your money to this person or business. Or, if you're sending someone a check because you didn't have time to go out and buy a real gift, type **Happy Birthday** in the Memo field. It's the little things that make a difference.

8. Enter the category.

Move the cursor to the Category field and type the category name for the expense you're paying with the check. If you don't remember the category name, scroll down the category list to find the category. Figure 5-2 shows the completed window for a check payable to Movies Galore, the local cable TV company.

Figure 5-2:
A completed
check.

![Write Checks: Checking window. Write checks from: Checking. Pay to the order of: Movies Galore. Date 8/31/2012. $ 25.50. Twenty-Five and 50/100 ************ Dollars. Bill Pay Address: Movies Galore, 123 Main Street, Pine Lake, WA 98765. Edit Address... Memo. Category: Bills & Utilities:Television. Record Check. Columns: Date, Type, Payee, Category, Amount. Row: 8/31/2012. New Check. Ending Balance: 8.66. Order Checks. Reports. Print. Done.]

You can assign a check to more than a single category by using the Split Transaction window. Using the Split Transaction window with the Write Checks window works the same way as using the Split Transaction window with the Transactions tab. (I describe using the Split Transaction window with the Transactions tab in Chapter 4.) Okay. So why do I bring this up? You use the Split Transaction window when a check pays more than one type of expense or is transferred to more than one account.

For example, if you're writing a check to pay your mortgage, with part of the check paying the actual mortgage and part of the check going into an escrow account for property taxes, you can use the Split Transaction window to describe the transaction's individual components. To split a check amount so that the amount is assigned to multiple spending categories, click the Split button (which looks like a sign for a fork in the road) or press Ctrl+S. Either way, Quicken displays the Split Transaction window for you to indicate the categories and categorized amounts that make up the check total. If you have questions about how split transactions work, refer to Chapter 4.

9. **Click the Record Check button.**

   Quicken records the check. It displays the current account balance and the ending account balance, and it even adds a Checks To Print total in the bottom of the window. If you're working with a monitor that supports a high screen resolution, you'll also see a Checks To Print window that lists all the nitty-gritty about the checks you have to print, as shown earlier in Figure 5-2. Shoot, when you're finished with one check, Quicken even scrolls the completed check off the screen and replaces it with a new, blank check that you can use to pay your next bill. It doesn't get much better than this, does it?

What if you make a mistake entering a check?

Don't worry. If you haven't yet printed the check, fixing mistakes is easy. If you press the PgUp and PgDn keys with the Write Checks window displayed, Quicken pages you through the check transactions. That way, you can display any check that you wrote — but have not yet printed — in the Write Checks window. Or, an even easier way if you've got a lot of checks is to double-click the check in the list that appears beneath the check form. (Quicken adds a check to this list when you click the Record Check button.)

With the check redisplayed, you can fix the mistake in two ways:

✔ If you incorrectly entered some bit of check information, move the cursor to the field with the incorrect data and just type over the data.

✔ If you're really mad or frustrated, you can delete the entire check by clicking the Delete button. (I should 'fess up here and suggest that you delete the check if you accidentally entered a check to me, for example.) Then you can re-enter the check — only this time, correctly.

Don't use this method to delete a check that you've already printed. To *void* a check that you've already printed, follow these steps:

1. **You must first go into the Spending tab. To display the register, you can click the Accounts bar hyperlink for the account.**

   The Accounts bar appears along the left edge of the Quicken program window.

2. **Find the check in the register, select the check, and void it by clicking the More Actions button and choosing the drop-down list's Void Transaction command.**

3. **Write something, such as** VOID, **in large letters across the face of the printed check.**

Printing a check you've entered

Printing checks is easy. Here's what you need to do:

1. **Load the checks into your printer.**

   You do so the same way you load any other paper into your printer. If you have questions about it, refer to your printer documentation. (Sorry I can't help more on this process, but with a million different printers on the market, I can't guess which one you have.)

2. **Click the Print button in the top of the Write Checks window and then choose the Checks command on the menu Quicken displays (or choose File⇨Print Checks or press Ctrl+P).**

   Quicken displays the Select Checks To Print: Checking dialog box, shown in Figure 5-3. At the top of the dialog box, Quicken shows how many checks you have to print and the total dollar amount for those checks.

3. **Enter the first check number.**

   Move the cursor to the First Check Number text box and type the number printed on the first check form you'll print. Figure 5-3 shows 1001, for example, so the first check form is numbered 1001. To quickly increase or decrease the check numbers, use + or – on the numeric keypad.

Figure 5-3:
The Select
Checks
To Print:
Checking
dialog box.

4. **Indicate which checks Quicken should print by selecting one of these options:**

   • *All Checks:* Select this option button if you want Quicken to print all the checks you've entered by using the Write Checks window, which is the usual case. (If you select this option, skip to Step 6.)

   • *Checks Dated Through:* Select this option button if you want to print all the checks through a certain date; then type that date in the text box. (If you select this option, skip to Step 6.)

   • *Selected Checks:* Select this option button if you want to pick and choose which checks to print.

5. **If you say that you want to select which checks to print, click the Choose button.**

   Quicken, with some annoyance, displays the Select Checks To Print window, shown in Figure 5-4. Initially, Quicken marks all the checks dated on or earlier than the current date by placing a check mark in the Print column. If you don't want to print a check, either leave the Print field for that check clear (unchecked) or click in the field to remove the check mark. When only the checks you want to print are marked to be printed, click Done to continue with this crazy little thing called check printing. Quicken, happy with your progress, redisplays the Select Checks To Print: Checking dialog box (refer to Figure 5-3).

Figure 5-4:
The Select
Checks To
Print win-
dow.

Select Checks to Print

Print	Date	Payee	Category	Amount
☑	8/31/2012	Movies Galore	Bills & Utilities:Television	25.50

Mark All   Clear All

Done

6. **Indicate which Quicken check form you're using.**

   Move the cursor to the Check Style drop-down list box, click the arrow
   so that the list drops down, and then select the check form you purchased: standard, voucher, or wallet checks.

7. **Tell Quicken if you're printing a partial page.**

   If you're printing a partial page, use the Checks On First Page option buttons to indicate the number of check forms on the partial page. Select
   the Three option button if you have three checks, the Two option button
   if you have two checks, or the One option button if you have one check.

8. **Indicate whether you want extra copies of the check form.**

   To do so, type the number of copies you want in the Additional Copies
   text box. (This text box appears only if you're set up for the voucher
   check style.)

   If you use Quicken for business to keep accounts payable files, make
   copies of checks to attach to the invoices that the checks pay. Then
   if a vendor calls later, starts hassling you, and asks which check paid
   an invoice, you can easily check your accounts payable files, quickly
   answer that question, and basically cover your *derrière*.

9. **Click OK and let the games begin.**

   If you're using a partial starting page of forms, your printer may prompt
   you to feed the first page of forms manually. When it finishes, Quicken
   asks whether it printed your checks correctly (as shown in Figure 5-5).

Figure 5-5:
The Did
Check(s)
Print OK?
dialog box.

Did Check(s) Print OK?

If checks 1001 through 1001 printed correctly, click OK
to continue. Otherwise, type the number of the first check
which printed incorrectly and then click OK.

First Incorrectly Printed Check: [   ]

OK   Help

10. **If the checks printed correctly, click OK. You're done. If the checks didn't print correctly, enter the number of the first check that printed incorrectly and click OK; then repeat Steps 3–9.**

11. **Sign the printed checks.**

    Then — and I guess you probably don't need my help here — put the checks in the mail.

What if you discover a mistake after you print the check?

This problem isn't as big as you may think.

If you've already mailed the check, you can't do a whole lot. You can try to get the check back (if the person you paid hasn't cashed it) and replace it with the correct check. (Good luck on this one.)

If the person has cashed the check, you can't get the check back. If you overpaid the person by writing the check for too much, you need to get the person to pay you the overpayment amount. If you underpaid the person, you need to write another check for the amount of the underpayment.

If you printed the check but haven't mailed it, void the printed check. First, write **VOID** in large letters — in ink — across the face of the check form. (Use a ballpoint pen if you're using multi-part forms so that the second and third parts also show as VOID.) Second, click on the Register tab, highlight the check, click the More Actions button, and then choose the Void Transaction command. (This option marks the check as one that has been voided in the system so that Quicken doesn't use the voided check in calculating your account balance.)

A few words about check printing

Check printing is kind of complicated at first, isn't it?

For the record, I'm with you on this one. But you'll find that printing checks does get easier after the first few times.

Pretty soon, you'll be running instead of walking through the steps. Pretty soon, you'll just skate around things like check-form alignment problems. Pretty soon, you'll know all this stuff and never have to read "pretty soon" again.

Oh, where, oh, where, do the unprinted checks go?

The register stores *unprinted checks* — those you've entered by using the Write Checks: Checking window but haven't yet printed. To identify them as unprinted checks, Quicken sets their check numbers as Print. After you tell Quicken to print the unprinted checks, Quicken prints the checks in your register that have **Print** in the check number field and replaces the word Print with the actual check number.

This information is of little practical value in most instances, but it results in several interesting possibilities. For example, you can enter the checks you want to print directly into the

register — all you need to do is enter the check number as **Print**. (Notice that you can't enter an address anywhere in the register, so this process isn't practical if you enter addresses that will be printed on your checks.) You also can cause a check you've printed once to print again by changing its check number from, say, **007** to **Print**. I can't think of many good reasons why you would want to change a check number. The only one I can think of is that you accidentally printed a check on plain paper and want to reprint it on a real check form.

Printing a Check Register

You can print a check register or a register for any other account. To print a register, follow these magic steps:

1. **Display the register by clicking the Accounts bar hyperlink for the account.**

2. **Click the Account Actions button to display its Account Actions menu, and then choose Print Transactions.**

   Quicken displays the Print Register dialog box, shown in Figure 5-6.

Figure 5-6: The Print Register dialog box.

3. **(Optional) Customize the printed register.**

   You can use the Print Register dialog box to give the printed register a title (just enter something into the Printed Title box) and to specify the range of transactions. If you check the Print Split Transactions box, Quicken prints the details of split transaction data.

4. Print the register.

Click the Print Register dialog box's Print button. Quicken displays the Print dialog box, shown in Figure 5-7. You don't have to fool around with this dialog box. If you want to print a register pronto, just click OK. Then again, if you're the sort of person who likes to fool around with this kind of stuff, carry on with the rest of these steps.

Figure 5-7:
The Print dialog box.

5. (Optional) Export the report to disk if you want.

To print the report to disk as a text file, select one of the following options in the Export To drop-down list:

- *Text File* if you want to create a text file, such as when you want to import the register into a word-processing program.

- *Tab-Delimited (Excel Compatible) Disk File,* such as when you want to import the register into a database program. (Oooh . . . fancy. . . .)

- *123 (.PRN) Disk File,* such as when you want to import the register into Lotus 1-2-3 or any spreadsheet program that will open 1-2-3 files (which, basically, means any spreadsheet program, including Microsoft Excel).

If you do indicate that you want a disk file, after you click the Export button to start the ol' exporting process, Quicken displays the Create Disk File dialog box (not shown). This dialog box asks for the filename that Quicken should create as part of printing the file to disk and asks where you want to store the file. Just enter the filename you want in — you guessed it — the File Name text box. (Use a valid filename, of course.) Use the Save In text box to indicate where you want to store the file. And what do you do with the disk file? You're on your own here. . . .

6. **(Optional) Tell Quicken which pages to print.**

   Use the Print Range option buttons and text boxes to limit the pages Quicken prints (refer to Figure 5-7). How? Select the Pages option button and then type the range of page numbers you want to print. That's simple enough, right?

7. **(Optional) Color your world.**

   If you have a color printer and want to print your register in color, select the Print In Color check box in the Print dialog box (refer to Figure 5-7).

8. **(Optional) Trade speed for quality.**

   Or you can select the Print In Draft Mode check box to tell Quicken it should print faster and spend less time worrying about the quality of the printing job (refer to Figure 5-7). In other words, you can use this check box to trade print quality for print speed. Life is full of trade-offs, isn't it?

9. **(Optional) Tell Quicken to scrunch the information so that it fits across the page.**

   Click in the Fit To One Page Wide check box to tell Quicken that you want its register information to fit across the width of the page (refer to Figure 5-7).

10. **Click OK.**

    Quicken finally prints the register. I'm not going to show a printed copy of the register here. All it is, really, is just a printed copy of the same account detail information you see on the Transactions tab.

Should you save a printed copy of your register?

Here's a question for you: Should you save a printed copy of your register? I don't know. The case for printing a copy of your register and then having it handy in case, well, just in case, is this: If your computer goes haywire and you need to re-enter your transactions or you need a hard-copy record of your transactions and for some reason don't have access to Quicken, having a printed register will make things much easier for you. You know what, though? I think that most people, if they religiously back up their Quicken data files (something I describe in Chapter 9), don't really need to print copies of their registers.

Now, I should say that if you're someone who likes to keep meticulous records of your income and spending, and you always double-check to make sure that you haven't left the iron on or even plugged in whenever you leave your house, you could print a copy of the register. And what I would suggest is that you print a copy of the register at the end of the year and then file this report away with your tax return.

By the way, I've been using Quicken since 1988 and have never needed a printed copy of my register. I've made frequent use of other reports. But never have I needed a hard, paper copy of my register. Anytime I have had a question, I've simply looked through the online version of my current register or archived files from previous years.

Chapter 6

Online and In Charge

● ●

● ●

Many banks now offer electronic banking services in a big, big way. This is a step toward providing a pretty impressive variety of online services to the general consumer (you and me). This chapter covers the Quicken electronic banking services: Online Account Access and Online Bill Payment.

What Are Online Account Access and Online Bill Payment?

I'm going to start with the basics — a definition of these two services.

Online services means that you can connect your computer to your bank's computer electronically through your Internet connection. You may think that doing so sounds scary, but Online Account Access and Online Bill Payment provide some very neat benefits:

✔ With **Online Bill Payment,** you can tell your bank or (in a pinch) the Intuit online financial services unit to make payments to specific individuals or businesses. In other words, rather than providing all this information in the usual way (on checks), you send the same information — the payees' names, their addresses, the amounts, and so on — and then the bank writes the checks. You can tell the bank to make automatic recurring payments for bills that you pay on a regular basis, such as a rent or mortgage payment. You can use Online Bill Payment at any bank.

✔ With **Online Account Access,** you can get transaction information — such as information about which checks and deposits cleared your account and what bank service fees you've been charged — from the bank's computer. You can also transfer money between accounts — such as from your savings account to your checking account and from your checking account to your credit card account (to pay a credit card bill). To use Quicken for Online Account Access, your bank must support the Quicken Online Account Access service.

Wise Whys and Wherefores

Neither Online Account Access nor Online Bill Payment is difficult to use. And despite the nightmares that people with delusional paranoia may develop about electronic banking, the service is safe, secure, and very solid. Nevertheless, before you, too, jump onto the Online Account Access and Online Bill Payment bandwagon, you should probably consider a few points:

✔ As I note in the preceding section, if you want to use the Online Account Access feature, your bank must be a part of the Quicken Online Account Access program. (See the next section for details on how to find out whether your bank qualifies.)

✔ To sign up for and use Online Account Access or Online Bill Payment services, you need an Internet connection.

✔ You should be fairly comfortable with Quicken, especially with account transactions and transferring money between accounts. (Therefore, if you're new to Quicken, you should at least record a handful of checks, make some deposits, and reconcile your account before venturing into Online Account Access. This ramping up of your Quicken skills should take, oh, I don't know, about two weeks.)

✔ Make sure that your records are completely up to date and reconciled with the last statements you received from the bank.

This stuff usually ain't free. I can't tell you how much these two services will cost because your bank sets the charges. A good guess is $10 to $20 per month — and that adds up over the course of a year. But in choosing to use Online Account Access or Online Bill Payment, do consider all the hidden costs of the normal way of banking and paying bills. Gasoline, time, and postage can all add up, and these almost hidden costs may make the costs of the online services appear more reasonable. (Besides, you won't have to deal with all that nasty glue on your tongue from licking envelopes.)

Banking with Online Account Access and Online Bill Payment

To begin using either the Online Account Access or the Online Bill Payment service, you have to sign up. If you want to use Online Account Access, you sign up with your bank. Just visit your bank's website or call your local branch and ask someone whether the bank supports Online Account Access with Quicken. (If your bank doesn't support Online Account Access, you can still sign up with Intuit for Online Bill Payment — choose Tools⇨Quicken Bill Pay⇨Learn About Quicken Bill Pay for details.) Then do whatever the folks at the bank tell you to do to sign up. You'll probably have to fill out an application, agree to pay some extra fees, and then wait a few days for a customer identification number and a *PIN,* or personal identification number.

After the bank does its preparation and sends you its welcome letter, you can set up Quicken for Online Account Access. To set up Quicken to use Online Account Access or Online Bill Payment services, display the account for which you want to activate online services. You can do this, for example, by following these steps:

1. **Click the account's hyperlink on the Accounts bar.**

2. **Tell Quicken you want to set up online banking or bill payment.**

   Click the Account Actions button and choose the Set Up Online command, shown in Figure 6-1. Quicken may display an Account Setup dialog box that asks which version of your bank's online banking service you're already set up to use. If you see this question, select the online banking service that corresponds with what you've set up. Then click Next.

3. **Identify yourself.**

   When Quicken displays the Quicken Account Setup dialog box that asks for your login information, supply your customer identification number and PIN.

Let me say a couple of more quick things about setting up Online Account Access or Online Bill Payment. Your bank or the Quicken folks may, as part of the application process, send you a letter asking for more information, a canceled check, or a signature. (If they do, of course, be sure to respond.)

Using Online Account Access and Online Bill Payment is extremely easy. You pay bills in pretty much the usual manner. You make account transfers in the same manner. And then you reconcile transactions with a mouse click.

Finding an online bank — online

You can determine which banks support Online Account Access by using
your Internet connection. To do so, start your web browser and then enter
the following web address into the browser's address box:

```
https://quickenonline.intuit.com/quickenweb/external/
              fi-select.jsf
```

Paying bills

You have three ways to record online payments. If you're comfortable using
the Write Checks window, you write a check in the usual way. You enter the
payee name, an amount, probably a category, and so on. Just make sure that
you select the Online Payment check box. The Online Payment check box
appears in the lower-right corner of the on-screen check form.

Honest Steve's evaluation of online services

I hate making financial record keeping more complicated. I like things simple. But all that said, I think Online Bill Payment and, in particular, Online Account Access are slick.

If you're using Quicken to keep your financial records, you get to pay your bills and reconcile your bank accounts for basically no extra work. Well, okay, you have to click your mouse an extra time. And initially, you need to provide addresses and account numbers for your payees (which takes about five minutes). So you do have to do a little extra work at the beginning. But Online Account Access saves you time and hassle when it comes to bill paying and banking.

The only catch — and this is a big one for some Quicken users — is that to use Online Account Access, your bank needs to have its act together. (Note that if your bank doesn't support Online Account Access with Quicken, you can still use Online Bill Payment by signing up for online payment with Intuit, as detailed at the Quicken.com website.)

Now, all that said, I want to close with two caveats. Here's the first one: Online Account Access isn't worth it if it means you end up banking at some poorly run bank. I, er, well, yeah, you see, I've been there. And it isn't pretty. To make a long, sorry story short, a long time ago, I had the experience of moving my banking from a well-run bank that didn't have Online Account Access to a poorly managed bank that did. Online Account Access is not — I repeat, is not — such a cool tool that you'll be happy banking at First National Idiots.

And now a second caveat: I have to tell you that online payments aren't, in my experience, as reliable as writing a regular check and then sending that check through the mail. I don't know why this is. But it's been my experience that online payments more frequently get lost, and they sometimes get delayed. I've been using online banking and bill payment for several years now, and a time or two a year, people or businesses call and say, "Dude, we never got your payment" or, "Dude, we got your check late — you owe us a late fee." In comparison, my experience is that the U.S. Postal Service almost never loses my mailed payments.

If you have questions about how the Write Checks window works, Chapter 5 shows you — among other things — how to use the Write Checks window to describe checks you want to print. You use the same basic procedure to describe online payments that you want to make.

If you're more comfortable using the register to record payments, you can make online payments with that, too. In the Num column, just specify the payment number as **Send**.

If you have questions about how the register works, you may want to read Chapter 4. Chapter 4 describes — in some detail, I might add — how the Quicken register works.

By the way, the first time you make an online payment to someone, Quicken asks for some information in the Set Up Online Payee dialog box: where the person lives or where the business is located, and what account number Quicken can use to identify the person or business. You can also describe online payees by choosing Tools➪Online Payee List, which displays a list of online payees. Then click the New button, which displays the Set Up Online Payee dialog box.

After you record a payment, you send it to the bank. To do so, choose the Tools➪One Step Update command.

Quicken connects, through the Internet, to your bank's computer. As part of making this connection, you need to provide a PIN. When Quicken finishes sending your payment instructions to your bank, it displays a summary that basically says you've connected to the bank's computer and sent it some payment instructions. At this point, you're done.

Note: The first time that you use Online Account Access, Quicken asks you to change your PIN.

Note: You can have Quicken regularly update your account information. To do this, choose the Tools➪Schedule Updates command and follow the on-screen instructions.

I need to make an important point here. You must send your payment instructions to the bank several days in advance of the time the bill needs to be paid. For obvious reasons, the bank needs a day or two to process the bill. And then the check probably has to go through the U.S. Postal Service. (I say "probably" in the preceding sentence because only a few payments get made electronically.)

Transferring money between accounts

As you may expect, you record Online Account Access transfers the same way that you record regular transfers — or at least in almost the same way. For online transfers, you can use the register in the normal way, but you need to specify that the transaction is an online transfer. You do this by activating the Num drop-down list box and selecting the Online Transfer entry.

If you have a credit card with a bank that supports Online Account Access and if you also set up the credit card for Online Account Access, you can pay your credit card bill by transferring money from a bank account to your credit card account. You probably already thought of this if you have a credit card account. But I thought I'd mention it anyway. (For more information about credit card accounts, refer to Chapter 11.)

Are you still with me?

Okay, I'm going to take a little breather here — just to make sure that you understand what's going on. When you boil everything down to its essence, online payments are really just payment instructions you send to your bank. And when you make an online transfer, you are effectively just calling the bank and saying, "Please transfer money from one account to that other account."

This makes sense, right? You're really just giving instructions to the bank. And then the bank (or actually the bank's computer) goes off and does whatever you've told it to do. It's pretty simple.

Is Online Account Access anything to get all excited about? Is it really as slick as some people think? I think so. Sure, it's not always cheap. But after you get going, you get away from that business of finding your checkbook, signing checks, finding stamps, and then, on occasion, running down to the post office to drop off some overdue bill.

Updating your Quicken accounts

One major advantage of Online Account Access is that you can get the most up-to-date information regarding your accounts. Let me explain: When you use the Tools menu's One Step Update or Schedule Updates command, your bank automatically sends current transactions to your computer. If Quicken can match the bank's records with your records, no problem. Everything is fine.

If Quicken can't match the bank records with your records, however, it lists the mystery transactions on the Downloaded Transactions tab of the account register window. You then examine them before they go into your records. You can add downloaded transactions from the bank's list to your register by clicking the transaction and then the Add to Register button.

By regularly downloading transactions into your online accounts and matching transactions between your Quicken records and the bank's records, you make reconciling your bank accounts a snap. In effect, by downloading and matching transactions, you get information about checks and debit card transactions that you've forgotten to record much earlier (because you don't have to wait until the end of the month). Note, however, that you should still reconcile your account in the usual way (described in Chapter 8).

Chapter 7

Reports, Charts, and Other Cool Tools

. . . .

In This Chapter

▶ Printing Quicken reports

▶ Using the Reports menu commands

▶ QuickZooming report totals

▶ Sharing information with a spreadsheet

▶ Editing and rearranging report information

▶ Creating a chart

▶ Using QuickReports

. . . .

Quicken enables you to summarize, slice, and dice register and account information in a variety of ways. This chapter describes how to use reports and produce graphs easily. This stuff is much easier to understand if you know how to print a transaction list first (a trick I describe at the end of Chapter 5).

Creating and Printing Reports

After you know how to print checks and transaction lists, all other printing in Quicken is easy, easy, easy.

Printing the facts, and nothing but the facts

The transactions you enter in the transaction list window or a transaction form and the checks you enter in the Write Checks window determine the information in a report. To print a report, just choose the Reports menu and tell Quicken which report you want to print.

Quicken produces a bunch of different reports. To make sense of what may otherwise become mass confusion, Quicken arranges all its reports into groups: Banking, Comparison, Investing (available when you've set up investment accounts), Net Worth & Balances, Spending, Tax, Rental Property (if you're using Quicken Rental Property Manager), and Business (if you're using Quicken Home & Business).

To see the reports in one of these groups, click the Reports command and then select the report group from the Reports menu. As you may know, those little triangles to the right of menu commands tell you that another menu follows.

Figure 7-1 shows the Banking group of reports. Pretty exciting stuff so far, don't you think?

To create a Cash Flow report (or any other report, for that matter) on the fly, choose the report on the appropriate menu. For example, to create the Cash Flow report, choose the Reports➪Banking➪Cash Flow command. Quicken then creates the report, placing it in a newly opened window. Figure 7-2, for example, shows the Cash Flow report. After you create a report, you can change the report date or date range by using the boxes at the top of the report.

Figure 7-1:
The Banking group of reports.

To find out what type of information a report includes before you create the report or to preview a report, choose Reports➪Reports & Graphs Center. This displays the Reports And Graphs window, shown in Figure 7-3. Select a report group by clicking a topic on the left side, and then select the report with the report group that you want to create. (In Figure 7-3, the Spending report group is selected and therefore shown. Within the Spending report group, the Spending By Category report is selected and therefore shown.)

Figure 7-2:
The Cash Flow in a report window.

Figure 7-3:
The Reports And Graphs window.

You can change the report date or date range by using the box(es) provided. Click the Show Report button to create the report. If you don't enter a new range of dates, Quicken assumes that you want to include transactions from the start of the current calendar year through the present date.

Reports that show account balances — such as the Account Balances report, the Net Worth report, the Balance Sheet report, or the Portfolio Value report — don't need a range of dates because these reports show account balances as of a specific date. In these cases, if you don't enter a date, Quicken assumes that you want account balances for the current system date from your computer's internal clock.

You can't see the entire on-screen version of a report unless your report is very small (or your screen is monstrously large). Press the PgUp and PgDn keys to scroll up and down and use Tab and Shift+Tab to move right and left. Or if you're a mouse lover, you can click and drag various pieces of the scroll bars.

To print the report Quicken shows, follow these steps:

1. **Click the Print button.**

   Quicken displays the Print dialog box (see Figure 7-4).

Figure 7-4:
The Print
dialog box.

2. **To accept the given specifications — which are almost always fine — just click Print.**

   You'll never guess what happens next: Quicken prints the report!

3. **(Optional) To modify the default printing suggestions, use the option buttons and text boxes in the Print dialog box to mix it up a bit and then click Print:**

   - *Print To:* The Print To option buttons let you tell Quicken where it should send the report it produces: to the printer or to a disk file. If you choose to print it to a file, Quicken displays another dialog box you use to specify where the print file should be located and what the print file should be named. (I describe how this print-to-file option works in Chapter 5, so I won't repeat the discussion here. If you want the scoop, refer to the section about printing a check register.)

   - *Print Range:* Printing a long report? Consider using the Print Range option buttons and text box to specify that you want to print only a specified range of pages. As you might guess (if you're a clever person), select the Pages option button and then specify the individual pages (separating each page by a comma) or the range of pages (separating the start and end page range with a hyphen). For example, the following page-range specification says, "Hey, Quicken, print pages 1, 4, and 5 and, oh shoot, I don't know, maybe the page range 34 through 41 as well." For this, you would type the following:

     1, 4, 5, 34–41

   - *Copies:* As you probably guessed, use the Number Of Copies text box to tell Quicken to print multiple copies of a report.

   - *Page Scaling:* For some reports — although not all — you can use the Page Scaling option buttons and text boxes to tell Quicken that it should try to squish the report onto a smaller number of pages. Ever the thoughtful software program, Quicken provides two squishing methods. You can select the Page Scaling Adjust To option button and then enter a squishing percentage. Or you can select the Page Scaling Fit To option button and then specify the report size as a certain number of pages wide by a certain number of pages tall.

   - *Print What:* The Print What check boxes let you flip-flop between printing a graph and printing a report of the Quicken data you've said you want to see a report on. The easiest way to see what this report option does is to select and deselect.

- *Orientation:* The Orientation option buttons allow you to specify how Quicken prints a report on pages: vertically (Portrait) or horizontally (Landscape). Again, if you're confused about this option, experiment by selecting the different buttons.

  Note: When you click a Print dialog box button or enter some value in a Print dialog box field, Quicken redraws the Preview box to show you what the report looks like with your new specification.

- *Ink Color:* If you use a color printer, Quicken provides Ink Color option buttons, which let you choose whether you want to print the report in expensive colored ink, in cheap black ink, or in shades of gray so that you can go all *film noire* about your finances.

- *Fonts:* The two Change Font buttons let you customize the look of your report by changing the font settings (point size, font, style, and so on) of the text used for your report's header text and body text. I feel kind of like a broken record saying this, but, dude, seriously — the way to most easily figure out what these options do is simply to experiment. You can't foul up or corrupt your Quicken data by fiddle-faddling with the Print dialog box settings. And this is true even if you do something truly visually outrageous.

- *Adjust Margins:* Click the Adjust Margins button to add margin-setting boxes to the Preview area in the Print dialog box. After Quicken adds these margin-setting boxes, you can change the printed report's margins by changing the margin settings.

Reviewing standard reports

Tables 7-1 through 7-8 describe the Quicken reports by group. (Some of these babies won't make sense unless you understand how to collect the information that goes into the report, as I describe in Chapters 13, 14, 15, and 16.)

Table 7-1	Quicken Banking Reports
Report	*Description*
Banking Summary	Summarizes spending totals by category.
Cash Flow	Summarizes the money that flows into and out of an account by income and expense categories and by transfers. Cash is king, dude, so this report includes only those transactions that you record in your bank, cash, and credit card accounts.

Report	Description
Cash Flow By Tag	Summarizes the money that flows into and out of an account not only by income and expense categories and by transfers, but, get this — also by tags. Perfect for the active real estate investor.
Missing Checks	Lists all the checks you've written and flags any gaps in the check number sequence. This report helps you identify missing checks.
Reconciliation	Summarizes an account reconciliation that you've performed. You don't need this report, really, unless you have a clinical anxiety disorder and need to prove to yourself or your accountant that you really did reconcile your account.
Transaction	Lets you list transactions in multiple accounts chronologically.

Table 7-2	Quicken Comparison Reports
Report	**Description**
Current Spending Vs. Average Spending By Category	Summarizes spending by category and compares category totals to the average category total over the last six months.
Current Spending Vs. Average Spending By Payee	Summarizes spending by payee and compares payee totals with the average payee total over the last six months.
Cash Flow Comparison	Lets you compare category totals from two periods. You can use this report to compare January's activity with February's activity, for example. *Remember:* Because you're comparing two periods, you need to enter two transaction date ranges.
Income And Expense Comparison By Category	Summarizes spending totals by category for two time periods.
Income And Expense Comparison By Payee	Summarizes spending totals by payee for two time periods.
Profit and Loss Comparison	Compares one period's income and expense with a previous period's income and expense. Note that this report only appears after you unlock the Business Tools features of Quicken.

Table 7-3	Quicken Investing Reports
Report	*Description*
Capital Gains	Lists all the realized gains on individual investments you hold. (A *capital gain* occurs when an investment is worth more than you paid for it. When you sell the investment, you realize the gain.)
Investing Activity	Shows investment transactions grouped by activity.
Investment Asset Allocation	Shows investments by asset class.
Investment Income	Summarizes income and expense categories for the transactions you record in your investment accounts.
Investment Performance	A power user report. This report calculates the internal rates of return delivered by each of the individual investments in your portfolio.
Investment Transactions	Lists recorded transactions for all your investment accounts.
Maturity Dates for Bonds and CDs	Produces a report that lists your bonds and certificates of deposit by maturity or redemption date.
Portfolio Value	Lists the current value of all securities in your investment accounts.
Portfolio Value & Cost Basis	Lists the current value and cost of all securities in your investment accounts.

Table 7-4	Quicken Net Worth & Balances Reports
Report	*Description*
Account Balances	Lists all accounts, their balances, and the difference between the sum of the asset accounts and the sum of the liabilities accounts, which the report identifies as your *net worth*.
Net Worth	Lists all accounts and their balances.

Table 7-5	Quicken Spending Reports
Report	*Description*
Itemized Categories	Lists transactions by category.
Itemized Payees	Lists transactions by payee.
Itemized Tags	Lists transactions by tags.

Report	Description
Spending By Category	Graphs spending and lists transactions by category.
Spending By Payee	Graphs spending and lists transactions by payee.
Current Spending Vs. Average Spending By Category	Summarizes spending by category and compares category totals with the average category total over the last six months.
Current Spending Vs. Average Spending By Payee	Summarizes spending by payee and compares payee totals with the average payee total over the last six months.
Income And Expense By Category	Summarizes income and spending by category.
Income And Expense By Payee	Summarizes income and spending by payee.
Budget	Summarizes income and expense categories and compares actual category totals for the year to budgeted category amounts. This report includes only transactions that you record in your bank, cash, and credit card accounts. (For this report to work, of course, you need to have a budget set up.)
Monthly Budget	Summarizes income and expense categories and compares monthly actual category totals to monthly budgeted category amounts. This report includes only transactions that you record in your bank, cash, and credit card accounts. (For this report to work, of course, you need to have a budget set up.)

Table 7-6	Quicken Tax Reports
Report	**Description**
Capital Gains	Lists all the realized gains on individual investments you hold. (A *capital gain* occurs when an investment is worth more than you paid for it. When you sell the investment, you realize the gain.)
Schedule A-Itemized Deductions	Lists and summarizes transactions that probably belong on your Schedule A tax form as itemized deductions: mortgage interest, property taxes, charitable contributions, and so on.
Schedule B-Interest And Dividends	Lists and summarizes interest and dividend income transactions that need to be reported on your Schedule B tax form.

(continued)

Table 7-6 *(continued)*

Report	Description
Schedule D-Capital Gains And Losses	Lists and summarizes capital gain and loss transactions that need to be reported on your Schedule D tax form.
Tax Schedule	Lists all transactions you've entered as tax-related and subtotals them by line item.
Tax Summary	Lists all transactions you've described as falling into tax-related categories.

Table 7-7   Quicken Rental Property Reports

Report	Description
Schedule E	Displays profit and loss data by property, which is what you need to complete the Schedule E tax form.
Cash Flow	Summarizes rental property cash income and cash expenses for a specified time period.
Cash Flow Comparison	Compares rental property category totals from two periods.
Tax Schedule	Shows all the individual transactions for each rental property income amount and deduction amount reported on your Schedule E tax form.

Table 7-8   Quicken Business Reports

Report	Description
Accounts Payable	Summarizes the vendor bills you've recorded but not yet paid.
Accounts Receivable	Summarizes unpaid customer invoices.
Balance Sheet	Reports on account balances at a point in time. If you've set up all your business assets and liabilities in Quicken, this account balances report works as a business balance sheet.
Cash Flow	Summarizes the money flowing into and out of business accounts by income and expense categories and by account transfers.

Report	Description
Cash Flow Comparison	Compares cash flows by category totals from two periods.
Missing Checks	Lists all the business checks you've written and flags any gaps in the check number sequence.
Payroll	Summarizes transactions that use *payroll* in the category name.
Profit And Loss Comparison	Compares one period's income and expense with a previous period's income and expense.
Profit And Loss Statement	Summarizes a business's revenues and expenses for a particular period of time.
Project/Job By Business Tag	Shows income and expenses by business tag.
Project/Job By Project	Shows income and expenses by job or project.
Schedule C - Profit or Loss from Business	Displays profit and loss data by business, which is what you need to complete the Schedule C tax form(s).
Tax Schedule	Shows all the individual transactions for each business income amount and deduction amount reported on your Schedule C tax form.

Finding the report you want

Okay, if you've read or even skimmed the reports I describe in Tables 7-1 through 7-8, you're probably a little overwhelmed. Quicken produces a bunch of different reports. How do you know which one provides the answers you want? What are you supposed to do? Sift your way through three dozen of these babies?

Thankfully, the answer is no. Quicken also provides something called EasyAnswer reports. In effect, EasyAnswer reports let you identify the question that you want a report to answer. After you identify the question, Quicken produces the appropriate report. Here's how this all works:

1. **Choose the Reports⇨EasyAnswer command**

   The Reports And Graphs Center command appears on the Reports menu.

2. **Select the EasyAnswer report category in the Reports And Graphs window.**

3. **Indicate your question.**

   To tell Quicken what your question is, click one of the questions, and then use the drop-down list boxes that accompany each question to further refine your question. For example, the "Where did I spend my money during the period…?" question lets you pick the period of time you're asking about: Last Year, Last Month, Current Year, Month to Date, and so on.

4. **Click Show Report.**

   Quicken produces a report that answers your questions. For example, if you ask, "Where did I spend my money last year?" Quicken produces a Cash Flow report that summarizes the previous year's income and expenses by category.

Going to the printing dog-and-pony show

You can do some neat things with the reports you create. I won't spend a bunch of time talking about these things, but I do want to give you a quick rundown of some of the most valuable tricks.

Got a question about a number? Just zoom it

If you don't understand where a number in a report came from, point to it with the mouse. When you point to numbers, Quicken changes the mouse pointer to a magnifying glass marked with a +. Double-click the mouse, and Quicken displays a list of all the transactions that make up that number.

This feature, known as QuickZoom, is extremely handy for understanding the figures that appear on your reports. If you had printed a report that summarized spending by payee and then had a question about the payments made to Movies Galore, the cable company, you could double-click the Movies Galore number in the Spending By Payee report, for example, and Quicken would display the report, like the one shown in Figure 7-5.

Ah, yes. Two cable TV bills. And you're not even buying the premium channels package. Yikes.

See a problem? Fix it

You can sometimes fix erroneous report data right in a report window. If you select a report transaction and Quicken enables the Edit button (shown in the upper-left corner of the report window), you can click the button to display an Edit menu. The menu lists editing commands you can use to delete the selected transaction or to change the category, payee, or memo information.

Figure 7-5:
The report
you get
after drilling
down deep
into the
data.

Got a question about register transactions? Use a mini-report

If you're looking at the Quicken register and you select either the Payee or Category field, Quicken adds a mini-report button to the end of the field. (The actual mini-report button looks like a small piece of paper.) If you click the mini-report button, Quicken creates a small report that summarizes the transactions falling into the same category or transactions with the same payee, as shown in Figure 7-6.

If you click the Show Report button, which appears in the mini-report window, Quicken creates a transaction report for the same information shown in the mini-report.

Sharing report data with spreadsheets

If you use Microsoft Excel, you can export the report to the spreadsheet program. Just click the Export This Report To One Of The Formats button and choose the Report To Excel Compatible Format option. Quicken displays a dialog box you use to name and locate a tab-delimited text file. (Any spreadsheet program worth its salt can open a tab-delimited text file.) You may need to use this feature if you want to use a spreadsheet to analyze the report data.

You can also copy the stuff that shows in a report window to the Clipboard. Just click the Export This Report To One Of The Formats button and choose the Copy Report To Clipboard command. Then, to use the copied report, start your spreadsheet (or other) program and choose Edit➪Paste to paste the stuff from the Clipboard. This process really isn't very hard, so go ahead and try it.

Figure 7-6:
The
mini-report
report.

Sharing report data in PDF files

You can create a PDF version of the report. To do this, click the Export This Report To One Of The Formats button and choose the Export To PDF Format option. Quicken displays a dialog box that you use to name and locate the PDF file it will momentarily create. A *PDF file* of the report is an electronic version of the report.

Editing and rearranging reports

You may notice that when Quicken displays the report window, it also displays rows of buttons, including Delete, Export Data, Preferences, Back, Forward, History, Print, Save Report, Find & Replace, and Customize (refer to Figure 7-2). Also appearing are the Date Range and the Subtotal By drop-down list boxes. Earlier in the chapter, in "Printing the facts, and nothing but the facts," I talk about what the Date Range drop-down list box does. So in the interest of fair play, I briefly discuss what the other buttons do. (Not all these buttons are available in every report document window. And sometimes Quicken uses different names to refer to them. I don't know why, really. Maybe it's just to keep you guessing.)

Customizing your reports

If you want to extract some financial tidbit, you can usually get what you want from one of the reports listed on the Reports menu, especially if you use the EasyAnswer feature to find the right report!

I should tell you something: Quicken is remarkably sophisticated in its reporting. You can customize any report you see on the Reports menu.

To customize these reports, click the Customize button to get to the nuts and bolts of your selected report.

I'm not going to describe the customization process. I feel kind of bad about this omission because a few people are probably out there who, late one night, will decide that they want to know how to filter, sort, and customize. Of course, there are also people who will decide late some night that they want to know how to replace the transmission on a 1971 Triumph Spitfire. And I'm not describing that here, either.

If you really want to customize your reports, just noodle around. You can't hurt anything.

If you do play around with these items, you can save any custom report specifications that you create. To do so, click the Save Report button at the top of the report window. Quicken displays a dialog box that asks you to supply a name for your customized report. (You can also provide a default report date range.) After you name the customized report, Quicken lists it whenever you choose Reports⇨Saved Reports & Graphs Center.

You really don't need to worry about these other buttons. Read through the discussion that follows only if you're feeling comfortable, relaxed, and truly mellow. Okay?

Back, Forward, and History

The Back and Forward buttons let you move back and forth between open report windows. The History button displays a list of the windows you've displayed; you can choose a previously displayed window by clicking it in the list.

Delete

The Delete button deletes the current report from the report list. You can use this button to, in effect, undo any changes you've made to a report and return to the default report specifications.

Export This Report To One Of The Formats

I talk about this option in the "Sharing report data with spreadsheets" and "Sharing report data in PDF files" sections, earlier in this chapter. Look there if you have questions.

Sort

The Sort button displays a list of sorting options that you can use for arranging information on the report. Enough said.

Save Report

Say you get into this customization thing. If you do, you should know that you can save your customized reports by clicking the Save Report button. When you click Save Report, Quicken displays the Save Report dialog box, shown in Figure 7-7. Mostly, Quicken displays this dialog box so that you can give your creation a name. You also use this dialog box to indicate in which financial activity center Quicken should save your report.

By the way, after you create a saved report, you can reproduce it by selecting the report from the My Saved Reports section of the Reports & Graphs Center.

What's the Preferences button for?

When you click the Preferences button, Quicken displays a Preferences dialog box with a bunch of boxes and buttons that let you change the way the window looks or works.

If I were a really great writer — the Stephen King of computer books, for example — I might be able to whip up a riveting discussion of how the Preferences dialog box works. I'm going to do both you and my publisher a favor, however, by making a suggestion: Just play with these option settings if you're interested. You'll find it more fun and a better learning experience.

Figure 7-7:
The Save
Report
dialog box.

Save Report

Save Report

Report name: Spending by Category

Description:

Save in: My Saved Reports

☐ Save report history

My Saved Reports contents:

OK   Cancel

Date Range

I briefly mention the Date Range box earlier in this chapter, but here I provide a slightly more detailed description. The Date Range box displays a drop-down list that you can use to specify what time period you want listed on your report: the current month, last year, the current quarter to date, and so on.

Column subtotaling

The Column drop-down list box displays a list that enables you to tell Quicken you want subtotal amounts by some criterion, as shown in Figure 7-8. Just select the criterion. Note that sometimes Column is replaced with Subtotal By.

Figure 7-8:
The Column drop-down list box.

Customizing

The Customize button works pretty much the same no matter which report shows in the document window.

When you click this button, Quicken displays a dialog box that lets you enter the report title and specify the range of dates the report should cover by using text boxes. It also lets you choose from a variety of other options, too, such as which accounts to use, which transactions to use, and how the report's information should be arranged.

Charts Only Look Tricky

I love charts. I know that sounds goofy. But *data graphics* open up wonderful opportunities for communicating. And Quicken charts are really easy to use.

In fact, many times, Quicken will add a small chart to a report window. Take a look at Figure 7-8, for example, and see what I mean. You can also display just a chart, however.

To produce just a Quicken chart, first produce the report you want and then click the Show Graph button that appears in the report window. That's it. Easy as rolling off a log.

Note: Not all reports provide data that can be plotted in a graph. Accordingly, you won't see a Show Graph button in every report window.

Figure 7-9 shows a picture of a bar graph of income and expense figures, but you'll have much more fun looking at your own data in a picture. By the way, you can drill down (described earlier in this chapter in "Got a question about a number? Just zoom it") through a chart to see a report that describes the data being plotted.

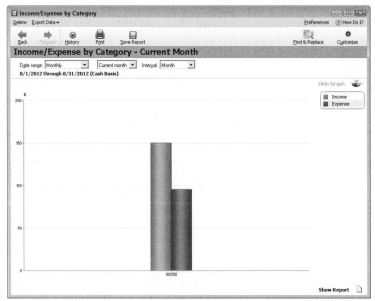

Figure 7-9:
The Income/
Expense
graph.

You can memorize customized graphs the same way you memorize customized reports. Just click the Save Report button at the top of the graph window. Then, when Quicken prompts you, give the graph a name. To later reuse the graph, select the graph from the My Saved Reports section of the Reports & Graphs Center.

Mini-reports: Last But Not Least

Before I forget, I need to tell you about one other variant of the Quicken reporting feature: Mini-reports. Ah, yes, Mini-reports. Here's the deal. Quicken supplies a quick-and-dirty report called, cleverly enough, a Mini-report. If you're working with the transaction list, you can produce a quick report that summarizes things, such as the checks written to a particular payee or the transactions assigned to a specific income or expense category.

To produce a Mini-report, first move the cursor to the field that you want to summarize in the report. Then right-click the field to display a shortcut menu. Typically, the second-to-last command will produce a Mini-report. The report shown in Figure 7-10, for example, is a Mini-report that shows the payments you've received from your Aunt Enid. She is *such* a sweetheart. (The name of the second-to-last command selected was, "Payments Received From Aunt Enid.")

Note: The *very last* command on the shortcut menu will usually (if selected) produce a mini-report, like that shown in Figure 7-6.

Figure 7-10:
Here's a
Mini-report.

Chapter 8

A Matter of Balance

I want to start this chapter with an important point: Balancing a bank account in Quicken is easy and quick.

I'm not just trying to get you pumped up about an otherwise painfully boring topic. I don't think balancing a bank account is any more exciting than you do. (At the Nelson house, we never answer the "What should we do tonight?" question by saying, "Hey, let's balance an account!")

My point is this: Because bank account balancing can be tedious and boring, use Quicken to speed up the drudgery.

Selecting the Account You Want to Balance

You need to tell Quicken which account you want to reconcile, or balance. But this step is easy. Just click on the account in the Accounts bar. When you do, Quicken displays the register view for the account (as shown in Figure 8-1).

Figure 8-1:
The register
view for an
account.

Balancing a Bank Account

Trust me when I say balancing a bank account is remarkably easy. In fact, I'll go so far as to say that if you have any problems, they'll stem from . . . well, sloppy record keeping that preceded your use of Quicken.

Telling Quicken, "Hey, man, I want to balance this account"

To tell Quicken that you want to *balance,* or *reconcile,* your account records with the bank's records, click the Account Actions button and then choose the Reconcile command. Quicken displays the Reconcile Details dialog box, shown in Figure 8-2.

Figure 8-2:
The
Reconcile
Details
dialog box.

Giving Quicken the bank's information

As you probably know, in a reconciliation, you compare your records of a bank account with the bank's records of the same account. You should be able to explain any difference between the two accounts — usually by pointing to checks that you've written but that haven't cleared. (Sometimes deposits fall into the same category; you've recorded and mailed a deposit, but the bank hasn't yet credited your account.)

The first step, then, is to supply Quicken with the bank's account information. This information comes from your monthly statement. Supply Quicken with the figures it needs as follows:

1. **Verify the opening balance.**

   Quicken displays a figure in the Opening Balance text box. If this figure isn't correct, replace it with the correct figure. To do so, move the cursor to the text box and type over the given figure. (If you're reconciling your account for the first time, Quicken gets this opening balance figure from your starting account balance. If you've reconciled before, Quicken uses the Ending Balance that you specified the last time you reconciled.)

2. **Enter the ending balance.**

   Move the cursor to the Ending Balance text box and type the *ending,* or closing, balance shown on your bank statement.

3. **Provide the statement's ending balance date.**

   Move the cursor to the New Statement Ending Date text box and type the ending date for the statement you're using to reconcile.

4. **Enter the bank's service charge.**

   If your bank statement shows a service charge and you haven't already entered it, move the cursor to the Service Charge text box and type the amount.

5. **Type a transaction date for the service charge transaction.**

   Quicken supplies its best guess for the date. If you're reconciling for the first time, Quicken uses the current system date from your computer's clock. If you've reconciled the account before, Quicken picks a date one month later from the last time you reconciled the account. If the date Quicken picks isn't correct, type the correct date.

   You can adjust a date one day at a time by using either the + or – key.

6. **Assign the bank's service charge to a category.**

   Quicken helps you out by displaying the Bank Charge category in the first Category text box — the one beneath the Service Charge text box. If you want to use a different category, click the down arrow in the Category text box to open the Category drop-down list box; then select a category by scrolling down the list and pressing Enter.

7. **Enter the account's interest income.**

   If the account earned interest for the month and you haven't already entered this figure, type the amount in the Interest Earned text box.

8. **Enter a transaction date for the interest income transaction.**

   You already know how to enter dates. I won't bore you by explaining it again (but see Step 5 if you're having trouble).

9. **Assign the interest to a category.**

   Type an appropriate income category for any interest — perhaps something like, er, **Interest Inc**.

10. **Tell Quicken that the bank statement is complete.**

    To do so, just click OK. Quicken displays the reconcile window, which I describe in the next section.

Explaining the difference between your records and the bank's records

Next, Quicken compares your register's account balance with the bank statement's ending account balance. Then it builds a list of checks and deposits that your register shows but that haven't yet *cleared* (haven't been recorded by the bank). Figure 8-3 shows the Reconcile: Checking window that Quicken displays to provide you with this information.

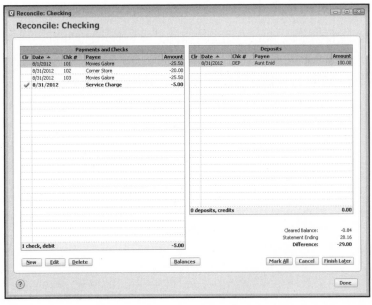

Figure 8-3:
The
Reconcile:
Checking
window.

As Figure 8-3 shows, the Reconcile: Checking window is basically just two lists — one of account withdrawals and one of account deposits. The window also displays some extra information at the bottom of the screen: the Cleared Balance (which is your account balance including only those transactions that you or Quicken have marked as cleared), the Statement Ending balance, and the Difference between these two figures.

Marking cleared checks and deposits

You need to tell Quicken which deposits and checks have cleared at the bank. (Refer to your bank statement for this information.)

1. **Identify the first deposit that has cleared.**

   You know how to do so, I'm sure. Just leaf through the bank statement and find the first deposit listed.

2. **Mark the first cleared deposit as cleared.**

   Scroll through the transactions listed in the right column of the Reconcile: Checking window, find the deposit, and then mark it as cleared by clicking it. Quicken places a check mark in front of the deposit and updates the cleared statement balance.

3. **Record any cleared but missing deposits.**

   If you can't find a deposit, you haven't entered it into the Quicken register yet. I can only guess why you haven't entered it. Maybe you just forgot. In any event, return to the Quicken register by clicking the Edit button and then enter the deposit in the register in the usual way — but type a **c** (for *cleared*) in the Clr column. This mark identifies the deposit as one that's already cleared at the bank. To return to the Reconcile: Checking window, click the Return To Reconcile button.

4. **Repeat Steps 1–3 for all deposits listed on the bank statement.**

5. **Identify the first check or other withdrawal that has cleared.**

   No sweat, right? Just find the first check or withdrawal listed on the bank statement.

6. **Mark the first cleared check or other withdrawal as cleared.**

   Scroll through the transactions listed in the left column of the Reconcile: Checking window, find the first check, and select it to mark it as having cleared the bank. Quicken inserts a check mark to label this transaction as cleared and updates the Cleared Balance.

7. **Record any missing but cleared checks or withdrawals.**

   If you can't find a check or withdrawal — guess what? — you haven't entered it in the Quicken register yet. Display the Quicken register by clicking the Edit button. Then enter the check or withdrawal in the register. Be sure to type a **c** (for *cleared*) in the Clr column to identify this check or withdrawal as one that's already cleared the bank. To return to the Reconcile: Checking window, click the Return To Reconcile button.

8. **Repeat Steps 5–7 for withdrawals listed on the bank statement.**

By the way, these steps don't take very long. It takes me about two minutes to reconcile my account each month. And I'm not joking or exaggerating. By two minutes, I really mean two minutes.

Making sure that the difference equals zero

After you mark all the cleared checks and deposits, the difference between the cleared balance for the account and the bank statement's ending balance should equal zero. Notice that I said *should,* not *will.* Figure 8-4 shows a Reconcile: Checking window in which everything is hunky-dory, and life is grand.

If the difference does equal zero, you're done. Just click the Done button to tell Quicken that you're done. Quicken displays a congratulatory message telling you how proud it is of you, and then it asks whether you want to print a Reconciliation report.

As part of the finishing-up process, Quicken changes all the cs to Rs. There's no great magic in this transformation. Quicken makes the changes to identify the transactions that have already been reconciled.

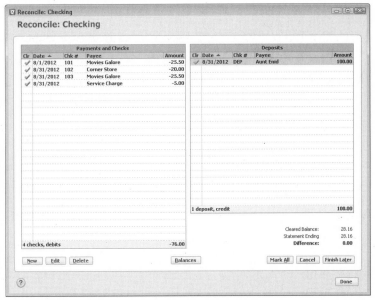

Figure 8-4:
The
Reconcile:
Checking
window
showing a
cleared
balance.

Can't decide whether to print the Reconciliation report? Unless you're a business bookkeeper or an accountant reconciling a bank account for someone else — your employer or a client, for example — you don't need to print the Reconciliation report. All printing does is prove that you reconciled the account. (Basically, this proof is the reason you should print the report if you *are* a bookkeeper or an accountant — the person for whom you're reconciling the account will know that you did your job and will have a piece of paper to come back to later if he or she has questions.)

If the difference doesn't equal zero, you have a problem. If you click Done, Quicken displays a message box that provides some cursory explanations as to why your account doesn't balance and then, if you indicate you want to soldier on anyway, Quicken displays the Adjust Balance dialog box (shown in Figure 8-5). This dialog box tells you, in effect, that you can force the two amounts to agree by clicking the Adjust button.

Figure 8-5:
The Adjust
Balance
dialog box.

Forcing the two amounts to agree isn't a very good idea. To do so, Quicken adds a cleared and reconciled transaction equal to the difference. (I talk about this transaction in the upcoming section, "Ten Things You Should Do If Your Account Doesn't Balance.")

If you want to reconcile later without saving your unfinished work, click Cancel in the Reconcile: Checking window and then click Yes when Quicken asks you whether you really want to quit without saving your work. The next time you click the Reconcile button, you'll have to start over from scratch.

If you can't get your account to reconcile but want to save your work, click the Finish Later button. Quicken leaves your reconciliation work basically half done. The transactions that you marked as cleared still show a c in the Clr field. And you still have an unexplainable difference between the bank statement and your register.

Either way, postponing a reconciliation and not choosing to adjust the bank account balance is usually the best approach. It enables you to locate and correct problems. (I give you some ideas about how to do so in the next section.) Then you can restart the reconciliation and finish your work. (You restart a reconciliation in the same way that you originate one.)

Ten Things You Should Do If Your Account Doesn't Balance

I have some suggestions for reconciling an account that's causing you problems. If you're sitting in front of your computer wringing your hands, try the following tips.

Make sure that you're working with the right account

Sounds dumb, doesn't it? If you have a bunch of different bank accounts, however, ending up in the wrong account is pretty darned easy. So go ahead and confirm, for example, that you're trying to reconcile your checking account at Mammoth International Bank by using the Mammoth International checking account statement.

Look for transactions that the bank has recorded but you haven't

Go through your bank statement and make sure that you have recorded every transaction that your bank has recorded. Cash machine withdrawals, special fees or service charges (such as for checks or your safety deposit box), automatic withdrawals, direct deposits, and so on, are easily overlooked.

If the difference is positive — that is, the bank thinks you have less money than you think you should — you may be missing a withdrawal transaction. If the difference is negative, you may be missing a deposit transaction.

Look for reversed transactions

Here's a tricky one. If you accidentally enter a transaction backward — a deposit as a withdrawal or a withdrawal as a deposit — your account won't balance. And the error can be difficult to find. The Reconcile: Checking window shows all the correct transactions, but a transaction amount appears positive when it should be negative or negative when it should be positive. The check you wrote to Mrs. Travis for your son's piano lessons appears as a positive number (a deposit) instead of a negative number (a check), for example.

Look for a transaction that's equal to half the difference

One handy way to find a transaction that you entered backward — *if* you only have one — is to look for a transaction that's equal to half the irreconcilable difference. For example, if the difference is $200, you may have entered a $100 deposit as a withdrawal or a $100 withdrawal as a deposit.

I don't want to beat a dead horse, but the sign (that is, positive or negative) of the difference should help you find the problem. If the difference is positive — the bank thinks you have less money than your register indicates — you may have mistakenly entered a withdrawal as a deposit. If the difference is negative — the bank thinks you have more money than your register says — you may be missing a deposit transaction.

Look for a transaction that's equal to the difference

While I'm on the subject of explaining the difference by looking at individual transactions, let me make an obvious point. If the difference between the bank's records and yours equals one of the transactions listed in your register, you may have incorrectly marked the transaction as cleared or incorrectly left the transaction marked as uncleared.

I don't know. Maybe that was too obvious.

Check for transposed numbers

Transposed numbers occur when you flip-flop two digits in a number. For example, you enter $45.89 as $48.59.

These turkeys always cause accountants and bookkeepers headaches. If you look at the numbers, detecting an error is often difficult because the digits are the same. For example, when comparing a check amount of $45.89 in your register with a check for $48.59 shown on your bank statement, both check amounts show the same digits: 4, 5, 8, and 9. They just show them in different orders.

Transposed numbers are tough to find, but here's a trick you can try. Divide the difference shown in the Reconcile: Checking window by nine. If the result is an even number of dollars or cents, you may have a transposed number somewhere.

Have someone else look over your work

This idea may seem pretty obvious, but I'm amazed at how often a second pair of eyes can find something that you've been overlooking.

If you're using Quicken at home, ask your spouse. If you're using Quicken at work, ask the owner or one of your coworkers (preferably that one person who always seems to have way too much free time).

Look out for multiple errors

By the way, if you find an error by using this laundry list and still can't balance your account, you should start checking at the top of the list again. You may, for example, discover — after you find a transposed number — that you entered another transaction backward or incorrectly cleared or uncleared a transaction.

Try again next month (and maybe the month after that)

If the difference isn't huge in relation to the size of your bank account, you may want to wait until next month and attempt to reconcile your account again.

Before my carefree attitude puts you in a panic, consider the following example. You reconcile your account in January, and the difference is $24.02. Then you reconcile the account in February, and the difference is $24.02. Then you reconcile the account in March, and, surprise, surprise, the difference is still $24.02.

What's going on here? Well, your starting account balance was probably off by $24.02. (The more months you try to reconcile your account and find that you're always mysteriously $24.02 off, the more likely it is that this type of error is to blame.)

After the second or third month, I think it's pretty reasonable to tell Quicken that it should enter an adjusting transaction for $24.02 so that your account balances. (In my opinion, this is the only circumstance that merits your adjusting an account to match the bank's figure.)

By the way, if you've successfully reconciled your account with Quicken before, your work may not be at fault. The mistake could be (drum roll, please) the bank's! And in this case, you should do something else. . . .

Get in your car, drive to the bank, and beg for help

As an alternative to the preceding idea — which supposes that the bank's statement is correct and that your records are incorrect — I propose this idea: Ask the folks at the bank to help you reconcile the account. (Check to see whether they charge for this service first, of course.) Hint that you think that the mistake is probably theirs. Smile a great deal. And one other thing — be sure to ask about whatever product they're currently advertising in the lobby. (This behavior encourages them to think that you're interested in that 180-month certificate of deposit, and they'll be extra nice to you.)

In general, the bank's record keeping is usually pretty darned good. I've never had a problem as a business-banking client or as an individual. (I've also been lucky enough to deal with big, well-run banks.)

Nevertheless, your bank may have made a mistake, so ask the people there to help you. (*Note:* Be sure to have them explain any transactions that you discover only by seeing them on your bank statement.)

Chapter 9

Housekeeping for Quicken

*O*kay, you don't have to worry about chasing dust bunnies in Quicken, but you do have to take care of little housekeeping tasks. This chapter describes these chores and how to do them right, with minimal hassle.

Backing Up Is Hard to Do

You should back up the files that Quicken uses to store your financial records. But you need to know how to back up before you can back up.

Backing up the quick-and-dirty way

You're busy. You don't have time to fool around. You just want to do a passable job backing up files. Sound like your situation? Then follow these steps:

1. **Insert a writable CD into the appropriate drive, or a flash drive into a USB port.**

   You can back up to any disc or storage device you can write to — this can be a writable CD or flash drive. You only need to know which letters your computer uses to label its drives. If you don't, consult the documentation that came with your computer.

2. **Verify that the file you want to back up is active.**

Expand the Accounts bar (if necessary) and then make sure that it displays one of the accounts in the file you want to back up. (If you don't remember setting up multiple files, don't worry. You probably have only one file — the usual case.)

3. **Start the backup operation by choosing File⇨Backup And Restore⇨Backup Quicken File on the menu bar.**

    Quicken displays the Quicken Backup dialog box, shown in Figure 9-1.

Figure 9-1:
The Quicken
Backup
dialog box.

4. **Identify the backup drive.**

    Select the Back Up On My Computer option button. Then verify that the disk letter shown in the text box is the one you want to use for backing up. If it isn't, click the Change button. When Quicken displays the Enter Backup File Name dialog box, shown in Figure 9-2, select the correct disk.

Figure 9-2:
The Enter
Backup File
Name dialog
box.

You can use any removable disk, including a flash drive, a recordable CD, or even a Zip disk.

5. **Click OK.**

You see a message on-screen that says, "Aye, Cap'n, I'm working just as fast as I can" (or something to that effect). Then you see a message that says the backup is complete. Don't worry. You'll never see a message that says, "She's starting to break up, Cap'n. She can't take warp 9 much longer." You will see a warning message if the file you want to back up is too large. In this case, you need to shrink the file, use a different disk, or use multiple disks.

As Figure 9-1 indicates, you can also back up Quicken online. When you select the Online option button and click OK, Quicken explains the service and gets you started. Just so you know, an online backup gets stored on Intuit's computers — Intuit makes Quicken — rather than on your computer's disks. Online backup works the same basic way as disk backup, except you need an Internet connection, and the online backup service costs money. The service costs from $9.99 to $149.99 a year at the time I'm writing this book, depending on the level of service you choose. I'm as cheap as the next guy, but I think the online backup option is truly something to consider. The prices seem cheap relative to the value of the data you're probably backing up. (This is especially true if you're using Quicken for a small business.)

Deciding when to back up

Sure, I can give you some tricky, technical examples of fancy backup strategies, but they have no point here. You want to know the basics, right? So here's what I do to back up my files. I back up every month after I reconcile. Then I stick the flash drive in my briefcase, so if something terrible happens at home, I don't lose both my computer and the backup disk with the data.

I admit that my strategy has a few problems, however. For example, because I'm backing up only once per month, I may have to re-enter as much as a month's worth of data if the computer crashes toward the end of the month. In my case, I wouldn't lose all that much work. However, if you have really heavy transaction volumes — if you write hundreds of checks per month, for example — you may want to back up more frequently than monthly, such as once weekly. If you use the same disk or set of disks to back up your Quicken file, Quicken will warn you before it replaces the old file with the new one. You can go ahead and let Quicken do this, as long as you're sure that you won't want to access the old file anymore.

A second problem with my strategy is only remotely possible but is still worth mentioning. If something bad does happen to the Quicken files stored on my computer's hard drive *and* the files stored on the backup disc, I'm up the proverbial creek without a paddle. I should also note that a removable disc may be more likely to fail or get lost than a hard drive. If this worst-case scenario actually occurs, I'll need to start over from scratch from the beginning of the year. To prevent this scenario from happening, some people — those who are religiously careful — make more than one backup copy of their Quicken files.

By the way, Quicken periodically prompts you to back up when you try to exit. (You'll see a message that basically says, "Friend, backing up is a darn good idea.") You can, of course, choose to ignore this message. Or you can take Quicken's advice and do the backup thing as I describe earlier in this chapter, in the section, "Backing up the quick-and-dirty way."

You know what else? Here's a secret feature of Quicken: Quicken adds a sub-directory called Backup to the Quicken directory. And Quicken will stick a backup copy of your files in this directory every few days. (Sorry to be vague on this point, but it's hard to be specific and concrete when it comes to undocumented features.) You can find out more on this later in this chapter in the section, "Losing your Quicken data when you haven't backed up."

Losing your Quicken data after you've backed up

What happens if you lose all your Quicken data? First of all, I encourage you to feel smug. Get a cup of coffee. Lean back in your chair. Gloat for a couple of minutes. You, my friend, will have no problem.

After you've sufficiently gloated, carefully do the following to reinstate your Quicken data on the computer:

1. **Get your backup disk.**

   Find the backup disk you created and carefully insert it or plug it in. (If you can't find the backup disk, forget what I said about feeling smug — stop gloating and skip to the next section.)

2. **Start Quicken.**

   You already know how to do this, right? By the way, if the disaster that caused you to lose your data also trashed other parts of your computer, you may need to reinstall Quicken. Shoot. I suppose it's possible that you may even need to reinstall Windows.

3. Choose File➪Backup And Restore➪Restore From Backup File on the menu.

Quicken displays the Restore From Backup File dialog box (not shown), which lets you restore from one of Quicken's automatic backup copies, from a backup copy you made using the File➪Backup And Restore➪Backup Quicken File command, or from an online backup. To restore using one of the automatic backup copies of the Quicken data file that Quicken has secretly previously made, simply select the automatic backup copy you want to use. Quicken then automatically restores the file for you — and you get to skip ahead to Step 6.

Alternatively, you can select the Restore From Backup button and then click the Browse button. Quicken looks at the selected folder or disk and displays a list of the files stored there, as shown in Figure 9-3. If your computer has another disk in it and this other disk has the backup copy of the file, use the Look In drop-down list box to select the other drive.

If you want to restore from an online backup copy of the Quicken data file, select the Restore From Online Backup button.

Figure 9-3:
The Restore Quicken File dialog box.

4. Select the file you want to restore and then click OK.

Use the arrow keys or the mouse to select the file that you want to restore.

If the file you select is the one Quicken used last, the program displays a message asking whether it's okay to *overwrite,* or replace, the file with the one stored on the disk.

When you restore a file, you replace the current, in-memory version of the file with the backup version stored on the disk. Don't restore a file for fun. Don't restore a file for entertainment. Restore a file only if the current version is trashed, and you want to start over by using the version stored on the backup disk.

5. **Click Restore Backup.**

   Quicken replaces the file it's currently using with the one from the backup disk. After it finishes, Quicken displays a message telling you that it has restored the file. You're almost done.

6. **Update the account registers as necessary.**

   Using the register windows for each of the accounts in a file, re-enter each of the transactions you recorded since you created the backup. Be sure that you update your accounts because you've almost certainly entered transactions since the last time you backed up.

Just to be on the safe side, you should back up the file after you complete this process. Using a new flash drive is probably a good idea, too. I have heard that lightning never strikes the same place twice, but I'm not sure that the old saying is true. If you have hard drive problems or another recurring problem, whatever fouled up your file this time may rear its ugly head again — and soon.

Losing your Quicken data when you haven't backed up

What do you do if you haven't backed up your files in a while and you lose all the data in your Quicken files? Okay. Stay calm. All may not be lost.

First, you can try restoring the files from the secret Quicken backup directory. To do so, you follow the same file restoration steps I cover in the preceding section, with one minor exception. After you choose the Restore From Backup command, look at the list of automatic (secret) backup files that Quicken has squirreled away on your computer.

Select the newest automatic backup file and then click OK. Quicken uses that file to restore the current file. As I alluded to earlier in this chapter, grabbing one of these secret backup copies of the Quicken data file may just work. And if it does, you should feel very lucky. Very lucky indeed.

Okay. So suppose that you've tried the approach described in the preceding paragraph, and it didn't work. What next?

You have to re-enter all the transactions for the entire year. Yeah. I know. It's a bummer. This method isn't quick, and it isn't pretty, but it works.

If you have copies of the registers, of course, you can use these as your information source to re-enter the information in your files. If you don't have copies of the registers, you need to use your bank statements and any other paper financial records you have.

If, for some unfortunate reason, the only copy you have of your Quicken data seems to have become corrupted, you can have Quicken try to rebuild the file. To do so, choose File⟹File Operations⟹Validate and Repair and enter the name of the file you want rebuilt in the File Name text box. You typically do this, however, only when instructed by Quicken or Intuit technical support people.

Working with Files, Files, and More Files

As part of setting up Quicken, you create what Quicken calls a *file:* a place where Quicken stores all your accounts (bank accounts, credit card accounts, investment accounts, and so on).

You can have more than one Quicken file at any time. Most people won't want to do this. But, for example, you can use different files to keep your personal financial records separate from business financial records.

Using multiple files does have a little drawback, however. You can't easily record, in one fell swoop, account transfer transactions between accounts in different files. You need to record the transaction twice — once in the *source account,* the file where the transaction originates, and again in the *destination account,* the file where you are transferring the transaction.

If the two accounts involved in a transfer are in the same file, just enter the account name in the Category text box. Quicken then records the transfer in the other account for you.

Setting up a new file

To set up a new file so that you can create accounts in it, follow these steps:

1. **Choose File⟹New on the menu bar.**

   Quicken displays the Create New File: Dude, Are You Sure? dialog box, shown in Figure 9-4.

2. **Select the New Quicken File option button and then click OK or press Enter.**

   Quicken displays the Create Quicken File dialog box, shown in Figure 9-5.

Figure 9-4:
The Create
New File:
Are You
Sure? dialog
box.

Figure 9-5:
The Create
Quicken File
dialog box.

3. **Enter a name for the Quicken file.**

   Position the cursor in the File Name text box and type some meaningful combination of letters and numbers. You don't need to enter a file extension because Quicken supplies the correct file extension — QDF — for you.

   Note: You can use the symbol characters on your keyboard, but doing so gets a little tricky. If you must use symbol characters in the filename, refer to the Quicken user documentation.

4. **Use the default file location.**

   Accept Quicken's suggestion to store the file in the QUICKEN directory. I can think of no good reason to put the file in another location.

5. **Click OK.**

   Quicken displays the Quicken home page with the Get Started button, shown in Figure 9-6.

Figure 9-6:
The Quicken
home page
with the
Get Started
button.

6. **Run the Setup.**

   To set up the new Quicken file, click the Get Started button. You might also want to click on the Setup tab and then read through the Setup tab's information and answer its questions. If you have questions about either of these steps, refer to Chapter 1.

Flip-flopping between files

You can work with only one file at a time. So, after you create a second file, you need to know how to flip-flop between your files. If you're recording business stuff, for example, you want to be using the business file. However, what if a transaction comes in that clearly is meant for your personal file and you want to enter it there immediately? Flip-flopping allows you to get from one file to another in no time.

Flip-flopping is easy:

1. **Just choose File⇨Open.**

   Quicken displays the Open Quicken File dialog box (see Figure 9-7).

Figure 9-7:
The Open
Quicken File
dialog box.

2. Pick the file you want from the File Name text box and then click OK.

Zap! You're in the new file.

If you really want to switch to another file with lightning speed, you can select the name of the other file directly on the bottom of the File menu, where Quicken lists the last four files you used.

When files get too big for their own good

You can enter a large number of transactions in a Quicken file; in fact, you can record tens of thousands of transactions in a single account or file. Wowsers!

In spite of these huge numbers, I can think of some good reasons to work with smaller files if you can. For example, working with files of a manageable size means that you can more easily and more quickly back them up. Also, fewer transactions mean that Quicken runs faster because more memory is available for Windows. (Windows likes lots of memory — the same way that some people like lots of ice cream.)

Note: Oh, jeepers. My technical editor wants me to remind you that there are good reasons to work with large files when you can. And, of course, he's right. Having several years of data at your fingertips, for example, is handy. With several years of data, you can easily get answers to all sorts of questions: how much money wealthy relatives have given you over the years, how much cable television has gone up in price, and so on.

If your files have gotten too big for their own good, you can knock them down to size by creating a new file that contains only the current year's transactions. You end up with a copy of the big file that you won't use anymore and a smaller, shrunken file with just the current year's transactions. Working with a smaller file probably means that Quicken will run faster. (The memory thing comes into play again.) And smaller files should make backing up easier because you can probably keep your files small enough to fit on just about any storage device.

Call me a Nervous Nellie — or a Nervous Nelson — but because shrinking a file involves wholesale change, I'd really feel more comfortable helping you through this process if you first back up the file you're about to shrink. I don't think that you need to be anxious about anything, but just in case something does go wrong during the shrinking process, I know that you want to have a backup copy of the file to fall back on.

To shrink a Quicken file, follow these steps:

1. **Choose File⇨File Operations⇨Year End Copy on the menu bar.**

   Quicken displays a portrait of Barry Nelson, the first actor to portray James Bond. No, not really — I just wanted to see whether you were awake. Actually, Quicken displays the Create A Year End Copy dialog box, shown in Figure 9-8.

Figure 9-8: The Create A Year End Copy dialog box.

2. **Describe what you want in the current data file.**

   Your next step in creating a year-end copy is to describe what information you want in the current data file, which is the Quicken file that you'll continue to work with. Like the Create A Year End Copy dialog box suggests, you have two choices: The Do Nothing choice leaves the Quicken data file alone. The Do Something (please!) choice creates a copy of the Quicken data file using only balances and transactions after a specified date. To shrink the current Quicken file, you predictably use the Do Something (please!) option by selecting the appropriate option button and then specifying the cutoff date.

   When you archive, you make a copy of the Quicken data file, but (typically) just through the end of the preceding year. You continue to work with the big, everything-is-still-there data file. Why archive? So that you can have a copy of the Quicken data file as it existed at a point in time. You might archive the Quicken data file on CD and store the archive file with your tax return, for example. By doing this, you'd be sure of always being able to later look at the Quicken data file that explained your tax deductions.

3. **Confirm the name in the Give The Archive File A Name And Location text box.**

   You can actually ignore the filename and folder location information that Quicken enters into the Give The Archive File A Name And Location text box. However, if you really must have it your way, you do have the option of replacing what Quicken suggests with another name. You can also click the Browse button and choose another folder location by using the dialog box that Quicken displays.

4. **Specify a starting date.**

   Using the Specify Starting Date text box, type a cutoff date. Nowadays, the folks at Quicken are calling this the This Archive Data File Will Contain Transactions Up To And Including text box, but you guessed that, didn't you? Quicken deletes all cleared transactions with dates that fall before this cutoff date from the current Quicken file. (***Remember:*** This file is the one you work with and want to shrink.) I chose 12/31/2011 as the cutoff date in Figure 9-8 so that I could create a new file for all 2012 transactions. (***Note:*** Quicken doesn't delete uncleared transactions, and it doesn't delete investment transactions.)

5. **Click OK.**

   Quicken creates an old-transactions "Old File" with the filename discussed in Step 3. If you told it to, Quicken also deletes all the old transactions from the current file so that your current file contains only the transactions that are dated after the cutoff date.

   Quicken then displays the dialog box shown in Figure 9-9, which tells you the file was successfully copied. Select the Current File option button if you want to use the current file you've just shrunk. Select the

Archive File option button if you want to use the old-transactions file.
Click OK after you make your choice.

Figure 9-9:
The File
Archive
dialog box.

If you want to see the old-transactions, or archive, file again, you can
select it in the Open dialog box (accessed by choosing File⇨Open). You
should *not* enter any new transactions in the old-transactions file, however, because these new transactions will change the old file's ending
account balance without changing the current file's beginning account
balance.

Using and Abusing Passwords

I have mixed feelings about Quicken passwords. Theoretically, they let you
lock up your Quicken data so that your rebellious teenagers (if you're using
Quicken at home) or the night janitors (if you're using Quicken in a business)
can't come in and print checks, process automatic payments, and just generally mess things up.

Using passwords sounds pretty good, of course. But before you set up a password and then start relying on it to protect your information, let me remind
you that a Quicken password only prevents someone from accessing your
data with Quicken. Using a password doesn't prevent someone from fooling
around with your computer itself. If the night janitors — or, heaven forbid,
your teenagers — are the nefarious types, they can erase your files with
Windows or scramble them with another program, such as a spreadsheet or
word-processing program. And they may even be able to get in and manipulate the data with another checkbook or accounting program.

Passwords come with one other little annoying problem, too. Darn it, you
have to remember them.

For these reasons, I think that passwords are best left to computer systems
that use them on a global basis to control access to all programs and to computer systems that can track all users (you, your teenagers, the night janitors, and anyone else) by name. Your PC doesn't fall into this category.

Setting up a file password

You still want a password? Okay. With much trepidation, I give you the following steps for setting up a password for a Quicken file:

1. **Select the file you want to protect with a password.**

   If the file you want to password-protect is not the active file, choose File⇨Open on the menu and then either double-click the file you want or select it and click OK.

2. **Choose File⇨Set Passwords For This Data File on the menu bar.**

   Quicken displays the Quicken File Password dialog box, shown in Figure 9-10.

Figure 9-10:
The
Quicken File
Password
dialog box.

3. **Enter the password into the New Password text box.**

   You can use up to 16 characters. Quicken differentiates between lowercase and uppercase characters, by the way, so Washington, wASHINGTON, and WASHINGTON are all different from its point of view. Quicken doesn't display the actual characters you type; it displays asterisks instead. If you type **Dog**, for example, it displays ✴✴✴. (Passwords require strict secrecy, you see.)

4. **Enter the password you want to use again — only this time into the Confirm Password text box — and then click OK.**

   Congratulations! You're done.

Assigning a password to a file doesn't prevent you from doing anything with the file that you would normally do. However, the next time you try to use this file — after you start Quicken or when you try to select the file by using the File⇨Open command — Quicken will ask you for the file's password. You need to supply the password to gain access to the file.

So what are transaction passwords?

If you choose File⇨Set Password For This Data File, you create a file password that a Quicken user needs to provide before he or she gets access to the Quicken data. In general, you use such a password, called a *file password,* to protect the access into a Quicken file.

However, you can also set a *transaction password* by choosing File⇨Set Password To Modify Transactions. A transaction password works a little differently from a file password. With a transaction password, the user has to enter the transaction password if he or she tries to enter a transaction that is dated before a specified date. You specify the date, called the *cutoff date,* when you set up the transaction password.

You would use transaction passwords, my guess is, when you want to "lock" the preceding year's records. In other words, if you don't want people to intentionally or accidentally change last year's transactions — because that would mean they're screwing around with things like your records of tax deductions you've claimed on a return — you use a transaction password.

Transaction passwords are okay, I guess. But I'm going to go out on a limb here and suggest something different: You can create and safely store backup copies of the Quicken file for last year or last month. Or you can keep the idiots from fooling around with your Quicken files. Jeepers, if somebody can't understand an instruction such as, "Use the current date," do you really want them mucking about in your books?

Changing a file password

After you set up a file password, you're not stuck with it forever. You can either change the password or remove it by choosing File⇨Set Password For This Data File.

If you've already set up a password, however, Quicken doesn't display the Quicken File Password dialog box shown in Figure 9-10. Instead, Quicken displays a mutated Quicken File Password dialog box that asks for the password you're now using and the new password you want to use in the future (as shown in Figure 9-11). Type the current password in the Old Password text box and the new password in the New Password and the Confirm Password text boxes. Then press Enter or click OK. From now on, you need to use the new password to gain access to the file. If you don't want to use a password anymore, just leave the New Password and Confirm Password text boxes blank.

And a final tip for you concerning Quicken passwords . . . If you lose your password, the Quicken technical support ninjas will retrieve your password-protected file for you. The cost for this service equals $9.95. (To initiate this service, visit http://quicken.intuit.com/support/. Select your version of Quicken and then search on the keywords *Quicken Password Removal Service.*)

Figure 9-11:
Change your
password
here.

Chapter 10

Compound Interest Magic and Other Mysteries

*T*he folks at Intuit provide several nifty little calculators (most are dialog boxes) with Quicken. I strongly encourage you to use these tools. At the very least, the calculators should make your work easier. And if you invest a little time, you should gain some enormously valuable perspectives on your financial affairs.

What's more, the most recent versions of some flavors of Quicken include a handful of more powerful financial planning wizards that I want you to know about. I won't walk you through the steps to using these wizards. But I do want to preview them in the same way that a restaurant critic tells you what you should and shouldn't order at some nice restaurant. You know what I mean. "Darling, you absolutely must try the *foie gras,* but do stay away from the chocolate mousse. It's abominable. . . ."

Noodling Around with Your Investments

My favorite Quicken calculator is the Investment Savings Calculator. I guess I just like to forecast portfolio future values and other similar stuff.

Using the Investment Savings Calculator

Suppose that you want to know how much you'll accumulate if you save $5,000 per year for 35 years in a stock mutual fund that you anticipate will earn 10 percent annually. Use the Investment Savings Calculator to estimate how much you should ultimately accumulate. To use it, follow these steps:

1. **Display the Savings Calculator.**

   Click the Planning tab to display its buttons. Click the Planning Tools button to display its list of calculators, and choose the Savings Calculator. Quicken displays the Savings Calculator dialog box (see Figure 10-1).

Figure 10-1:
The Savings
Calculator
dialog box.

2. **Enter what you've accumulated as your Starting Savings Balance.**

   Move the cursor to the Starting Savings Balance text box and then type the amount of your current investments. If this amount is zero, for example, type **0**.

3. **Enter the Annual Yield that you expect your investments to earn.**

   Move the cursor to the Annual Yield text box and type the percent. If you plan to invest in the stock market and expect your savings to match the market's long-term return of about 10 percent, for example, type **10** (don't type **.10**).

4. **Indicate how long you plan to let your investments earn income.**

   Use the Save For text box to indicate how many time periods (years, months or whatever) you'll save. Then use the Save For drop-down list box to select the time period appropriate to your investment planning. (Usually, you'll select Years, as Figure 10-1 shows.) For example, if you select Years in the drop-down list box and you plan to let your investments grow for 35 years, you type **35**.

5. **Enter the anticipated inflation rate.**

   Move the cursor to the Inflation Rate text box and type the inflation rate. By the way, over the 20th century, the inflation rate averaged just over 3 percent.

6. **Enter the amount you plan to add to your investments every period.**

   Move the cursor to the Regular Contribution text box and type the amount you plan to add. Figure 10-1 shows how to calculate an individual retirement account's (IRA's) future value, assuming a $5,000 annual contribution.

7. **Indicate whether you plan to increase your annual contribution as a result of inflation.**

   Select the Increase Based On Inflation Rate check box if you plan to annually increase — by the annual inflation rate — the amount you add to your investment portfolio. Don't select the check box if you don't want to inflate the payments.

8. **After you enter all the information, click Calculate.**

   The Ending Savings Balance field shows how much you'll accumulate in present-day, uninflated dollars: $481,587.80. Hmmm. Sweet.

If you want to know the amount you'll accumulate in future-day, inflated dollars, deselect the Show In Today's $ check box.

To get more information on the annual deposits, balances, and so on, click the View Schedule button, which appears at the bottom of the Investment Savings Calculator dialog box. Quicken whips up a quick little report showing the annual deposits and ending balance for each year you plan to add into the savings. Try it. You may like it.

Trying to become a millionaire

So you want to be a millionaire someday.

To find out how to realize this childhood dream, use the Calculate option buttons, which appear in the Savings Calculator dialog box (refer to Figure 10-1). With these option buttons, you click the financial variable (Ending Savings

Balance, Regular Contribution, or Starting Savings Balance) you want to calculate. For example, to determine the annual amount you need to contribute to your investment so that your portfolio reaches $1,000,000, here's what you do:

1. **Select the Regular Contribution option button.**

2. **Select the Inflate Contributions check box.**

3. **Enter all the other input variables.**

    Remember to set the Ending Savings Balance text box to 1000000 (the Ending Savings Balance field becomes a text box after you select the Regular Contribution option).

    The Investment Savings Calculator computes how much you need to save annually to hit your $1,000,000 target.

Starting from scratch, it'll take 35 years of roughly $2,800-per-year payments to reach $1,000,000.00, as shown in Figure 10-2. (All those zeros look rather nice, don't they?) Note that this calculation assumes a 10 percent annual yield and that you adjust your contributions for inflation.

Figure 10-2:
The secret to your success: $2,800 per year for 35 years.

"Jeepers, creepers," you say. "This seems too darn good to be true, Steve."

Well, unfortunately, the calculation is a little misleading. With 3 percent inflation, your million bucks will be worth *only* $355,383.59 in current-day dollars. (To confirm this present value calculation, select the Ending Savings Balance option button and then the Show In Today's $ check box.)

> ## A timing assumption you should know
>
> The Savings Calculator assumes that you'll add to your portfolio at the end of the period — what financial planners call an *ordinary annuity*.

One of my pet ideas is that it really is possible for most people to become millionaires. There are just three tricks to doing so. First, make sure that you use tax-advantaged investments like 401(k) plans and IRAs. Second, invest this money into a very low-cost, super-diversified mutual fund like the Vanguard Target Retirement 2050 fund to make sure that, over time, your returns average out to the average. Third, use Quicken and your computer to make smarter financial decisions — by doing this, you can rather easily free up an extra $50, $100, or even $200 per month. I talk about this subject in Chapter 18.

The Often Unbearable Burden of Debt

To help you better manage your debts, Quicken provides a neat Loan Calculator that computes loan payments and balances.

Using the Loan Calculator to figure payments

Suppose that one afternoon, you're wondering what the mortgage payment is on one of those monstrous houses: tens of thousands of square feet, acres of grounds, cottages for the domestic help, and so on. You get the picture — something that's a really vulgar display of wealth.

To calculate what you would pay on a 30-year, $5,000,000 mortgage if the money costs 5 percent, use the Loan Calculator:

1. **Display the Loan Calculator.**

   Click the Planning tab. Click the Planning Tools button to display Quicken's list of financial calculator tools. Then choose the Loan Calculator. Quicken displays the Loan Calculator dialog box. (See Figure 10-3 for a picture of this handy tool.)

Figure 10-3:
The Loan
Calculator
shows that
you can't
afford that
huge man-
sion.

2. **Enter the loan amount.**

   Move the cursor to the Loan Amount text box and type the amount of
   the loan. (If you're checking the lifestyle of the ostentatious and vulgar,
   type **5,000,000.**)

3. **Enter the annual interest rate.**

   Move the cursor to the Annual Interest Rate text box and type the interest rate percent. If a loan charges 5 percent interest, for example, type **5**.

4. **Enter the number of years you want to take to repay the loan.**

   Move the cursor to the Number Of Years text box and type the number
   of years you plan to make payments.

5. **Indicate how many loan payments you plan to make per year.**

   Move the cursor to the Periods Per Year text box and type the number
   of loan payments you plan to make per year. If you want to make
   monthly payments, for example, type **12**.

6. **Indicate how frequently the lender will calculate, or *compound*,
   interest.**

   Move the cursor to the Compounding Period box and select the interest
   compounding period. If a loan uses monthly compounding, for example,
   select Monthly. (By the way, just so you know, most loans use compounding periods equal to the payment period. Some don't. But
   most do.)

If you click Calculate or move the selection cursor, Quicken calculates the
loan payment and displays the amount in the Payment field. Hey, wait.
$26,841.08. That doesn't seem so bad, does it? I mean, you could almost make
an annual — oh, never mind. That's a monthly payment, isn't it? Yikes!

I guess if you have to ask how much the mortgage payment is, you really can't afford it.

To get more information on the loan payments, interest and principal portions of payments, and outstanding loan balances, click the View Schedule button, which appears on the face of the Loan Calculator dialog box. Quicken whips up a quick loan amortization schedule showing all this stuff.

Calculating loan balances

To calculate the loan principal amount, select the Loan Amount option button under Calculate in the Loan Calculator dialog box. Then enter all the other variables.

For example, those $26,841.08-per-month payments for the monster mansion seem a little ridiculous. So calculate how much you can borrow if you make $2,000-per-month payments over 30 years and the annual interest rate is 4.25 percent:

1. **Select the Loan Amount option button.**

2. **Type** 4.25 **in the Annual Interest Rate text box.**

3. **Type** 30 **in the Number Of Years text box.**

4. **Type** 12 **in the Periods Per Year text box.**

5. **Type** 2000 **in the Payment Per Period text box.**

After you click the Calculator button or move the selection cursor, the Loan Calculator computes a loan amount of $406,553.73, as shown in Figure 10-4.

Figure 10-4:
The Loan
Calculator
dialog box.

The Refinance Calculator

You won't read about the Refinance Calculator here — but not because I'm lazy. Believe it or not, I enjoy writing about things that help you make better financial decisions. The Refinance Calculator merely calculates the difference in mortgage payments if you make new, lower payments; then it tells you how long it would take the savings from these lower payments to pay back the refinancing costs you incur.

For example, if you save $50 per month because you refinance and it costs $500 to refinance, the Refinance Calculator tells you that it would take ten months of $50-per-month savings to recoup your $500.

You know what? Although you may want to know how long it would take to recoup the refinance costs, that information doesn't tell you whether refinancing is a good idea. Deciding whether to refinance is very, very complicated. You can't just look at your next few payments, like the Refinance Calculator does. You also need to look at the total interest you would pay with the old mortgage and the new mortgage.

I can't think of any good reason to use the Refinance Calculator; it just doesn't do what it purports to do.

So that I don't leave you hanging, however, let me give you two general rules to help you make smarter refinancing decisions:

✔ First, if you want to save interest costs, don't use refinancing as a way to stretch out your borrowing. That is, if you refinance, make sure that you make payments large enough to pay off the new mortgage by the same time you would have paid off the old mortgage. In other words, if you have 23 years left on your old mortgage, don't go out and get a 30-year mortgage. Find a lender who will let you pay off the new mortgage in 23 years.

✔ Here's a second trick, if you can find a willing lender. Ask the lender to calculate the *annual percentage rate* (APR) on the new mortgage, assuming that you'll pay off the mortgage by the same time you would have paid off the old mortgage. (An APR includes all the loan's costs — interest, points, miscellaneous fees, and so on — and calculates an implicit interest rate.) If the APR on the new loan is lower than the current loan's interest rate, refinancing would probably save you money.

Let me issue one caveat. When you base your refinancing decision on the comparison between the new loan's APR and the current loan's interest rate, you assume that you'll live in your current house until the mortgage is paid.

I hope this information helps. As I said, mortgage-refinancing decisions are tough if you truly want to save money.

The Retirement Calculator

I think that this section is the most important one in this book. No joke. Your financial future is much too consequential to go for easy laughs or cheap shots.

The dilemma in a nutshell

By the time the 30-something and 40-something crowd reaches retirement, Social Security coverage almost certainly will be scaled back.

But the problem isn't just Social Security. Most employer-provided pension plans are *defined contribution plans,* which add specific amounts to your pension (such as 2 percent of your salary), rather than *defined benefit plans,* which promise specific pension amounts (such as $1,000 per month). As a result, although you know that someone will throw a few grand into your account every so often, you don't know how much you'll have when you retire.

The truth about Social Security

Though the Social Security Administration recently suspended regularly sending out a Personal Earnings and Benefits Summary, sometimes known by the acronym PEBS, past statements you've received and hopefully retained show you how much you can expect to receive in the way of retirement savings based on your past earnings, assuming you continue to earn similar amounts in the future. The statement also typically tells you that if Congress does nothing, there will only be money to cover *x* percent of your benefits at some point a few decades in the future. For example, the statement may have said something along the lines of "Blah, blah, blah, and if Congress does nothing to fix the funding challenges faced by the nation's aging workers, in 2037 the trust fund will be depleted, and Social Security tax receipts will be only enough to pay 76 percent of the retirees' and other recipients' benefits...." Okay, that's a bummer. I know.

But think about the worst-case scenario. If Congress really does nothing, the Social Security Administration now tells you, implicitly through the PEBS statement, by what amount your benefits will be cut. The last PEBS that I received during the summer of 2010, for example, suggested that the trust fund runs out of money in roughly 27 years, and, at that point, benefits will have to be cut back to 76 percent of their current levels. For example, someone who would have gotten $1,000 per month will get only $760. Okay, that's not good. But as long as you're not depending solely on Social Security, it isn't quite a financial meltdown either. You can save just a bit more money yourself and more than make up the difference. To give you an idea about the relative challenge of this personal solution, with twenty years of work left, you need to save about $66 a month to make up the difference. If you're not currently taking advantage of an employer-provided pension fund with a match, most of this money can come from your employer and through tax savings.

More about timing

The Retirement Calculator assumes that you or your employer will add to your retirement savings at the end of the year — what financial planners call an *ordinary annuity*. If you or your employer adds to your retirement savings at the beginning of the year, you earn an extra year of interest. As a result, your after-tax income will be more than Quicken shows.

So what does all this mean? In a nutshell, you need to think about your retirement now. Fortunately, the Quicken Retirement Calculator can help you.

Retirement planning calculations

Imagine that you decide to jump into your employer's *401(k)* thing (a type of profit-sharing plan), and that it allows you to plop $6,000 into a retirement account that you think will earn about 9 percent annually.

Fortunately, you don't need to be a rocket scientist to figure this stuff out. You can just use the Retirement Calculator:

1. **Display the Retirement Calculator.**

   Click the Planning tab. Click the Planning Tools button. Choose the Retirement command. Quicken displays the Retirement Calculator dialog box, shown in Figure 10-5.

2. **Enter your current age.**

   Move the cursor to the Current Age text box and type a number. You're on your own here, but let me suggest that this is a time to be honest.

3. **Enter your retirement age.**

   Move the cursor to the Retirement Age text box and type a number. Again, this is purely a personal matter. (Figure 10-5 shows this age as 65, but you should retire when you want.)

4. **Enter the age to which you want to continue withdrawals.**

   Move the cursor to the Withdrawal Until Age field and type a number. I don't want to beat around the bush here. This number is how old you think you'll be when you die. I don't like the idea any better than you do. Let me say, though, that ideally you want to run out of steam — there, that's a safe metaphor — before you run out of money. So go ahead and make this age something pretty old — like 95.

Retirement Calculator

Retirement Calculator

Calculate: ⦿ Annual retirement income
○ Annual contribution
○ Current savings

Current age: [40]
Retirement age: [65]
Withdrawal until age: [95]

Current savings: [0.00]
Annual yield: [9.000%]
Inflation Rate: [4.000%]
Annual contribution: [6,000.00]
☐ Increase based on inflation rate

Other retirement income: [24,000.00] per year
(Social Security, etc.)
Annual retirement income after taxes: 33,838.07
☑ Show in today's $
(no inflation adjustment)

Tax Assumptions: Retirement tax rate: [15.000%]

⦿ Tax sheltered investment
○ Non-sheltered investment - Current tax rate: [28.000%]

[Calculate] [View Schedule]

(?) [Done]

Figure 10-5:
The
Retirement
Calculator
dialog box.

5. Enter what you've already saved as your current savings.

Move the cursor to the Current Savings text box and type your current retirement savings: for example, if you have some IRA money or you've accumulated a balance in an employer-sponsored 401(k) account. Don't worry if you don't have anything saved — most people don't.

6. Enter the annual yield that you expect your retirement savings to earn.

Move the cursor to the Annual Yield text box and type the percent. In the little example shown in Figure 10-5, I say the annual yield is 9 percent. This is, I'll remind you, slightly less than the average return that the stock market produces over long periods of time.

You can use the long-term return the stock market delivers as your expected yield if you're taking a do-it-yourself approach, investing in a diversified portfolio of stocks (such as through mutual funds), and you're really watching your investment expenses — such as would be the case if you're using low-cost index funds to keep costs low. If you're working with a financial planner that charges you, say, 1 percent a year, obviously, your return will be 1 percent less in effect. Also, if you're investing some portion of your money into lower-risk investments like bonds, that approach, although perhaps very prudent, will slightly reduce your annual yield.

7. Enter the anticipated inflation rate.

Move the cursor to the Inflation Rate text box and type the inflation rate. By the way, in recent history, the inflation rate has averaged just above 3 percent (refer to Figure 10-5). I use 4 percent in Figure 10-5 to be just a bit more conservative.

8. Enter the annual amount added to your retirement savings.

Move the cursor to the Annual Contribution text box and type the amount that you or your employer will add to your retirement savings at the end of each year. In the example, I say that I plan to add $6,000 (refer to Figure 10-5).

9. Enter any other income you'll receive — such as Social Security.

Move the cursor to the Other Retirement Income (SSI, and so forth) text box and type a value. (Figure 10-5 shows $24,000.) Note that this income is in current-day, or uninflated, dollars. By the way, if you didn't save a copy of your last future Social Security benefits (this is the PEBS statement I talk about in the "The truth about Social Security" sidebar, earlier in this chapter), you can visit the Social Security Administration (SSA) website at www.ssa.gov and use their retirement estimator to get a good working estimate of your future retirement benefits.

10. Indicate whether you plan to save retirement money in a tax-sheltered investment.

Select the Tax Sheltered Investment option button if your retirement savings earn untaxed money. Select the Non-Sheltered Investment option button if the money is taxed. *Tax-sheltered investments* are such things as IRAs, annuities, and employer-sponsored 401(k)s and 403(b)s. A *403(b)* is kind of a profit-sharing plan for a nonprofit agency.

As a practical matter, tax-sheltered investments are the only way to ride. By deferring income taxes on your earnings, you earn interest on the money you otherwise would have paid as income tax.

11. Enter your current marginal tax rate, if needed.

If you're investing in taxable stuff, move the cursor to the Current Tax Rate text box. Then type the combined federal and state income tax rate that you pay on your last dollars of income.

12. Enter your anticipated retirement tax rate.

Move the cursor to the Retirement Tax Rate text box, and then . . . hey, wait a minute. Who knows what the rates will be next year, let alone when you retire? I think that you should type **0**, but remember that the Annual Retirement Income After Taxes is really your pretax income (just as your current salary is really your pretax income).

13. **Indicate whether the annual additions will increase.**

    Select the Inflate Contributions check box if the additions will increase annually by the inflation rate. (Because your salary and 401(k) contributions will presumably inflate if there's inflation.)

14. **After you enter all the information, click Calculate and take a peek at the Annual Retirement Income After Taxes field.**

    Figure 10-5, for example, shows $33,838.07. Not bad really. If you want to see the after-tax income in future-day, inflated dollars, deselect the Show In Today's $ check box but leave the Inflate Contributions check box checked.

To get more information on the annual deposits, balances, income, and so on, click the View Schedule button, which appears on the face of the Retirement Calculator dialog box. Quicken whips up a quick little report showing the annual deposits, income, and ending retirement account balances for each year you plan to add to and withdraw from your retirement savings.

If you're now bummed out about retirement

First, don't feel depressed. At least you know *now* if your golden years seem a little tarnished. After all, you acquired Quicken to help you sort out your finances. Now you can use Quicken and your newly gained knowledge to help improve your financial lot.

Basically, retirement planning depends on just three things:

- ✔ The number of years that the retirement savings will accrue interest
- ✔ The *real yield* (that is, adjusted for inflation) you earn — in other words, the annual yield minus the predicted inflation
- ✔ The yearly payments

Anything you do to increase one of these variables increases your retirement income.

If you invest, for example, in something that delivers higher real yields, such as the stock market, you should see a big difference. (Of course, you usually bear more risk.) Or if you wait an extra year or two to retire, you wind up making more annual payments and earning more interest. Finally, if you boost the yearly payments (for example, by participating in an employer-sponsored 401(k) or 403(b) plan, where your employer matches a portion of your contribution), you'll see a huge change.

Noodle around with the variables. See what happens. You may be surprised.

Retirement roulette

Use the Calculate option buttons in the Retirement Calculator (refer to Figure 10-5) to determine a retirement income variable. You can calculate current savings, annual contribution, or, as I describe earlier in the section, "Retirement planning calculations," the annual after-tax income.

To calculate the yearly payment required to produce a specific level of retirement income, for example, select the Annual Contribution option button. Then enter all the other variables — including the desired after-tax income — and click Calculate. The Retirement Calculator figures how much you need to save to hit your target retirement income.

Cost of College

Ouch. I have a couple of daughters, so I know how you feel. Man, oh, man, do I know how you feel.

The College Calculator

Suppose that you have a child who may attend college in ten years, and you haven't started to save yet. If the local university costs $20,000 per year and you can earn 9 percent annually, how much should you save?

The College Calculator works like the Retirement Calculator:

1. **Display the College Calculator.**

   Click the Planning tab. Click the Planning Tools button. Choose the College Calculator command. Quicken displays the College Calculator dialog box, shown in Figure 10-6.

2. **Enter the annual college costs.**

   Move the cursor to the Annual College Costs text box. Then type the current annual costs at a school Junior may attend. Figure 10-6 shows this amount as $20,000.

3. **Enter the number of years until enrollment.**

   Move the cursor to the Years Until Enrollment text box and type a number. For example, if Junior will start college in ten years, type **10**.

4. **Enter the number of years enrolled.**

   Move the cursor to the Number Of Years Enrolled text box and type a number. Assuming that Junior doesn't fool around, type **4** or **5**.

Figure 10-6:
Use the
College
Calculator
dialog box
to determine
whether
you'll have
to take out
a second
mortgage
to pay for
Junior's
college
education.

5. **Enter the amount of the current college savings.**

   Move the cursor to the Current College Savings field and type an amount. Figure 10-6 shows this amount as $20,000. Perhaps Grandpa has really come through for little Junior on this.

6. **Enter the annual yield that you expect the college savings to earn.**

   Move the cursor to the Annual Yield text box and type the percent. Figure 10-6 shows the yield as 9 percent.

7. **Enter the inflation rate anticipated in college tuition.**

   Move the cursor to the Inflation text box and type the inflation rate percent. Figure 10-6 shows this rate as 4 percent.

8. **Indicate whether you plan to increase your annual contribution as a result of inflation.**

   Select the Adjust Based on Inflation Rate check box if you plan to annually increase — by the annual inflation rate — the amount you save. Figure 10-6 shows this check box selected.

After you enter all the information, click Calculate or move the selection cursor. The Annual Contribution field shows how much you need to save each year until the child graduates from college.

Just to beat this thing to death, Figure 10-6 shows that the lucky student will attend five years at a college that currently costs $20,000 per year and that you expect to earn 9 percent annually and anticipate 4 percent annual inflation. Given these cold hard facts, you need to start saving $3,663.95 every year.

Because I'm a CPA, I want to offer you a quick tax-planning tip. If you do embark on a serious college savings program for a child or grandchild, take a look at the Sec. 529 college savings plans that are offered by most banks, brokers, and mutual fund companies. With a Sec. 529 plan, neither you nor the future college student gets taxed on the interest the college savings earn as long as the money is ultimately used for college expenses.

To get more information on the annual deposits, tuition, and balance, click the Schedule button, which appears on the face of the College Calculator dialog box. Quicken whips up a quick little report showing the annual deposits, tuition, and ending college savings account balances for each year you add to, and Junior withdraws from, the college savings money.

If you're now bummed out about college costs

Look at the positive side: You now understand the size of the problem and the solution.

College planning depends on four things:

- College costs
- The number of years that the savings earn interest
- The *real yield* (that is, adjusted for inflation) you earn — in other words, the annual yield minus the predicted inflation
- The yearly payments

I don't mean to sound like a simpleton, but you can ease the burden of paying for a college education in four basic ways:

- Reduce the years spent in school
- Reduce the annual costs (find a less expensive school)
- Invest in things that deliver higher yields
- Boost the yearly payments

You should consider especially the first two factors: years in school and annual costs because out-of-the-box thinking in these areas can pay off handsomely. Some high schools, for example, pay for students to attend community college — which means that these students get up to two years of college paid for by the local school district. High school advanced placement classes may have the same effect. And note that college costs vary widely. I think the best deal that I've recently heard about is the not-for-profit, online Western Governors University, which costs roughly $6,000 a year to attend.

Note that students who get their high schools to pay for community college classes and then go to a school like Western Governors for two years pay maybe $12,000 for their college education.

Use the Calculate option buttons (refer to Figure 10-6) to compute a specific financial variable. Select the variable you want to calculate and then input the other values. The College Calculator computes the flagged variable.

Finding a less expensive school isn't necessarily the same thing as looking for the cheapest tuition fees. Another huge factor these days is whether a program takes four years or five years to complete. A cheap-tuition school that requires five years may be more expensive than, say, a good private school that gets a student out — and working — in four years.

Planning for Taxes

Quicken also comes with a very powerful, very useful Tax Planner. The Tax Planner helps you make a precise estimate of the taxes that you'll owe. To use the Tax Planner, take the following steps:

1. **Display the Tax Planner.**

   Click the Planning tab. Click the Tax Tools button. Choose the Tax Planner command. Quicken displays the Tax Planner window. To move past the introductory information, click Let's Get Started and then click Next. Quicken shows the second page (see Figure 10-7).

   Note: Quicken may display a dialog box that asks whether you want to learn how TurboTax can help with year-round tax planning. Click No if you see this message. You have my help.

2. **Verify the tax year and filing status.**

   In the upper-left corner of the Tax Planner window, notice that the tax year (labeled *Year*) and the filing status (labeled *Status*) appear. These are probably correct. Quicken can guess the year by looking at your computer's clock. It determines your filing status based on information that you supply when you set up Quicken. But if one of these bits of information is wrong, click the Year or Status hyperlink. The hyperlinks are those bits of text along the left edge of the Tax Planner window. Quicken displays the Tax Planner Options text boxes, which let you specify the Tax Year and the Filing Status and choose a Scenario.

   Note: A *Scenario* is just a set of income tax inputs. You may have only one Scenario. Or you may have several Scenarios based on different guesses about your income and deductions.

Figure 10-7:
The second
page of the
Tax Planner
window.

3. Enter the wages and salaries that you and your lovely or handsome spouse expect.

Click the Wages hyperlink. Then, when Quicken displays the Wages text boxes, type your wages and, if you're married, those of your spouse. Quicken totals your wages and then makes a first rough calculation of the amount you'll owe in taxes. Of course, Quicken needs to collect some more data before this number is accurate, so don't freak out yet.

You can move to the next set of input text boxes by clicking the Next hyperlink and to the previous window of input text boxes by clicking the Previous hyperlink. The Next and Previous hyperlinks appear near the bottom of the Tax Planner window. (You may have to scroll down to see them on your computer.)

4. Enter the other income you'll have from interest, dividends, capital gains, and so on.

To record the other income that you'll need to pay taxes on, click the Interest/Dividend Inc, Business Income, Capital Gains, and Other Income hyperlinks and provide the information that Quicken requests. Some of these numbers are pretty easy to guess. Some of them aren't. You can also look at last year's tax return or at the year-to-date information you've already collected by using Quicken.

5. Identify any adjustments to your gross income.

Click the Adjustments hyperlink and then, using the Adjustments to Income text boxes, identify or estimate any adjustments to gross income that you'll have. Most people make only one adjustment — contributions to a deductible IRA. Self-employed individuals, however, also typically have several other adjustments, including half of their self-employment tax (which Quicken automatically calculates and enters), a portion of any health insurance paid, and Keogh and SEP pension contributions.

6. **Estimate your itemized deductions.**

   Click the Deductions hyperlink and then use the Standard and Itemized Deductions text boxes to estimate your deductions for expenses, such as state and local taxes, mortgage interest, and charitable contributions. Alternatively, if you'll probably or possibly use the standard deduction, carefully check any of the boxes that Quicken uses to determine which standard deduction you should use.

7. **Tell Quicken how many personal exemptions you'll claim.**

   Click the Exemptions hyperlink and then specify the number of dependents you'll claim on your return. The basic rule is that you get one exemption for every person in your family (you, your spouse if you're filing jointly, and your kids) as long as they live in your house. I should mention, however, that things become tricky if you have shirt-tail relatives (your Aunt Enid, for example) living at your house, if your kids live away from home or are married, or if some of the kids in the house have divorced parents. If you have questions because one of these situations sounds vaguely familiar, get the IRS preparation instructions and read the part about who is and is not a dependent.

8. **Indicate whether you owe any other taxes or have tax credits you can use to reduce your taxes.**

   Click the Other Tax, Credits hyperlink and then use the Other Taxes & Credits text boxes to describe any of the federal taxes you'll pay in addition to the usual federal income tax. The other taxes, by the way, typically include just two taxes: self-employment tax (which is the tax that self-employed people pay in place of Social Security and Medicare tax) and, in special cases, the alternative minimum tax. A bunch of different tax credits exist. You can very possibly look at your prior years' returns to see if they apply (typically) in your situation.

9. **Enter any estimated taxes you've paid or any federal income taxes your employer has withheld from your paycheck.**

   Click the Withholding hyperlink and use the Withholding text boxes to record how much money you've paid through withholding. Then click the Tax Payments hyperlink and use the Estimated Tax Payments text boxes to record how much you've paid in estimated tax payments and to guess how much you'll pay in the coming months.

10. **Return to the Tax Planner Summary and review the Quicken program's calculations.**

   After you complete the preceding steps, click the Tax Planner Summary hyperlink and review the calculations that Quicken makes. Quicken estimates the total tax you'll pay (which is useful and interesting in itself), the estimated refund or payment you'll have to make, and one other particularly useful bit of information — your marginal income tax rate (which Quicken labels *Marginal Rate*). If you want to print a copy of the Tax Planner's information and calculations, click Print (in the upper-right corner of the window).

Knowing your marginal income tax rate enables you to make more precise investment calculations. For example, the Retirement Calculator — described earlier in the chapter in the section cleverly titled, "The Retirement Calculator" — uses your marginal income tax rate to make more precise calculations. You can also use the marginal income tax rate to calculate the after-tax return that taxable investments deliver. Simply multiply the taxable return by the factor (1 – marginal tax rate).

The Other Planning Tools

In the preceding pages of this chapter, I talk about the personal financial planning tools that are most useful. Before I wrap up my discussion, let me quickly mention that Quicken provides some other interesting and, for some people, useful tax and financial planning tools.

For example, the Projected Balances and Savings Goals commands also appear on the Planning Tools menu. The Projected Balances command projects bank account balances using withdrawals and deposits that Quicken can guess about because you've set up bill or income reminders. (I talk about reminder transactions in Chapter 12). The Savings Goals lets you define and then monitor your progress toward achieving some savings goal (such as down payment money for a car or house).

If you open the Tax Tools menu, you'll notice Deduction Finder, Itemized Deduction Finder, Capital Gains Estimator, Tax Withholding Estimator, Online Tax Tools, and TurboTax commands. These calculation tools walk you through specific tax accounting and planning projects — and may be helpful to some taxpayers.

At the top of the Planning window, Quicken provides links to two other planning tools, too: Debt Reduction and Lifetime Planner. Click these links to begin walking through the steps for working your way out from under your debts or planning for personal finances. For what it's worth, in my opinion, most people won't be interested in taking the time to use these planning wizards. But if you're really serious or worried or compulsive about one of these topics, well, it just may be worth your time to explore a bit.

Part III
Home Finances

The 5th Wave   By Rich Tennant

"I'm not sure — I like the mutual funds with rotating dollar signs, although the dancing stocks and bonds look good, too."

In this part . . .

Are you going to be using Quicken for your personal financial stuff? If so, you should know that this program offers more than just the checkbook-on-a-computer business that I describe in Part II. Quicken can help you manage and monitor such things as credit cards, home mortgages, and investments. If this stuff sounds interesting, keep reading.

Chapter 11

Credit Cards, Petty Cash, and PayPal

*Y*ou can use Quicken to track your credit cards and even the cash in your pocket in much the same way that you use Quicken to keep a checkbook. Tracking these items uses a nearly identical process — with a few wrinkles.

First, however, I need to discuss whether you should even bother.

Tracking a Credit Card

Of course, if you do carry a credit card balance — and about 50 percent of people do — you can set up a Quicken credit card account and use it for tracking credit card purchases. If you just need to keep track of how much you charge during the month (even if you're going to pay the balance in full), you must also set up a credit card account and use it. I should make one other point: In order to track not just what you charge (by using spending categories) but also *where* you charge it (by using the Payee field), you must set up a credit card account and use it.

I don't use Quicken to track my credit card purchases because I pay my credit card balance in full every month. (Don't feel bad if you don't — it's like a natural law that CPAs like me must do this.) Therefore, I don't have an open credit card balance to track. What's more, when I pay the monthly credit card bill, I can easily use the Split Transaction window to describe my spending categories: $3.53 on food for lunch, $52.64 for car repair, and $217.54 for books (my personal weakness). If you're in the same boat — meaning you use a credit card but you don't carry a balance — you don't need anything special to track your credit card purchases. And, of course, you don't need to use Quicken to tell you your account balance because it's always zeroed-out at the end of the month.

How to Set Up a Credit Card Account

If you want to track credit card spending and balances with Quicken, you must set up a special credit card account. (In comparison, you use bank accounts to track other things, such as the money that flows into and out of a checking account.)

Adding a credit card account

To set up a credit card account, you follow roughly the same steps as you do to set up a bank account. Here's what you do:

1. **Display the Quicken home page.**

   You can do this by clicking the Home tab. Figure 11-1 shows the Quicken home page.

2. **Click the Add An Account button.**

   The Add button appears in the lower left-hand corner, by the way. (I mention this because the button is a little hard to spot.) Quicken displays the Add Account dialog box.

Figure 11-1:
The Quicken home page window.

3. **Tell Quicken you're setting up a credit card account.**

   Select the Credit Card option button when Quicken asks what type of account you want to set up (see Figure 11-2). Then, click Next to display the Quicken Account Setup dialog box (or boxes) that ask about the financial institution foolish enough to issue you a credit card.

Figure 11-2:
The first Quicken Account Setup dialog box asks what type of account you want to set up.

4. Identify the financial institution.

Quicken displays one or two dialog boxes that ask for the name of the credit card issuer. The first "identify your financial institution" dialog box, shown in Figure 11-3, lets you enter the issuer name or part of the name into a text box or, alternatively, lets you pick your bank from Quicken's list of popular banks. After you identify the bank issuing the credit card, Quicken prompts you to provide your online username and password. If you don't want Quicken to make online connections to your bank, you can click the Advanced Setup hyperlink (at bottom of dialog box) to indicate you don't want to identify your credit card issuer. When Quicken displays the dialog box that asks whether you want to download transactions or manually enter them, select the Enter Transactions Manually option button and click Next.

Figure 11-3: This Add Account dialog box asks for your financial institution.

5. Name the account and then click Next.

Why not? Move the cursor to the Account Name/Nickname text box and type a name. After you click Next, Quicken displays the Add Account dialog box that lets you provide the account balance on a specific date, as shown in Figure 11-4.

6. Enter the date on which you will start keeping records for the credit card account.

You should probably choose the date of your last statement, like Quicken suggests. Move the cursor to the Statement Ending Date text box and type the date in *MM/DD/YYYY* format. September 1, 2012, for example, should be entered as **9/1/2012**.

Figure 11-4:
The dialog box that lets you provide the account balance on a specific date.

7. Enter the balance you owed at the end of the last credit card billing period after making your payment. Then click Next.

Move the cursor to the Statement Ending Balance text box and type the balance value by using the number keys. After you click Next, Quicken displays a message that the account setup is complete. Just click Finish. Quicken finally gets the message and redisplays the Quicken home page (refer to Figure 11-1).

Note: As you complete the credit card account setup, Quicken may also display a message that urges you to sign up for your credit card company's online banking services. For now, ignore this. If you later want to sign up, just tell your bank, and it'll help you get set up.

Selecting a credit card account so that you can use it

To tell Quicken that you want to work with an account, you use the Accounts bar. Just click the credit card account's name.

You can also use the Accounts List window to get to the new credit card account — or to any other account, too. To get to the Accounts List window again, choose Tools⇨Accounts List and then select the account you want to work with.

After you select the account you want, Quicken displays the register for that account so that you can begin recording transactions (which I describe in the next section).

How to Enter Credit Card Transactions

After you select a credit card account, Quicken displays a special version of the register, as shown in Figure 11-5.

Touring the credit card register

The credit card register works like the regular register that you use for a bank account. You enter transactions into the rows of the register. After you record a charge, Quicken updates the credit card balance and the remaining credit limit (if you entered the optional credit limit information when you set up the account).

You can use the same techniques and commands as you do for your regular ol' bank account register. I talk about these in earlier chapters, so I won't regurgitate those discussions here.

Figure 11-5:
The credit card ver- sion of the Quicken register.

Recording a credit card charge

Recording a credit card charge is similar to recording a check or bank account withdrawal. For the sake of illustration, suppose that you charge $30.57 for dinner at your favorite Mexican restaurant. Here's how you record this charge:

1. **Enter the charge date.**

   Move the cursor to the Date field (if it isn't already there) and type the date using the *MM/DD* format. For example, enter September 1, 2012, as **9/1**. You usually don't have to type the year because Quicken retrieves the current year number from the little clock inside your computer. Or, if you want, get crazy — click the box that remotely resembles a calendar at the end of the field, and Quicken displays a pop-up calendar (see Chapter 4 for more information) from which you can select the appropriate month and day.

   Don't bother with the Ref field. Quicken supplies it so that you can record the credit card reference number — a bit of data that's usually about 20 characters long. You, my friend, have better things to do with your time, however. So just skip the field.

2. **Record the name of the business you paid with a credit card.**

   Move the cursor to the Payee field and type the name of the person or business you paid. If the restaurant is Florencia's Cantina, for example, type **Florencia's Cantina** into the Payee field.

3. **Enter the charge amount.**

   Move the cursor to the Charge field and type the total charge amount — **30.57** in this example. Don't type a dollar sign, but do type the period to indicate the decimal place and cents.

4. **Enter the category.**

   Move the cursor to the Category field, open the drop-down list box, and select the appropriate category. You may categorize a restaurant charge as Food & Dining:Restaurants, for example, if you're using Quicken's suggested categories and subcategories.

5. **(Optional) Enter a memo description.**

   Move the cursor to the Memo field and type the specific reason you're charging the item, such as a special date with your spouse or an important business meeting. The Memo field — just so you know — appears only when the register display is set to Two-Line Display mode.

6. **Record the charge and click the Save button.**

   Quicken beeps and then calculates both the new credit card balance and the remaining credit limit. Quicken then moves the cursor to the next slot in the register.

Figure 11-6 shows the charge at Florencia's. Good food and reasonable prices — you can't ask for much more than that.

Figure 11-6:
The
charge at
Florencia's
Cantina.

Changing charges you've already entered

Use the arrow keys or click the mouse to highlight the charge that you want
to change. Use Tab and Shift+Tab or the mouse to move the cursor to the
field that contains the misinformation you want to fix. You can then fix the
entry and record the transaction by clicking the Save button. That's easy
enough, isn't it?

Paying credit card bills

If you're tracking the credit card account balance with a credit card account
like the one I'm describing here, Quicken provides two ways for you to pay a
credit card bill.

Note: If you're not using a credit card account in Quicken, you record the
check you send to pay a credit card bill in the same way you record any
other check. And that means you don't have to read anything I'm about
to say.

A most bodacious way to pay a credit card bill

This method is pretty simple, so don't blink your eyes because you may miss the action.

Look at your credit card statement. Decide how much you want to pay. Select the bank account on which you'll write the check. Then write the check and record it in the bank account register — but as a transfer to the credit card account.

You're done. If you have questions, take a peek at the selected check transaction shown in Figure 11-7. It pays $30.57 of the credit card balance. The only trick — if you want to call it that — is that the credit card account is specified as the account to which the money is transferred. (You can see the other account by right-clicking the transaction and choosing Go To Transfer, or you can click on the other account's QuickTab, of course.)

If you could look at the credit card account register now — of course, you can't because you're not sitting in front of my computer — you would see that this check reduces the credit card balance by $30.57.

Figure 11-7:
A check transaction that pays a credit card balance.

A less bodacious way to pay a credit card bill

You can also tell Quicken that you want to pay some portion of the credit card bill as part of reconciling the credit card's account balance. What will happen is that after you reconcile the credit card account, Quicken will (or may) ask whether you want to make a payment. If you say you do, Quicken prompts you to describe the payment.

I think that this method is slightly more difficult. But if you want to reconcile your credit card account, think about using this second method. If you're reconciling a credit card statement and paying some portion of the credit card balance at the same time, you may find this method more convenient. Who knows?

I describe how to reconcile a credit card account in the very next section.

Reconciling That Crazy Account

You know that trick in which you compare your checking account records with your bank's records of your checking account? The one in which you calculate the difference between what you think is your account balance and what the bank thinks is your balance? And this difference is supposed to equal the total of the transactions floating around out there in the system? You can use this same trick on your credit card account.

To reconcile a credit card account, first get your credit card statement. Next, display the credit card account in a transaction list window.

What the nasty credit card company says

To tell Quicken what that nasty credit card company says, follow these steps and put on some music if you can't seem to get the rhythm thing right:

1. **Click the Account Actions button in the transaction list window and choose the Reconcile command.**

   Quicken displays the Reconcile: Credit Card dialog box, as shown in Figure 11-8.

2. **Enter the charges and cash advances that your statement shows.**

   Move the cursor to the Charges, Cash Advances text box and then type the number.

3. **Enter the payment and credits that your statement shows.**

   You know the drill: Move the cursor to the Payments, Credits text box and type the number.

Figure 11-8:
The
Reconcile:
Credit Card
dialog box.

4. **Enter the new balance shown on the credit card statement.**

   Now I bet this is a surprise. Go ahead and type the figure in the Ending Balance text box — even if you just can't believe you charged that much.

5. **Enter the ending statement date.**

   I don't know why Quicken is now collecting this piece of information. For more than ten years, Quicken has been able to reconcile your credit card account (and any other account) without this snidbit of data.

6. **Enter the monthly interest charge by using the Finance Charges text box.**

   Pause for a moment of silence here if this topic makes you sad, sad, sad.

7. **Assign the monthly interest to the appropriate spending category, such as Interest Exp.**

   Move the cursor to the Category text box and type the category name. (Are you getting bored yet? I know: move and type . . . move and type . . . all I ever seem to say is "move and type.") Remember that you can click the little down arrow at the end of the text box to see a list of categories to select from.

8. **Click OK.**

   Quicken displays the Reconcile: Credit Card window (see Figure 11-9). Use this window to tell Quicken which credit card charges and payments appear on your statement. (This step is akin to looking at a bank statement and noting which checks and deposits have cleared the bank.)

Figure 11-9:
The
Reconcile:
Credit Card
window.

Ouch! Did I really spend that much?

After you give Quicken an overview of your credit card situation, you can note which charges have cleared and which charges have not.

If you're comfortable whipping through a bank reconciliation, you can probably do this reconciliation with your eyes closed. If you need some help, leave your eyes open so that you can read these steps:

1. **Find the first charge listed on the credit card statement.**

2. **Mark the charge as cleared.**

   Charges are listed in the left list box. If you charged a bunch of stuff, scroll through the transactions listed in the Charges window until you find the charge. After you see a charge that appears on your credit card statement, click it. Or select the charge by using the arrow keys and then press the spacebar. Quicken adds the check mark symbol in front of the list entry in the Clr column to mark this charge as cleared and then updates the cleared statement balance.

3. **Enter any missing charges.**

   If you can't find a charge, you probably didn't enter it in the Quicken register yet. Open the credit card account register by clicking on its tab and then enter the charge into the register in the usual way — except enter a **c** (the letter *c*) into the Clr column by clicking in the Clr field. By doing so, you identify the charge as one that's already cleared. After you finish, click the Return To Reconcile button to return to the Reconcile: Credit Card window.

4. **Repeat Steps 1–3 for charges listed on the credit card statement.**

   Or until you're blue in the face.

5. **Find the first payment or credit listed on the credit card statement.**

   Any payments and credits appear in the right list box.

6. **Mark the payment or credit as cleared.**

   Scroll through the transactions listed in the Payments window until you find the first payment or credit and then select it. Or select the credit and then press the spacebar. Quicken adds the check mark symbol in front of the list entry to mark the payment or credit as cleared and then updates the cleared statement balance.

7. **Enter any missing payments or credits.**

   If you can't find the payment or credit — you probably know what I'm going to say — it means you haven't entered it into the Quicken register yet. Open the credit card account register by clicking on its tab, and then enter the payment or credit into the register in the usual way, but put a **c** in the Clr column. When you finish, click the Return To Reconcile button to return to the Reconcile: Credit Card window.

8. **Repeat Steps 5–7 for payments or credits listed on the credit card statement.**

If you record a transaction wrong, do this

As you're looking through the credit card statement, you may discover that you incorrectly recorded a transaction. If this happens, display the credit card register so that you can make the necessary fixes.

Oh, that explains the difference

After you mark all the cleared charges and payments, the difference between the cleared balance for the credit card and the statement's ending balance should be zero.

Figure 11-10 shows how this looks. By the way, reconciling with fictitious data is darned easy.

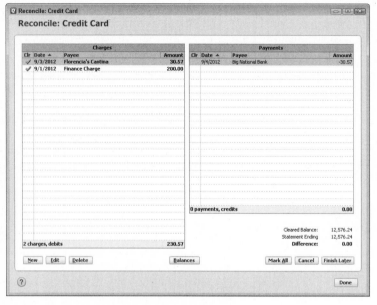

If you're ready to finish

If the difference does equal zero, you're cool. You're golden. You're done. (Sort of makes you sound like fried chicken, doesn't it?)

All you need to do is click Done to tell Quicken that you're done. Quicken asks you whether you want to make a credit card payment. Jump ahead to the "Paying the bill as part of the reconciliation" section for help doing just that.

If the difference doesn't equal zero, you have a problem. If you clicked Done in spite of the problem, Quicken displays a message that has some cursory explanation as to why your account doesn't balance. This message also tells you that you can force the two amounts to agree by pressing Enter.

Forcing the two amounts to agree isn't a very good idea, though. To make the balances agree, Quicken adds a cleared transaction equal to the difference. (Quicken asks for a category if you choose the adjustment route.)

Despite the ease of making adjustments, you should still correct the error responsible for the difference.

Chapter 8 provides some ideas for trying to figure out why a bank account that should balance doesn't. You can apply the same list of tips to credit card reconciliations if you're in a bad way.

If you want to postpone the inevitable

You can postpone reconciling the account by clicking the Finish Later button. When you click this button, you abandon your reconciliation work. Transactions that you mark as cleared still show the c in the Clr text box. You still have an inexplicable difference between the credit card statement and your register. Even so, postponing a reconciliation is usually better than forcing the cleared balance to equal the credit card statement balance. By postponing a reconciliation, you can hopefully find the problem or problems and fix them. Then you can restart the reconciliation and finish your work. (You restart a credit card reconciliation in the same way that you originally start one.)

When you finish, Quicken redisplays the Transactions tab. You may notice that when you mark credit card transactions as cleared, Quicken puts a c in the Clr column of the credit card register. When you finish reconciling the credit card account, Quicken changes all these cs to Rs. None of what Quicken does here is magical. Quicken just makes this change to identify the transactions that have already been through the reconciliation process. (The c shows that a transaction has been marked as cleared. The R shows that a transaction has been reconciled.)

Paying the bill as part of the reconciliation

After you finish reconciling the credit card account, Quicken does two things. First, if some of the stuff in the credit card register doesn't agree with the credit card statement, Quicken displays a message box to alert you to these, er, discrepancies. It then suggests you let Quicken bring your records into agreement with the statement (see Figure 11-11). To synchronize your records with the credit card statement, verify that Quicken is using a reasonable expense category to "categorize" the discrepancy and then click Adjust.

Figure 11-11:
The Adjusting Register To Agree With Statement dialog box.

Adjusting Register to Agree with Statement

In order to bring your records into balance with the statement, Quicken is about to make the following entry in your register.

Missing charges adjustment

30.57   Category (optional):

Help   Adjust   Cancel

Quicken also does a second thing after you finish reconciling a credit card account. Quicken asks whether you want to pay the bill. Figure 11-12 shows the Make Credit Card Payment dialog box, which is the tool that Quicken uses to collect the necessary data. You simply identify the bank account on which you want to write the check and indicate whether you'll use a printed check or a handwritten check. Quicken then records a check that pays the credit card balance into the register. You can edit, print, and do whatever else you want to do with this check in the usual way.

Figure 11-12:
The Make Credit Card Payment dialog box.

The Online Banking Hoopla

As I briefly mention in Chapter 6, Quicken supports online banking. If you have your credit card with a credit card company — probably a bank — that is set up to handle Quicken online banking, you can grab your credit card statement directly from the credit card company. If you have a checking account at the bank that issued the credit card, you can also pay your credit card bill simply by transferring money from your checking account to your credit card. (This feature is actually pretty slick, I have to say.)

The big hoopla concerning this feature — at least as it relates to credit cards — is that you don't have to enter the credit card transactions into a register. Rather, you retrieve them by using an Internet connection.

Should you even bother?

Is the online-banking-with-a-credit-card-thing a feature that you should look into? Does it really save you time? Is it a good deal? Inquiring minds want to know, so I'll tell you what I think. (I should point out that what I'm about to say next is just my humble opinion.)

I think that online banking in general is well worth the fee you probably have to pay for the service when you consider the time savings. You'll probably pay only a few dollars a month. (What you pay depends on the bank issuing the credit card.)

Something bothers me about the whole deal, however: You really just receive an electronic version of your statement, which means — at least from my perspective — that you're more likely not to see erroneous transactions. And reconciling your bank statement against, well, your bank statement isn't going to make a whole heck of a lot of sense. (Golly, gee, Batman, the charge to Edna's Pet School appears on both statements, too!)

How to use Online Account Access with your credit card

Okay, so you've listened to my side of the story, but you still want to use the Quicken Online Account Access feature with your credit card — and your bank is one that provides this service. "What next?" you're wondering.

Here's the answer: You set up online credit card accounts the same way you set up online bank accounts. *Note:* For more information about the Quicken Online Account Access feature, see Chapter 6.

Petty Cash and Mad Money

You can track petty cash in your business as well as the petty cash in your wallet by using a special Quicken cash account. To track the cash, you must set up a cash account and then enter the increases and decreases into the cash account's register. Sure, this stuff isn't exactly rocket science, but shoot, I thought I'd just quickly go over it to show you how easy it really is. Okay?

Adding a cash account

To set up a cash account, you follow roughly the same steps as you do for setting up a bank account. Because you've probably already set up a bank account, you can move quickly through the following steps to set up a cash account:

1. **Display the Quicken home page.**

   Click on the Home tab. Quicken displays the Quicken home page (refer to Figure 11-1). You remember this puppy.

2. **Click the Add An Account button to set up a new account.**

   Quicken, of course, is no fool, so it displays the Add Account dialog box. The Add An Account button appears in the lower-left corner of the window.

3. **Set up a cash account.**

   You can guess how to do this, can't you? You indicate you want to set up a cash account and then simply step through Quicken's questions about the account you want to set up. You need to give the account a name, for example, such as *cash* or *pocket money.* And you need to provide a starting balance value using the faithful, familiar Add Account dialog box, as shown in Figure 11-13.

Figure 11-13:
The final
Quicken
Add
Account
dialog
box used
for cash
accounts.

4. **Click Next and then Done.**

   When you finish describing the cash account, click Done. Quicken displays the new cash account in a register window.

Tracking cash inflows and outflows

After you set up a cash account, you can use it to track the cash you receive and spend in the same way that you track the deposits and checks for a bank account.

To record your cash inflows and outflows, use the QuickTab for the account, which should appear on the Accounts bar. Figure 11-14 shows the cash account version of the register. Until you start entering transactions, only the first opening balance transaction shows.

Figure 11-14:
The cash
account
version of
the register.

To record the amount of money you spend, fill in the Date, Payee, and Spend fields. To record the amount of money you receive, fill in the Date, Payee, and Receive fields. To track the reasons that you're receiving and spending the cash, use the Memo and Category fields.

Recording checks you cash instead of deposit

By the way, you don't necessarily need to set up a cash account if you like to spend cash (rather than, say, write checks or charge on a credit card). If you just cash a check and you do have a bank account set up, you can record the transaction in another way that may be simpler: Just use the Split Transaction window to show both the income category (Salary, for example, for an individual) and how you're going to use the money.

For example, if you cash a $1,000 check and you plan to use the $1,000 for spending money, you may show a positive $1,000 in the Net Salary category and a negative $1,000 in the Entertainment:Amusement spending category. Figure 11-15 shows this trick.

Figure 11-15:
A zero-
amount
transaction
is one handy
trick.

Note that the transaction shown in Figure 11-15 produces a transaction that equals zero. This is correct. Cashing a check that you never deposited doesn't affect your checking account balance. But by filling out the Split Transaction window, as shown in Figure 11-15, you do end up recording both the $1,000 of income and the $1,000 of expense.

Don't worry. I won't ask why you're carrying around $1,000 in cash.

Updating cash balances

You can update a register's cash balance to reflect what you actually have in petty cash, your wallet, under the mattress, in the cookie jar, or wherever else you keep your cash, by taking the following steps:

1. **Display the cash account register.**

2. **Click the Account Actions button and choose Update Balance.**

   Quicken displays the Cash Account: Update Balance dialog box, as shown in Figure 11-16.

Figure 11-16:
The Cash
Account:
Update
Balance
dialog box.

3. **Enter the actual cash balance in the New Balance text box.**

4. **Enter a date in the Adjustment Date text box.**

5. **Choose the category that you want to update in the Category For Adjustment drop-down list box.**

   After you click the arrow to the right of the drop-down list box, you get a list of all the categories that you have set up.

6. **After you finish, click OK.**

   Quicken updates the cash account's balance.

And that, my friend, is that.

PayPal Can Be Quicken's Friend

One final point before I end this discussion.

If you use PayPal, you can and should use Quicken to track the money flowing into and out of your PayPal account. Fortunately, tracking a PayPal account with Quicken is pretty dang easy.

To track PayPal using Quicken, you just want to remember these three points:

✔ A PayPal account is really just another bank account, albeit a special sort of bank account. Accordingly, you want to set up a Quicken PayPal account in the same way that you set up any other Quicken bank account. (Refer to Chapter 2 for additional information about setting up a bank account.)

✔ If you use your credit card to pay money into the PayPal account, you're actually transferring money from your credit card account to your PayPal account. To record this transfer, you record a credit card charge into your credit card register (similar to the charge made to Florencia's Cantina shown in Figure 11-6). However, rather than use a Quicken category, you specify the PayPal account.

✔ You should reconcile your PayPal account just like any other bank account or credit card account. During this reconciliation, be sure to record any PayPal charges.

And one final snidbit for people who really want to push the envelope: PayPal will allow you to download your transaction history into a QIF file, which can then be imported into Quicken using the File⇨File Import⇨QIF File command. You may want to refer to Quicken's and PayPal's online help for more information.

Chapter 12

Other People's Money

A while back, a popular, financial self-help writer used to argue that one of the secrets to financial success is using other people's money: the bank's, the mortgage company's, the credit people's, your brother-in-law's. . . . You get the idea.

Me? I'm not so sure that using other people's money is the key to financial success. Borrowing other people's money can turn into a nightmare.

Quicken can help you here. No, the folks at Intuit won't make your loan payments for you. But in a way, they do something even better: They provide you with a tool to monitor the money you owe other people and the costs of your debts.

Should You Bother to Track Your Debts?

I think that tracking your debts — car loans, mortgages, student loans, and so on — is a good idea when lenders fail to tell you the amount that you're paying in annual interest or the amount you owe after each and every payment.

If your lenders are doing a good job at keeping you informed, I don't think that using Quicken for this purpose makes much sense. Heck, it's their money. They can do the work, right?

Let me make one more observation. If lenders have half a clue, they send you a United States 1098 tax form at the end of every year. The number shown on that form equals your tax deduction if the interest stems from a mortgage, business, or investment loan. Note that personal interest expenses aren't deductible anymore, so you shouldn't track them unless you really want to be mean to yourself.

How Do You Get Started?

To track other people's money with Quicken, you must set up a *liability account.* Setting up one of these babies is easy. Just remember that you must set up a liability account for every loan or debt you want to track: one account for your mortgage, another for your car loan, still another for your student loan, and so on.

Setting up a liability account for an amortized loan

An *amortized loan* is one on which you make regular, equal payments. Over time, the principal portion of each payment pays off, or *amortizes,* the loan principal. If you borrowed money to purchase a house, a car, a Winnebago, or anything else that's really expensive and that you pay off over several years, chances are that your loan is of the amortizing variety.

Setting up a loan account requires a few dozen steps, but none of the steps are difficult. And none takes that much time to complete. As long as you have your loan information handy — the loan amount, interest rate, balance, and so on — setting up this type of account is a snap.

Here's the recipe for setting up a liability account:

1. **Click the Add An Account button.**

   The Add An Account button appears in the lower-left corner of the Accounts bar.

2. **Tell Quicken you want to set up a loan account.**

   When Quicken displays the Add Account dialog box, click Loan and then Next. Quicken displays the Loan Setup dialog box (see Figure 12-1).

3. **Provide some basic background information. Then click Next.**

   Use the Loan Type option buttons to specify whether you're borrowing money or lending money. Use the New Account text box to name the new loan account something clever like *mortgage* or *car loan.* And use the Have Any Payments Been Made? option buttons to indicate, well, whether you've started making payments yet. After you click Next, Quicken displays another set of boxes and buttons, shown in Figure 12-2.

Figure 12-1:
The Loan
Setup dialog
box.

4. **Enter the date that you borrowed the money in the Opening Date text box; or, if your loan has a grace period (like a student loan), enter the date when your loan enters the repayment period.**

   Quicken needs to know this date so that it can calculate the interest the loan started to accrue when you borrowed the money. The program suggests the current system date as the Opening Date, but this is probably wrong.

Figure 12-2:
Another
Loan Setup
dialog box.

5. **Enter the original loan balance.**

   Enter the original loan amount into the Original Balance text box. You can get this amount, if you're unsure, from the original loan documents.

6. **Enter the loan term in years in the Original Length text box.**

   If you set up a 30-year mortgage, for example, type **30**. You may have to perform one tiny trick when entering this figure: If you set up a loan that includes a balloon payment, enter the number of years over which the loan will be fully paid — not the number of years used for calculating the loan payment. For example, loan payments may be calculated based on a 30-year term, but the loan may require a balloon payment at the end of 7 years. In that case, type **7** in the Original Length text box.

7. Indicate how often the bank calculates loan interest.

Use the Compounding Period text box to specify how often the bank calculates interest on the loan. The interest-compounding period usually equals the payment period.

8. Describe how often you make a loan payment by using the Payment Period options.

If you make regular monthly payments, for example, select the Standard Period option button, open the Standard Period drop-down list box, and choose Monthly. If you can't find an entry in the Standard Period drop-down list box that describes how often you make payments, select the Other Period option button and then type the number of payments you make each year in the Payments Per Year text box.

9. Click Next.

Quicken displays another set of boxes and buttons on the Loan Setup dialog box (shown in Figure 12-3).

Figure 12-3: More buttons and boxes you can use to describe the amortized loan.

10. (Optional) Describe the balloon payment (if you have one).

The balloon payment option buttons and boxes let you alert Quicken to any balloon payment you must make in addition to the last regular loan payment. If the loan doesn't have a balloon payment, ignore this stuff and make sure that the No Balloon Payment option is selected.

If the loan does have a balloon payment, select the Amortized Length option button; then use the Amortized Length text box and drop-down list box to specify the number of years or months (or whatever) over which the loan is amortized. If you know that you have a loan payment (and know the loan payment amount) but don't know what the amount is or when it occurs, select the Calculate option button in the Balloon Information area.

11. **Enter the Current Balance if you've made any payments.**

    If you indicated that you've already made payments on the loan, specify how much you still owe on the loan after making the last payment by using the Current Balance text box. If you don't know the current balance, call the lender and ask for it. If you haven't made any payments yet, skip to Step 12. You know the drill by now. Just move the cursor to the text box and pound a few number keys.

12. **Enter the date as of which the current balance is, well, current.**

    Use the As Of field to indicate the date for which you've entered the current balance. All the standard date entry and date-editing tricks apply to this text box. You can press the + and – keys, for example, to move the date ahead and back by one day. And you can click that icon at the right end of the As Of text box to display a pop-up calendar.

13. **Specify the interest rate.**

    Enter the loan's interest rate into the Interest Rate text box in the Payment section in this window. The loan interest rate, by the way, isn't the same thing as the _APR,_ or annual percentage rate. You want to enter the actual interest rate used to calculate your payments. Enter the interest rate as a decimal amount. For example, don't type **7⅝**; instead, type **7.625**. You should be able to get this rate from the lender or the prospective lender.

14. **(Optional) Describe the payment in more detail (if necessary).**

    If you've entered all the loan information that Quicken has requested in the preceding steps, you can just select the Calculate option button in the Payment area. Quicken then calculates the loan payment by using the loan balance, term, balloon payment information, and interest rate you entered. If you haven't entered all this information — say, you left out the balloon payment information because you don't know what it is — select the Payment Amount (P+I) option button and then enter the loan principal and interest amount into the Payment Amount (P+I) text box. If necessary, edit the next payment date in the Due On drop-down list box.

15. **Click Done.**

    If you asked Quicken to calculate anything for you, a dialog box pops up, telling you that Quicken did so. Click OK. Make sure that the Quicken calculations make sense and then click Done again. Quicken displays the Set Up Loan Payment dialog box (shown in Figure 12-4).

16. **Verify the principal and interest payment calculated by the program.**

    If it's wrong, you can keep going, but let me point out a minor yet annoying problem. You probably entered one of the loan calculation inputs incorrectly, such as the loan balance, loan term, or the interest rate. Fortunately, these errors are only a minor bummer. Later in this chapter (in the "Fixing loan stuff" section), I describe how to restart.

Figure 12-4:
The Set
Up Loan
Payment
dialog box.

17. (Optional) Indicate any amounts you pay besides principal and interest.

Click the Edit button. Quicken displays the Split Transaction dialog box (see Figure 12-5), which you can use to describe any additional amounts the lender requires you to pay. In the case of a mortgage, for example, you may be required to pay property taxes or private mortgage insurance. After you enter the information and click OK, Quicken calculates the full payment and redisplays the Set Up Loan Payment dialog box (refer to Figure 12-4).

Figure 12-5:
The Split
Transaction
dialog box.

18. Indicate how you make payments in the Type drop-down list box.

Choose one of the payment transaction types listed in the Type drop-down list box. *Payment* means that you handwrite checks; *Print Check* means that you print checks by using Quicken; and *Online Pmt* means that you use Quicken Online Banking to make electronic payments.

If you print checks by using Quicken and want to put the payee's address on the check, click the Address button in the Set Up Loan Payment dialog box. Quicken displays a dialog box that you can use to input the payee's address, as shown in Figure 12-6. When you finish providing name and address information, click OK and go get another cup of coffee. When you come back, Quicken will have redisplayed the Set Up Loan Payment dialog box.

Figure 12-6:
The Edit Address Book Record dialog box.

19. Type the lender's name in the Payee text box.

The *payee* is just the name of the person or business that loaned you the money.

20. (Optional) Type a memo description.

Does the lender always get mixed up when you send the check? Stick the loan account number in the check's Memo text box. I refrain from using this text box to comment on the fairness of the bank's interest rate, to mock the intelligence of the loan payment processors, or to perform other emotionally gratifying, but generally unproductive, acts.

21. Type the date of your next loan payment in the Next Payment Date text box.

22. Enter the interest category.

Open the Category For Interest drop-down list and choose the appropriate category.

Quicken lets you *schedule* (have Quicken automatically enter) or *memorize* (just have Quicken remind you to enter) loan payments and electronic payments. I assume that you don't want to be doing this kind of stuff — at least not yet. If I'm assuming incorrectly, click the Payment Method button. Then fill in the dialog box that appears. It's not all that difficult. If you're still confused, I explain how you can use the Calendar to schedule loan payments later in this chapter.

23. Ignore the Loan website text box.

Or, heck, I don't care. Go ahead and enter the lender's website address if you want to have the information stored someplace handy within Quicken.

24. With the Set Up Loan Payment dialog box displayed, click OK.

Quicken removes the Set Up Loan Payment dialog box and asks whether any asset is associated with the loan. If you want to associate an asset with your loan, Quicken walks you through the steps for setting up an asset account. But you know what? Don't worry about setting up an asset account. It actually isn't worth it. Just click No. Quicken displays a new Net Worth tab, or window. You probably want to see the new liability you've set up in its own register, so click the new account. Quicken displays a register window with any of the loan's transactions, as shown in Figure 12-7.

By the way, I want to apologize to you for describing a 24-step process. I couldn't do anything about it, but I feel bad anyway.

Figure 12-7:
The Liability:
Mortgage
transaction
list.

Fixing loan stuff

Nobody's perfect, right? You may have made a tiny little mistake in setting up either the loan or the loan payment. This mistake doesn't need to be a major financial or personal crisis, however. Just display the loan account's transactions (such as by clicking the account name in the Accounts bar), click the Account Actions button, and then choose the Loan Details command. Quicken displays the View Loans dialog box, as shown in Figure 12-8.

Figure 12-8: The View Loans dialog box.

Hey, can I mention one other thing about the View Loans dialog box? See those two tabs labeled Payment Schedule and Payment Graph? You can probably guess what they do, but if you click the Payment Schedule tab, an amortization schedule shows the interest and principal portions of each loan payment. If you click the Payment Graph tab, Quicken displays a line chart that shows how you pay off the loan balance over time. You may want to take a minute and experiment with these two tabs. They're pretty neat.

Changing loan or loan payment information

If you want to change something about the loan, click the Edit Loan button. Quicken displays the Edit Loan dialog box. It works like the Loan Setup dialog boxes in Figures 12-1 and 12-2. Make the changes and click OK.

To change something about the payment, click the Edit Payment button. Quicken displays the Edit Loan Payment dialog box. Make your changes and click OK.

Working with adjustable-rate loans

Before I wrap up this discussion, let me mention a few other things. If you have a variable-rate loan, you can click the Rate Changes button to display the Loan Rate Changes dialog box (shown in Figure 12-9). This dialog box has a very simple purpose: It lists the interest rates you entered for a loan and the dates these interest rates were used in loan calculations.

Figure 12-9:
The Loan Rate Changes dialog box.

If you want to record new interest rates — because you have a variable-rate loan and the interest rate changes, for example — follow these steps in the Loan Rate Changes dialog box:

1. **Indicate that you want to record a new interest rate.**

   Click the New button in the Loan Rate Changes dialog box or right-click in the dialog box and choose New on the shortcut menu that appears. Quicken displays the Insert An Interest Rate Change dialog box, shown in Figure 12-10.

Figure 12-10:
Changing a loan's interest rate.

2. **Provide the effective date of the interest rate change.**

   Use the Effective Date text box to indicate when the new interest rate becomes effective. You can either type in a date or open the drop-down list box and select a date from the calendar.

3. **Give the new interest rate.**

   Type the new interest rate in the Interest Rate text box. When you move the selection cursor to a new box, Quicken refigures the loan payment and sticks the new loan payment figure in the Regular Payment text box.

4. **Click OK.**

Removing and adding loans

You can delete (remove) and add loans by using the Loan Summary tab in the View Loans window (refer to Figure 12-8).

Delete a loan that you no longer need or shouldn't have added in the first place by clicking the Choose Loan button and selecting the loan account. Then click the Delete button. Quicken then warns you that you're about to delete your loan and asks you whether you want to save the account for your records. Saving the account keeps the account available in your Accounts window but eliminates it in your View Loans window. You can hide the saved account later if you want it to disappear from your Accounts window. (To do so, choose Tools⇨Account List, click the account when Quicken displays the Account List window, and then check one of the Hide This Account boxes.)

You can add loans in the View Loans window, too (refer to Figure 12-8). To do so, click the New Loan button in the View Loans window. Quicken displays the Loan Setup dialog box and walks you through the sequence of steps that I describe earlier in the "Setting up a liability account for an amortized loan" section to set up the loan. For example, you fill in both the Loan Setup dialog box (refer to Figures 12-1 and 12-2) and the Set Up Loan Payment dialog box (refer to Figure 12-4).

Delivering a Pound of Flesh (Also Known as Making a Payment)

After you set up a liability account, you're ready to hand over a pound of your flesh — that is, make a payment. Before you say that this phrase is just some sort of populist bull-dweeble, I want to remind you that this metaphor comes from Shakespeare's *The Merchant of Venice,* in which a loan is guaranteed with a pound of human flesh. Ouch.

Recording the payment

After you set up the loan and the loan payment, you're ready to record the payment in (drum roll, please) the register.

I'm trying to make the old Quicken register more exciting for you because you're probably becoming pretty darn familiar with it. And familiarity, as they say, breeds contempt.

Anyway, complete the following steps to record a payment:

1. **Display the loan's register.**

   Click the loan account in the Accounts bar.

2. **Display the View Loans dialog box.**

   To do so, click the Account Actions button and choose the Loan Details command from the menu Quicken displays.

3. **Click the Make Payment button.**

   Quicken displays a message box that asks whether the payment you're making is a regular payment (one the lender expects) or an extra payment (perhaps to amortize the loan more quickly). After you select the payment type, Quicken displays either the Make Regular Payment or the Make Extra Payment dialog box. Figure 12-11 shows the Make Regular Payment dialog box; the Make Extra Payment dialog box looks almost exactly the same.

Figure 12-11:
The Make Regular Payment dialog box.

4. **Describe the loan payment.**

   I'm not going to give you the blow-by-blow account here. If you've gotten this far, you don't need my help. (Mostly, as you know, you just type stuff in boxes.)

5. **Click OK.**

   Quicken enters the loan payment in the liability register and bank account register. You're done.

Handling mortgage escrow accounts

I should talk about one minor, mortgage record-keeping annoyance — mortgage escrow accounts.

If you have a mortgage, you know the basic procedure. Although your mortgage payment may be $599.55 per month, your friendly mortgage company (while insisting that it trusts you completely) makes you pay an extra $125 per month for property taxes and other such things. In other words, even though you're paying only $599.55 per month in principal and interest, your monthly payment to the mortgage company is, according to this example, $724.55 ($599.55 + $125).

The mortgage company, as you probably know, saves this money for you in an *escrow* account or a set of escrow accounts. A couple of times yearly, the mortgage company pays your property taxes; and, a time or two per year, it pays your homeowner's insurance. If you have private mortgage insurance, it may pay this fee every month as well. And so it goes.

The question, then, is how do you treat this stuff? Like with most things, you can take the easy way (which is rough, dirty, and unshaven) or the hard way (which is precise, sophisticated, and cumbersome).

You can choose whichever method you want. It's your life.

The rough, dirty, and unshaven method

Suppose that you do pay an extra $125 per month. You can treat this extra $125 as another expense category, such as Tax:Property or Other Housing or Property Expenses. (I'm just making up these categories. If you can think of better ones, use your own.)

Nice. Easy. No fuss. These words and phrases pop into my head when I think about the rough, dirty, and unshaven method of mortgage escrow record keeping. Figure 12-12 shows a sample Split Transaction window filled out this way. If the Split Transaction window seems like too much fuss, mosey on over to Chapter 4, where I give you the rundown on using it.

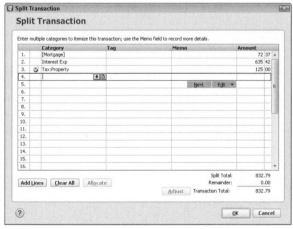

Figure 12-12: A mortgage payment with an escrow account treated as an expense.

I use the rough, dirty, and unshaven method. Let me make a confession, though. This approach doesn't tell you how much moolah you have stashed away in your escrow accounts. It also doesn't tell you how much you really spend in the way of homeowner's insurance, what you're entitled to claim as a property tax deduction, or how much they're bleeding you for private mortgage insurance.

To get these figures, you have to peruse the monthly and annual mortgage account statements — that is, if you get them. Or you have to call the mortgage lender and rattle a cage or two.

Still, with all its shortcomings, I like the easy-to-use, rough, dirty, unshaven method.

The precise, sophisticated, and cumbersome approach

You say you can't live with the uncertainty, the stress, the not knowing? Then I have another approach just for you.

You can set up an *asset account* for each escrow account for which the mortgage company collects money.

You set up asset accounts like you set up a checking account. And, in fact, you should think of escrow accounts essentially as special checking accounts into which your lender deposits money collected from you so that it can pay your property taxes and insurance.

Because I explain this "setting up a checking account" process in Chapter 1, I'll just cover it quickly. You set up an asset account with its starting balance equal to the current escrow account balance. To do so, follow these steps:

1. **Display the Quicken home page or some other Quicken tab that shows the Accounts bar along the left edge of the window.**

2. **Click the Add An Account button to indicate that you want to create a new account.**

3. **As you step through the seemingly interminable account setup process, identify the account as an asset account and give it a name.**

4. **Tell Quicken how much money is in the account as of a specific date.**

   If you've set up an account or two in your time, this process should take you about 40 seconds.

After you set up your asset account and record its current balance, you're ready to cruise. Record payments in the escrow as account transfers whenever you record the actual loan payment.

You need to do one other thing. When you set up an escrow account, you must record the payments that the bank makes from your escrow account to the county assessor (for property taxes) and to the insurance company (for things such as homeowner's and private mortgage insurance). You don't know when these payments are really made, so watch your monthly mortgage account statements.

When the mortgage company disburses money from the escrow account to pay your first property tax assessment, for example, you need to record a decrease equal to the payment for property taxes and then categorize the transaction as a property tax expense. This process isn't tricky in terms of mechanics. The account increases after every loan payment and decreases after a disbursement.

Basically, the Asset Account register mirrors the Checking Account register. The only difference is that the Payment and Deposit fields are labeled Decrease in the latter and Increase in the former. To get to this account's register, click its name in the Accounts bar.

This second approach doesn't seem like all that much work, does it? And if you use this approach, you can track escrow balances and escrow spending precisely. You can, for example, pull your property tax deduction right from Quicken. Jeepers, maybe I should try the sophisticated approach next year.

Your Principal-Interest Breakdown Won't Be Right

Not to bum you out, but your principal-interest breakdown will often be wrong. You may calculate interest expense as $544.55 when your bank calculates it as $544.56. A few pennies here, a few pennies there, and pretty soon, your account balance and interest expense tallies are a few pennies off.

So you can't change the world

You can try calling the bank, telling whomever you talk to what a bozo he (or she) is, and then demanding that someone there correct your balance. (If this approach works for you, let me know.)

Or (and this method is really more practical) you can adjust your records to agree with the bank's records. Here's how:

1. **Display the register for the liability.**

   To get to this account's register, you just click the account name on the Accounts bar.

2. **Click the Account Actions button and choose the Update Balance command.**

   (Go ahead. Tap your keys very hard if you're angry that the bank won't adjust its records.) Quicken displays the Update Balance dialog box, shown in Figure 12-13.

Figure 12-13:
The Update
Balance
dialog box.

Update Balance

New Balance 99,901.00

Adjustment Date 11/1/2012

OK   Cancel

3. **Enter the correct account balance (that is, the one that the bank says is correct).**

   Type the correct figure in the New Balance text box. (The amount probably comes from the year-end or month-end loan statement.)

4. **Enter the last day of the month or year for which you're making the adjustment.**

   Enter a transaction date in the Adjustment Date text box. (You must use a transaction date that sticks the adjustment transaction — which fixes the principal-interest split — into the right month or year.)

5. **Record the adjustment.**

   When the Update Account Balance dialog box correctly describes the needed adjustment, click OK.

Slightly smarter adjustments

The Update Balance dialog box (shown in Figure 12-13) adjusts the loan balance to whatever value you indicate, but then it forgets to categorize this adjustment. That's okay, I guess. But if you want to be slightly smarter about this adjustment, you should adjust the interest expense category. But let me explain.

When you record loan payments, you split the loan payment between the interest expense category and a principal account transfer that reduces the liability. When the liability gets reduced either too much or not enough — this would be the case if you need to adjust the liability balance — you must fix the liability balance *and* the principal-interest split.

Let me give you an example. Suppose that over the course of a year, you record $0.17 too little interest expense — and, therefore, record $0.17 too much principal reduction, despite your best efforts to be accurate. You need to increase the liability account balance by $0.17 in this case, but you also need to increase the interest expense figure by $0.17.

If you want to be just a little bit more obsessive compulsive than Quicken is, you can do so. Simply display the loan account register, select the adjustment transaction, and then use the appropriate interest expense category for Adjustment.

Automatic Payments

Quicken has a couple of nifty features — Scheduled Transactions and the Calendar — that can help you with automatic loan payments.

The Calendar and Scheduled Transactions features may be useful in other instances as well. For example, a business may use the Scheduled Transactions and Calendar features to schedule and plan employee payroll checks, tax returns, and deposits. But I think that they're both most useful in the case of a loan. So I talk about them both here.

Scheduling a bill reminder

If a payment occurs regularly — the payment might be for a loan or some other regular bill, like your cable TV service — you can tell Quicken to remind you about the payment, or you can set it up as a scheduled payment. When you do so, Quicken either reminds you or automatically records the payment for you based on a schedule.

Follow these steps to set up such a reminder or scheduled transaction:

1. **Display the Calendar window.**

   To display the Quicken Calendar window, you can press Ctrl+K. Or, you can choose the Tools⇨Calendar command. Either way, Quicken displays the Calendar window, shown in Figure 12-14. The figure shows a calendar for the current month and, optionally, a list of memorized payees.

   Note: If you can't see the list of transactions along the right edge in the Calendar window, click the Options button and then choose the Show Memorized Payees List command from the menu Quicken displays. By dragging payees from the list to the Calendar, you add transactions to the register one at a time, using previously recorded transactions.

Figure 12-14:
The
Calendar
window.

2. **Display the first month for which you want to schedule the transaction.**

   Using the left-arrow and right-arrow buttons, select the starting month for the reminder or scheduled transaction. You can also enter a date into the Go To Date box and click the Go button. Quicken displays the month you want to schedule a payment for inside the Calendar window.

3. **Click the Add Reminder button and choose Bill Reminder from the menu.**

   Quicken displays the first Add Bill Reminder dialog box (not shown), which you use to enter the payee name. You can also click the button at the right end of the Pay To box to drop down a list of previous payees and then select one.

4. **Use the second Add Bill Reminder dialog box to describe the recurring payment.**

   Click Next to continue from the first Add Bill Reminder dialog box to the second Add A Bill Reminder dialog box (see Figure 12-15), which you'll use to describe the recurring payment.

5. **Verify that the Pay To and Amount Due fields are correct.**

   They probably are. But I have kind of a compulsive personality. Because I've been telling you to check all this other stuff, I thought I'd also suggest that you check these fields. Quicken uses the last payment amount to the payee as the suggested amount due, by the way.

Figure 12-15:
The Add
A Bill
Reminder
dialog box.

6. **Check the payment scheduling stuff.**

   Verify that the Due Next On text box and labeling show the correct date for the first payment. If Quicken doesn't show the current due date, click the button that shows a picture of a stubby little pencil to display a pop-up box with boxes that let you specify how often the payment should be made, which day of, say, the month the payment is due, and the date payments should stop.

7. **Identify how the payment should be made.**

   Open the From Account drop-down list box and then select the appropriate account.

8. **Categorize, tag, and bag.**

   If you're scheduling a reminder for a transaction you've already correctly recorded once, the Category, Tag, and Memo fields should show the correct information. You should still check them, however. You don't want to have Quicken copy some old error you made. Note that the Tag field only appears if you've enabled the Show Tag Field option in the Register section of the Quicken Preferences window. Quicken opens text boxes to make changes to the Category, Tag, and Memo fields when you click.

9. **Click Done.**

   Quicken adds the payee's transaction to the Calendar.

Note: When you schedule payments, you may implicitly break your budget. If you've set up a budget and scheduling a payment does "break" the budget, Quicken alerts you. Quicken also asks (in the nicest way possible) if you want to update your budget. For more information about budgeting, refer to Chapter 3.

Scheduling income and transfer reminders

If you click the Add Reminder button, shown in the lower left-hand corner of the Calendar window (see Figure 12-14), Quicken actually displays a menu of three commands: Bill Reminder, Income Reminder, and Transfer Reminder.

While I'm only going to describe in step-by-step detail the Bill Reminder command (see preceding paragraphs), you can use the Income Reminder and Transfer Reminder commands in the same basic way as you use the Bill Reminder command. The Income Reminder command lets you schedule reminders to record recurring income or deposit transactions such as from a regular payroll check. The Transfer Reminder command lets you schedule reminders to record recurring transfers such as mortgage payments from your checking account.

Another way to schedule transactions

Quicken allows you to automatically schedule the adding of transactions. To create these scheduled transactions, you choose Tools⇨Manage Bill & Income Reminders. Quicken displays the Bill and Income Reminders window (see Figure 12-16).

Figure 12-16:
The Bill and
Income
Reminders
window.

To create a scheduled transaction, click the Create New button and select the Bill Reminder, Income Reminder, or Transfer Reminder command. After you choose the transaction you want to schedule, Quicken displays a dialog box (not shown) that you use to describe an automatically scheduled transaction. Note that you can automatically schedule any kind of transaction — loan payments, insurance premiums, child support, or whatever. (I'm describing the automatically scheduled transactions feature here in this chapter, though, because loan payments are one of the most common ways to use this Quicken feature.) If you have questions about how bill, income, or transfer reminders work, refer to the earlier discussion, "Scheduling a bill reminder." But know that income and transfer reminders work very, very similarly to bill reminders.

The Create New menu's Scheduled Transaction Group command deserves a bit more discussion, though, so let me briefly touch on that subject. If you choose Scheduled Transaction Group from the menu Quicken displays when you click the Create New button, Quicken displays the Create Transaction Group dialog box (see Figure 12-17).

Figure 12-17:
The Create
Transaction
Group
dialog box.

A scheduled transaction group is a collection of transactions that you schedule together — such as all the bills you need to pay on the first of the month or out of your second paycheck.

To create a scheduled transaction group, use the Create Transaction Group dialog box to name the group, pick the account from which you'll use funds, and then provide payment date and frequency information.

The Create Transaction Group dialog box provides a list of memorized transactions that you can use to indicate which transactions belong in the group. Check the box for each transaction you want to add.

Checking out the Calendar

The bar along the top of the Calendar (refer to Figure 12-14) provides some other tools that you may want to use. I'm not going to spend much time on them; you'll have more fun trying them out yourself than you would reading about them. Nevertheless, let me give you a bird's-eye view:

- ✔ The **Add Note** button lets you post a note on a calendar day. You use this feature to create reminder notes that will also appear in the Alerts area of the Cash Flow Center. For example, you may want to post a note saying Remember Wedding Anniversary on the big day. After you click this button, Quicken displays a dialog box in which you type the message. Then you click Save My Butt. The program also marks the calendar day with a little yellow square — a miniature stick-on note. Click the square to read the message.

- ✔ The **Options** button displays a menu of commands that let you specify which transactions should appear in the Calendar, add an account balance graph in the Calendar window, and fiddle with the memorized transactions list. The transactions shown in that list box along the right edge of the Calendar window, by the way, are memorized transactions. (Chapter 4 briefly discusses memorized transactions.)

Chapter 13

Tracking Tax-Deferred Investments

*I*nvestment record keeping is something that more of us need to think about. More of us are investing as the population ages and we prepare for retirement. And the craziness in the financial markets in 2008 and again in 2011 means that we probably all need to save more.

Fortunately, Quicken provides great tools for managing your investments, including your tax-deferred investments. And this chapter talks about those tools. But first, I should talk about whether you even need to do this.

Deciding to Use Investment Features

The Quicken investment record-keeping feature lets you do three important things:

✔ Track your interest and dividend income

✔ Track real and potential capital gains and losses

✔ Measure an investment's performance by calculating the annual return from an investment

If you're a serious investor, these things probably sound worthwhile. But before you invest any time learning how Quicken investment record keeping works, be sure that you need all this power.

Are your investments tax-deferred?

If your investments are *tax-deferred* — if, for example, you're using individual retirement accounts (IRAs), Simple-IRAs, Roth accounts, or 401(k)s — you don't really need to track investment income and capital gains and losses. Tax-deferred investments have no effect on your personal income taxes in the United States. You get a tax deduction for the money you stick into IRAs, for example, and anything you take out is taxable. (Or in the case of a Roth IRA or Roth 401(k), you don't get a deduction for amounts you stick into the account, but then you also don't get taxed on amounts taken out of the account — which means that you don't need to closely account for Roth IRA investments, at least for tax accounting reasons.)

With tax-deferred investments — like deductible IRAs, 401(k)s, and Simple-IRAs — you record all that you should need to know via your checking account. Checks earmarked for investment are categorized as *IRA Deductions,* for example, and investment account withdrawals deposited into your checking account are categorized as *IRA Distributions.* In other words, you don't need to set up special accounts for tracking your investments. Your bank accounts track everything you need to keep track of.

Note: For purposes of this chapter, 529 plans are also tax-deferred investments, but a 529 plan works a little differently. In a 529 plan, you save money for someone else's college costs — probably a child or grandchild. You don't get a tax deduction when you put money into the 529 plan, but the investment earnings are *not* taxed as they are realized. And later, when the plan beneficiary (again, probably your child or grandchild) withdraws money, the withdrawals aren't taxed as long as the money is used for college costs. In a sense, a 529 plan works like a Roth account — except the money goes for college and not for retirement.

Are you a mutual fund fanatic?

I want to make a related point. If you're a fan of mutual funds, you don't need Quicken to measure the funds' annual returns. Fund managers provide these figures for you in quarterly and annual reports. In fact, part of what you're paying the mutual fund manager for is record keeping and performance management.

Accordingly, if you're investing in mutual funds through a tax-deferred account, you probably *really* don't need to be going to the extra work of figuring out the Quicken investment recording stuff.

Some investors don't need Quicken

Let me give you an example of someone who doesn't need to use the Quicken program's investments feature — me. Once upon a time, I bought and sold common stocks, fooled around with half a dozen mutual funds, and learned firsthand why junk bonds are called junk bonds. (Apparently, junk bonds are more risky. And so fluctuate wildly in value.) For more than the last decade, and even though my investment account has grown steadily through compound interest and additional savings, I've simplified my financial affairs considerably.

I don't invest directly in stocks, bonds, or mutual funds these days; instead, I stick money into an IRA. My investments don't produce taxable dividends or interest income, nor do they produce taxable or tax-saving capital gains or losses. Money I put into the IRA is tax deductible. And money I ultimately take out of the IRA will be taxable.

I'm also sticking with a handful of mutual funds, but I don't need to calculate the annual return — that's what mutual fund managers do. So I don't need to figure, for example, what my shares of Vanguard Total Stock Market Portfolio (my favorite mutual fund) delivered as an annual return when I include both the 1 percent dividend and the 8 percent price change.

Because I don't need to track investment income, or track capital gains and losses, or calculate the progress of my investment portfolio, I don't need Quicken investment record keeping for my personal use.

Many investors do want Quicken

Of course, many people — including mutual fund investors using tax-deferred investment options like 401(k) plans, 403(b) plans, and individual retirement accounts — do want to track their investments with Quicken in spite of the laziness I'm trying to promote. Accordingly, I'm going to describe how to track tax-deferred accounts with Quicken.

Furthermore, if you have a taxable portfolio stuffed full of individual stocks and bonds, you're going to want to use Quicken to track your other taxable investment accounts anyway. And if you're going to go to that work, it's not much additional effort to track tax-deferred investments with Quicken, too.

How to pick a mutual fund

Would you mind terribly if I took a minute and provided a handful of tips about how to pick a mutual fund? I guess I'm thinking that maybe, just maybe, my observations might be useful to you. I am not, after all, trying to earn a commission by selling you some financial product or service, so maybe I can be a bit more objective. I'm also rather over-educated (with a couple of master's degrees — one in finance and one in taxation). And I've been a CPA for, jeepers, 26 years, am a former registered investment advisor but am not trying to sell you investments, and, most interestingly, have seen countless real-life examples of people's investing successes and mistakes. . . .

Here, then, are my tips:

1. Carefully watch your investment expenses, including both commissions and the mutual fund management fees. Why? Despite what you may have been told, you almost never get extra investment returns by paying extra for investment advice or financial planning. And note that every bit of financial research — the kind that finance professors do — supports this statement. Usually, you want to pick the cheapest mutual fund alternative. Almost always, that's an index fund. And one other note: Remember that paying a 2 percent fee on investments earning 8 percent means you're giving up 25 percent of your profit to the mutual fund or financial advisor. That's like a 25 percent tax!

2. Use tax-deferred investment accounts like 401(k)s, 403(b)s, and IRAs for your investments. Income taxes can be a huge drag on your investment returns. And over the decades that you'll be investing, minimizing your income taxes will add at least

tens of thousands of dollars and potentially hundreds of thousands of dollars to your wealth.

3. To diversify, use an inexpensive index fund, one per investment category. For example, you can diversify by investing in one index fund that invests in the U.S. stock market, another index fund that invests in corporate bonds, another that invests in real estate investment trusts, and so on. Diversification reduces your investment risk.

4. Consider one of the new target retirement funds such as those offered by Vanguard, T. Rowe Price, or Fidelity. With one of these babies, you don't worry about trying to diversify. You don't worry about asset allocation or rebalancing. You don't worry about adjusting your investment mix as you get older. You just pick a single fund that's tied to your retirement year. For example, if you will retire in 2025, you would buy the target retirement that assumes you'll retire in 2025. That's it. That's the last investment decision you need to make.

5. For goodness' sake, don't trade, attempting to buy low and sell high. Trading rarely works. And it's always expensive. Be a long-term investor who buys inexpensive mutual funds and holds them for the long term.

6. Invest some time and money in beefing up your investment knowledge. You can do this by reading pretty much anything that Burton Malkiel or John Bogle has written. I particularly like and recommend Burton Malkiel's *A Random Walk Guide to Investing* (published by W. W. Norton & Company).

Tracking a Tax-Deferred Investment

If you need to track a tax-deferred investment, you need to know how to set up a tax-deferred account and then record your investment activities.

If you'll use Quicken to track any of your investments, you shouldn't skip this section. Understanding how tax-deferred investment works makes tracking taxable investments much, much easier for you.

Setting up a tax-deferred investment account

Setting up an investment account to track a tax-deferred investment account works the same way as setting up any other account:

1. **Display the Accounts List window.**

   Choose Tools⇨Accounts List to do this.

2. **Click the Add An Account button.**

   Quicken dutifully displays the first Quicken Add Account dialog box that you use to add a new Quicken account (see Figure 13-1). You've likely seen this dialog box a million times by now. It just asks you to identify the type of account you want to add.

Figure 13-1:
The first Add Account dialog box.

3. **Identify the type of investments in the account and then click Next.**

   You select the appropriate Investing options button to indicate you're adding an investment account — Brokerage, IRA or Keogh Plan, 401(k) or 403(b), or 529 Plan — and then click Next.

   Just to quickly identify what these different account types actually are, a *529 plan* is a college savings account that complies with Sec. 529 of the Internal Revenue Code. The *401(k)* and *403(b)* accounts are retirement accounts that comply with Sec. 401(k) and Sec. 403(b) of the Internal Revenue Code. The *IRA* and *Keogh* account type is for individual retirement accounts (IRA) and Keogh accounts (an old retirement savings account option). The standard brokerage account option is the catchall account type for investment accounts that *aren't* tax-favored retirement or college savings accounts. (I talk about this type of account in Chapter 14.)

4. **Identify the financial institution.**

   After you specify which type of investment account you're setting up, Quicken displays the second Add Account dialog box, which asks for the name of the bank or broker holding your investments. This dialog box lets you enter the bank or broker name or part of the name in a text box or, alternatively, lets you choose from a list of popular banks by clicking the bank or institution's name. If you do identify the bank or financial institution, Quicken prompts you to provide the online username and password used for electronically accessing your account information. Alternatively, you can click the Advanced Setup hyperlink at the bottom of the dialog box to indicate you don't want to identify your bank or broker. Quicken then displays another version of the second Add Account dialog box, which lets you click the I Want To Enter Transactions Manually button to indicate you want to enter investment transactions manually.

   Note: Quicken really wants you to electronically grab your transactions from the bank or financial institution. But manually entering the transactions usually works well when you're just starting out with Quicken.

5. **Click Next, name the investment, and then click Next again.**

   Quicken displays the third Add Account dialog box (shown in Figure 13-2). Move the cursor to the Account Name/Nickname text box and type a name for the account. If you're setting up an account to track an individual retirement account, you might type **IRA**.

   After you click Next, Quicken displays the fourth Add Account dialog box.

Figure 13-2:
The third
Add
Account
dialog box.

6. **Provide the last statement date and then click Next.**

The fourth Add Account dialog box (see Figure 13-3) asks for the date of the statement you're using to enter your investment information. This date is the starting date, in essence, for your investment record keeping with Quicken. Enter the date and then click Next.

Figure 13-3:
The fourth
Add
Account
dialog box.

7. Describe the cash balance or money market balance (if any) associated with the account and then click Next.

As you probably already know if you're investing through a broker, some investment accounts have a cash account associated with the main investment account. The cash in this account, of course, provides the money you use for additional investments. And when you receive cash from selling some investment or from some dividend, the money goes into this account.

To describe this cash account, use the Cash and Money Market text boxes to give the opening balances. You can probably guess this, but at the risk of being redundant, the information that you provide to set up a cash account or money market fund mirrors the information you provide to set up a regular ol' checking account.

8. (Optional) Identify the account owner.

If prompted by Quicken, indicate who owns the tax-deferred investment account — you or your spouse. Click Next to display the sixth Add Account dialog box (see Figure 13-4).

9. Name the security, provide the ticker symbol, and then click Next.

This sixth dialog box does two things for you:

- First, it collects the investment's ticker symbol (if available) so that you can download share prices several times during the day and drive yourself half mad with anxiety (see Figure 13-4). If you don't know the ticker symbol, click the Ticker Symbol Lookup button to display a Quicken.com web page that lets you find the ticker symbol.

Figure 13-4:
The sixth
Add
Account
dialog box.

- Second, it asks you to name the security held in the investment account you're setting up, using the Security Name box. This won't make sense in some cases — such as when you're holding a single certificate of deposit in an IRA. But in other cases — like when you've set up an IRA with a mutual fund company and you've invested in three different mutual funds within the IRA — separately identifying the different securities within the account will make sense.

After you click Next, Quicken displays the seventh Add Account dialog box, shown in Figure 13-5.

Figure 13-5:
The seventh Add Account dialog box.

10. **Provide a total shares count.**

Enter the number of shares you hold of each security you identified in Step 9.

11. **Click Next.**

Quicken displays a dialog box summarizing the investment that you've just entered. If something seems amiss, click the Back button to find the Add Account dialog box where you entered some incorrect bit of information. If everything seems okay, click Done. For some types of tax-deferred investment accounts, Quicken may also ask for additional information. For example, if you set up an IRA account, Quicken asks about the type of IRA you're setting up and if the IRA belongs to you or to your spouse. Answer any questions by clicking the Yes or No button as appropriate. Then click Done again. This time, click harder — like you really mean it.

12. **Review the new (partially described) investment.**

To check your work so far, click the Investing tab. Quicken displays the Portfolio window, which shows your new investment account and provides a bit of additional, investment-related information (see Figure 13-6).

Figure 13-6:
The
Investing
tab shows
the newly
set up
investment
account.

Recording your initial investment

After you set up an investment account and describe the securities in the account, you can record an initial purchase of the investments.

Of course, you need to know the original price of those first shares. So dig through that kitchen drawer where you stuff bank statements, financial records, and those kooky birthday cards from Aunt Enid.

When you find the proper paperwork that shows the number of shares you purchased and the price per share, here's what you do:

1. **Open the investment account, if it isn't already open.**

   Open the investment account by clicking the account name in the Accounts bar.

   If the Investing tab isn't shown, choose View➪Tabs To Show➪Investing.

2. **Tell Quicken you want to enter cost basis data.**

   Click the Enter hyperlink in the Cost Basis column. If the Cost Basis column doesn't show the Enter Cost hyperlink, click the plus (+) symbol next to the Security Name you chose for the mutual fund. After you click the hyperlink, Quicken displays the Enter Missing Transactions dialog box, shown in Figure 13-7.

Figure 13-7:
The Enter
Missing
Transactions
dialog box.

3. Click the Enter Missing Transaction button.

Quicken displays the Buy – Shares Bought dialog box, shown in Figure 13-8.

Figure 13-8:
The Buy –
Shares
Bought
dialog box.

4. In the Transaction Date text box, enter the date you first purchased the fund shares.

Move the cursor to the Transaction Date text box and enter the date by using the *MM/DD/YYYY* format. ***Note:*** You don't have to enter a two-digit month or day number if a single digit makes sense. Enter July 18, 1989, for example, as **7/18/89**. You may also select the date from the pop-up calendar.

5. **(Optional) Enter a memo description.**

   If you want to tie the purchase to a confirmation order number, for example, enter the data in the Memo text box. I suppose that you could use this text box to record anything: *Kilroy was here. Save the Whales. Don't tread on me.*

6. **Indicate the size of your purchase.**

   To enter the total number of shares, move the cursor to the Number Of Shares text box. (Fractional shares are okay.)

7. **Indicate what you paid per share.**

   With the cursor in the Price Paid text box, enter the amount you paid for the lot. After you supply Quicken with the adjusted cost basis, it calculates the total cost.

8. **Record the initial purchase of mutual fund shares by clicking the Enter/Done button.**

   Quicken redisplays the Enter Missing Transactions dialog box (refer to Figure 13-7).

9. **(Optional) Repeat Steps 2–8, if necessary.**

   You need to repeat Steps 2–8 to record any other lots you purchased. For example, if you own 1,000 shares of Vanguard 500 Index, but you accumulated these shares by buying shares ten different times over the last ten years, you need to record ten separate lots. The last time through the steps, if you're setting up a tax-deferred investment account that you didn't really need to set up, you can ask yourself why you didn't listen to me when I said you don't need and therefore don't want to do this for tax-deferred investments.

After you describe each lot that makes up your holdings of the mutual fund investment, the Enter Missing Transactions dialog box shows that there aren't any placeholders for missing transactions because the Shares placeholder and the Cost placeholder should both equal zero (see Figure 13-9). You can click Done.

If you make a mistake entering a transaction, you can click the Edit or Delete button to the right of the transaction to change or remove the erroneous data.

Buying investments

As you buy additional investments — by contributing additional amounts to your retirement account or by reinvesting dividends and capital gain distributions — you record the transactions for the investment account.

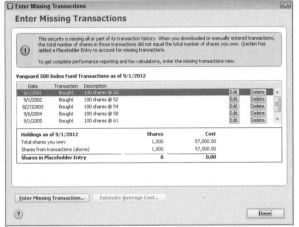

Enter Missing Transactions

Figure 13-9:
The Enter
Missing
Transactions
dialog box
after one
enters all
the missing
transac-
tions.

By writing a check

If you buy shares by writing a check, display the investment window (by clicking the Investing tab and then the investment account), and then record the purchase by following these steps:

1. **Click the Enter Transactions button.**

   Quicken displays the dialog box used to enter investment transactions.

2. **Select Buy – Shares Bought in the Enter Transaction drop-down list box.**

   Quicken displays the Buy – Shares Bought version of the investment transaction entry dialog box, shown in Figure 13-10.

Figure 13-10:
The Buy –
Shares
Bought
dialog box.

3. **Enter the purchase date in the Transaction Date text box.**

4. **(Optional) Enter a description in the Memo text box.**

5. **Enter the bank account on which you'll write the check that pays for the shares.**

   Select the account name in the From drop-down list box.

6. **Indicate the size of your purchase by using the Number Of Shares and the Price Paid text boxes.**

   Tell Quicken the size of your investment by giving the number of shares purchased and the price paid per share.

7. **Enter the commission or fee that you paid.**

   Move the cursor to the Commission text box and enter the commission or fee you paid to purchase the shares. (The amount shown in the Total Cost text box includes this figure.)

8. **Record the purchase.**

   Click the Enter/New button if you want to record the transaction and enter another new transaction, or click the Enter/Done button if you want to record just the single transaction. Quicken records your purchase of new shares. You are now a capitalist. Congratulations.

By reinvesting dividends, interest, or capital gains

When you reinvest your dividends, interest, or capital gains, you also must record your reinvestment transactions. Essentially, you're buying new shares using the dividend or capital gain proceeds you could have received. To record the reinvestment of investment profits, display the investment window (by clicking the Investing tab and then clicking the investment account), and then follow these steps:

1. **Click the Enter Transactions button.**

   Quicken displays the dialog box used to enter investments transactions.

2. **Select Reinvest – Income Reinvested in the Enter Transaction drop-down list box.**

   Quicken displays the Reinvest – Income Reinvested version of the investment transaction entry dialog box, shown in Figure 13-11.

3. **Enter the purchase date (in this case, the reinvestment date) in the Transaction Date text box.**

4. **(Optional) Type a brief explanation of the transaction in the Memo text box.**

5. **Use the Amount and Shares columns to describe the reinvestment.**

   Take another look at Figure 13-11. No, really, go ahead. I'll wait. See those rows labeled Dividend, Interest, Short-Term Cap Gain Dist, Mid-Term Cap Gain Dist, and Long-Term Cap Gain Dist? And see the columns labeled Amount and Shares? Use these rows and columns to record the amounts of dividends, interest, and capital gains distributed to you by the mutual fund and to record the numbers of shares you purchase by reinvesting these amounts. For example, if you receive $100 of dividends and use this amount to purchase two shares, you enter **100** in the Dividend Amount box and **2** in the Dividend Shares text boxes, respectively.

6. **Record the reinvestment transaction.**

   Click the Enter/New button if you want to record the transaction and enter another new transaction, or click the Enter/Done button if you want to record just the single transaction.

Figure 13-11 shows $450 of dividends being reinvested in the mutual fund by buying 4 more shares and $4,500 of long-term capital gains being reinvested by buying 40 shares.

Recording your profits

Perhaps regularly, you'll receive distributions directly from the investment account's investments that you don't immediately reinvest. Instead, you'll deposit these proceeds into the investment accounts' cash account or money market account.

To record these kinds of distributions, you follow a process very similar to those I describe in the preceding set of steps. For example, to record an income transaction directly into the investment account, follow these steps:

1. **Click the Enter Transactions button.**

   Display the investment window — by clicking the Investing button and then clicking the Enter Transactions button. Quicken displays the dialog box used to enter investment transactions.

2. **Select Inc – Income (Div, Int, Etc.) in the Enter Transaction drop-down list box.**

   Quicken displays the Inc – Income (Div, Int, Etc.) version of the investment transaction entry dialog box. The Inc – Income (Div, Int, Etc.) version of the investment transaction entry dialog box closely resembles the Reinvest – Income Reinvested dialog box, so I won't show it here.

3. **Enter the distribution date in the Transaction Date text box.**

4. **Use the Transfer Account drop-down list to identify the account into which you'll deposit the check that the mutual fund company sends you.**

5. **(Optional) Type a brief description of the distribution in the Memo text box.**

   Be creative — type your wedding anniversary, the name of your dog, or even a piece of data related to the dividend or distribution.

6. **Indicate the dividend or capital gains distribution amount.**

   Enter the amount in the appropriate amount text box. A dividend, I hope you can guess, goes into the Dividend box. A short-term capital gain goes into the Short-Term Cap Gain Dist box, and so on.

7. **Record the dividend or distribution transaction.**

   When you click either the Enter/New or the Enter/Done button, you record the dividend. If you click the Enter/New button, Quicken leaves the dialog box open so that you can enter some other transactions.

Selling investments

Selling mutual fund shares works basically the same way as buying them — only in reverse. To record the sale of shares held in an investment account, perform the following actions:

1. **Click the Enter Transactions button.**

   Display the investment window by clicking the Investing Center button and then clicking the Enter Transactions button. Quicken displays the dialog box used to enter investment transactions.

2. **Select Sell – Shares Sold in the Enter Transaction drop-down list box.**

   Quicken displays the Sell – Shares Sold version of the investment transaction entry dialog box, shown in Figure 13-12.

Figure 13-12:
The Sell – Shares Sold dialog box.

3. **Enter the sale's date in the Transaction Date text box.**

4. **(Optional) Type a brief description of the sale in the Memo text box.**

5. **If you're selling all your shares, click in the Sell All Shares In This Account check box.**

6. **Give Quicken the number of shares you're selling.**

   Use the Number Of Shares box to specify the number of shares you're selling (if you didn't click in the Sell All Shares check box in Step 5).

7. **Indicate the price per share that you received by using the Price Received text box.**

   With a little luck, your selling price is more than you paid.

8. **Enter the commission or fee you paid to sell the shares in the Commission text box.**

   No wonder Bernie, your broker, does so well, huh? He makes money even if you don't.

Quicken calculates whatever you don't enter. For example, if you tell Quicken how many dollars you sell (by using the Price Received text box), it calculates the number of shares you sell by dividing the total sales amount by the price per share. If you tell Quicken how many shares you sell (using the Number Of Shares text box), it calculates the total sales amount by multiplying the number of shares by the price per share. I guess this feature is handy.

9. **Enter the bank account into which you're going to deposit the sale's proceeds.**

    Open the To drop-down list box and select the appropriate account. (Probably, you'll deposit the proceeds into the associated cash account.)

10. **Click one of the Enter buttons.**

    Quicken records your sale.

Correcting a mistake

If you make a mistake, don't worry — it's not a problem. You can edit an investment transaction. To edit a particular transaction, you first need to display the investment transactions list. To do this, click the investment account in the Accounts bar. Quicken displays the Investment Transactions window (see Figure 13-13).

Figure 13-13:
The Investment Transactions list.

To edit one of the transactions you see listed for the investment account, double-click the transaction. Quicken opens the dialog box you originally used to record the transaction (such as the one shown in Figure 13-14), and you use it to make your changes.

If you don't see the transaction listed, use the Date Range box to specify that you want to see all transactions for the account.

Figure 13-14:
The Edit
Sell –
Shares Sold
dialog box
appears
when you
indicate you
want to edit
a shares
sold
transaction.

For example, you can click in the fields with the incorrect entries, fix them, and then record the new, corrected transaction.

Working with slightly tricky investment transactions

I haven't described every possible investment transaction that you're likely to encounter in a typical tax-deferred investment account — although I have described every one I've encountered in the past 10 or 12 years. You should know, however, that Quicken does let you record three additional, common-to-tax-deferred-investment-account transactions by specifying several almost magical actions: shares out, stock split, and reminder transactions.

How do I remove shares from an account?

You can tell Quicken to remove shares from an account — without moving the money represented by the shares — to some other account. Why would you want to remove shares from an account using a *shares-removed* transaction? I can think of two situations:

✔ You erroneously added shares to the account with the shares added transaction action and now you need to remove them.

✔ You're using an investment account to record old investment activity, such as activity from last year.

The first instance is self-explanatory because you're simply correcting an error that you made. In the second case, however, you don't want to transfer the proceeds of an investment sale to a cash account because the money from the sale was already recorded as a deposit at some point in the past.

You can record a shares-removed transaction directly into Quicken by clicking the Enter Transaction button and choosing Remove – Shares Removed in the Enter Transaction drop-down list box. Then fill in the rest of the fields in the dialog box the same way that you would for a regular ol' sell transaction. The only difference is that you won't give a transfer account for the sale proceeds — because there aren't any proceeds.

What? The stock split and then doubled?

Stock splits don't occur very often; however, when they do occur, the company issuing the shares, in effect, gives you a certain number of new shares (such as two) for each old share you own.

To record a stock split, you click the Enter Transactions button and select Stock Split in the Enter Transaction drop-down list box. When Quicken displays the Stock Split version of the dialog box used to enter investment transactions (see Figure 13-15), you indicate the ratio of new shares to old shares. For a two-for-one split, for example, you indicate that you get two new split shares for each old unsplit share. The whole process is pretty easy.

Figure 13-15: The Stock Split version of the investment transaction entry dialog box.

Quicken, will you remind me of something?

A *reminder* transaction is the electronic equivalent of a yellow stick-on note. If you put a reminder transaction in an investment account, Quicken gives you a reminder message on the reminder date. You can't goof up anything by trying out reminders, so if you're curious, enter a reminder transaction for tomorrow and see what happens.

You can post a reminder note by clicking the Enter Transaction button, selecting Reminder Transaction in the Enter Transaction drop-down list box, and filling in the dialog box that Quicken displays (see Figure 13-16).

Figure 13-16: The Reminder Transaction version of the investment transaction entry dialog box.

You might want to use reminder transactions to record due dates for contributions to retirement accounts or for required minimum distributions amounts or dates.

Reconciling an account

You reconcile a tax-deferred investment account the same basic way that you reconcile a bank account. The only real difference — and it doesn't affect reconciliation mechanics — is that you focus on investment shares and not on account balance dollars. To begin reconciling a tax-deferred investment account, display the Investing tab, click the Account Actions button, and choose the Reconcile command. If you have questions about what to do next, refer to Chapter 8. It describes how you reconcile a bank account, but the same procedures apply to both tax-deferred and regular investment accounts.

Trying reports

I just want to say one thing about Quicken reports as they relate to your investments — both tax-deferred investments and taxable investments: *Remember that the reports are available.* (For more information, see Chapter 7.)

Using menu commands and other stuff

For the most part, the commands and menus available for an investment account (no matter whether you're talking tax-deferred or taxable) are the same as those available for all the other accounts Quicken supplies. I write about the commands that I think are most helpful to new users in the preceding chapters of this book. If you have a question about how the Void Transaction(s) command works, for example, refer to the Index, which directs you to a specific discussion of that command.

Updating Securities Prices

You can collect current market prices and store this information with your accounts (both tax-deferred and taxable).

To automatically update security prices, just display the Investing tab and click the Portfolio button. Then, when Quicken displays the Portfolio tab (see Figure 13-17), click the Update button and choose the One Step Update command. Quicken will grab nearly current security prices from the Quicken.com website.

To manually update the market price for a security, you also need to display the Portfolio view of the Investing tab. But once you've done that, just use the arrow keys or click the mouse to select the security. Then move the cursor to the Quote/Price text box and enter the current price.

Using either the automatic or manual updating of pricing information, Quicken recalculates the Market Value field on the Portfolio tab as well as the Market Value figure at the bottom of the register window.

If you invest exclusively in tax-deferred investments, the information in this chapter should be all you need. If you also invest more actively using taxable accounts, you may want to turn to Chapter 14. It describes how you use a Quicken investment account to track a typical brokerage account.

Figure 13-17:
The Portfolio view of the Investing tab, or window.

The Investing tab

You can do more with the Investing tab (refer to Figure 13-17) than just update share prices or play peekaboo with your various investments.

For starters, the Investing tab lets you slice and dice portfolio information. The Show drop-down list box lets you customize how Quicken reports on your investment holdings. The Group By drop-down list box lets you group your investment accounts into categories (industries, sectors, asset classes, and so on). The As Of field lets you specify the date on which you want to see and set market prices and values. And the Customize button displays a dialog box that lets you add all sorts of information to the Investing tab — information that can give you all sorts of insights into how you're doing with your investing.

Interested in digging even deeper? No problem. Click the Performance or Allocations button to get additional information. The Performance button, for example, displays a screenful of information about the historical cost and market value of your investments. The Allocations button breaks down your investments into asset classes (big company stocks, little company stocks, bonds, and so forth).

The Update button displays a menu of commands you can use to keep your portfolio data current as well as get current and historical prices of securities. (Go ahead and experiment with the Update button's commands: You can't hurt anything.)

I'm not going to go into more detail here about what all these extra bells and whistles do, however. If you're interested in this stuff, just take the time to explore these commands. You *will* gain some interesting insights into your financial investments.

Chapter 14

Stocks and Bonds

. . . .

In This Chapter

▶ Setting up a brokerage account

▶ Describing the securities in a brokerage account

▶ Transferring cash to and from a brokerage account

▶ Buying stocks and bonds from a brokerage account

▶ Recording income from securities held in a brokerage account

▶ Recording margin interest, miscellaneous income and expenses, and return of capital

▶ Updating securities prices

▶ Adjusting your brokerage cash balance

▶ Adjusting your brokerage account shares

. . . .

*A*fter you understand how Quicken handles tax-deferred investments, working with a regular taxable brokerage account (and the extra complexity that such an account typically includes) is a snap.

 If you haven't yet used Quicken for tax-deferred investment record keeping or read Chapter 13, I recommend you at least skim Chapter 13. That chapter provides some useful information about the fundamentals of investment record keeping with Quicken.

Setting Up a Brokerage Account

Setting up a brokerage account is similar to setting up a regular tax-deferred account. Because I describe this process in painstaking detail in Chapter 13, I don't repeat the discussion here.

The one bit of information that I will note is this: During the investment account setup process, when Quicken asks you what kind of account you're setting up, specify that you're setting up a standard brokerage account.

Recording your initial share balances

If you've already read or skimmed Chapter 13 (which talks about using Quicken to track tax-deferred investments), you may remember a section titled, "Recording your initial investment." That little section explains how to tell Quicken what you paid for the mutual fund shares, stock shares, and so forth, held in your tax-deferred investment account.

Okay. So here's the deal. Just as you need to describe your starting share balances when you set up a tax-deferred investment account, you need to describe your starting share balances when you set up a standard brokerage investment account. In other words, if you own three stocks in your broker-age account — IBM, GE, and Boeing — you need to describe how much you paid and when you purchased your IBM, GE, and Boeing shares.

Rather than copy that earlier discussion (I'd literally be copying and past-ing material from Chapter 13), let me refer you to the "Recording your ini-tial investment" section in Chapter 13. Go through the nine-step process described there for each stock you hold.

Working with brokerage accounts

Brokerage accounts work like tax-deferred accounts, which I describe in Chapter 13, except for a handful of minor differences.

Essentially, only three general differences exist between tax-deferred invest-ment accounts and brokerage investment accounts:

- Brokerage accounts typically use more extensive security lists (whereas tax-deferred investment accounts don't).

- Brokerage accounts have cash accounts (whereas tax-deferred invest-ments usually don't).

- Brokerage accounts let you record a handful of goofy transactions that tax-deferred investment accounts don't (because they don't make sense in the context of conventional tax-deferred investments).

I spend the next few paragraphs of this chapter describing features that are unique to brokerage accounts.

Setting up security lists

Typically, a brokerage account probably contains more than one type of *secu-rity*. You may have shares of Boeing, General Motors, or Google. You name it, and someone owns it.

Therefore, a brokerage account uses a list of securities — and you, as the investor, need to create and maintain the list of securities (stocks, bonds, and so on) that your account holds.

To do so, set up the brokerage account (as described in the first part of this chapter) and then complete the following steps:

1. **Choose the Security List command.**

   Display the Investing tab, click the Tools button, and choose the Security List command. Quicken displays the Security List window, shown in Figure 14-1. Note that any mutual funds you've already set up appear in the list as securities.

Figure 14-1:
The Security
List window.

2. **Click the New Security button in the Security List window.**

   Quicken displays the first Add Security To Quicken dialog box, shown in Figure 14-2.

3. **Enter the stock symbol for the security in the Ticker Symbol text box.**

   If you don't know the symbol, make sure that you have the name of the security correct and then click the Look Up button to search for the ticker symbol at Quicken.com.

4. **Click Next to continue.**

   Quicken retrieves information about the stock whose ticker symbol you entered and displays it in another Add Security To Quicken dialog box.

Figure 14-2:
The first Add
Security To
Quicken
dialog box.

5. **Click Done.**

   Quicken adds the security to the security list and redisplays the Security List window. If you have additional securities, you can add them by repeating Steps 2–4. Also, you can add securities on the fly while you're recording the purchase of a security for the first time. When you do this, Quicken starts this little "Oh, let's add another security to the list" process for you at Step 3.

Before I quit this discussion of the security list, let me just make a couple of observations for your benefit. See those buttons along the right and top edges of the Security List window? (Go ahead and flip back to Figure 14-1.) You can use them to do useful stuff. For example, click Edit to change security information. Click the Report button to display a report of transactions for the security. Click the Delete button to remove the selected security from the list. Finally, use the Watch List and Hide check boxes to add a security to your watch list or to hide the selected security. Just thought you'd want to know.

Working with cash

One of the big differences between a brokerage account and a traditional tax-deferred investment account is that a cash management, or *money market*, account is always, always attached to the brokerage account — and is actively used.

When you initially set up a brokerage account, your money goes into this account. (The broker bought you a muffin and coffee in this meeting, remember?)

You purchase your first shares with the cash from this account. And when you sell shares, all cash proceeds go into this account.

Transferring cash to and from an account

Because you work with cash in a brokerage account, you need to know how to record the cash that flows into and out of the account.

To transfer cash to an account, follow these steps:

1. **Display the investment account's window.**

   You can do this in more than one way, as luck would have it, but one easy way is to click the investment account on the Accounts bar. The investment account window should look something like the one shown in Figure 14-3. (If you're lucky.)

2. **Indicate that you're transferring money.**

   Click the Enter Transactions button. Quicken displays the dialog box shown in Figure 14-4. Choose Cash Transferred Into Account in the Enter Transaction drop-down list box.

Figure 14-3: The Transaction List shows the activity within an investment account.

Figure 14-4:
The dialog
box used
to record
transfers
into an
account.

3. **Record the transaction date, amount, and account.**

   To record the amount of a cash transfer, confirm the transaction date (shown in the Transaction Date text box), enter the dollar amount in the Amount To Transfer text box, and then specify the checking account supplying the cash in the Transfer Account drop-down list box. Then click the Enter/New or the Enter/Done button. (If you click Enter/New, Quicken records the transaction but leaves the dialog box open so that you can record some more transactions.)

To transfer cash from an account, follow these steps:

1. **Display the investment account window.**

2. **Indicate that you're transferring money from an account.**

   Click the Enter Transactions button. Quicken displays the dialog box shown in Figure 14-5. Choose Cash Transferred Out Of Account in the Enter Transaction drop-down list box.

3. **Record the transaction date, amount, and account.**

   To record the amount of a cash transfer, again confirm the transaction date (using the Transaction Date text box), enter the dollar amount in the Amount To Transfer text box, and specify the checking account receiving the cash in the Transfer Account drop-down list box. Then click either the Enter/New or the Enter/Done button.

Figure 14-5:
The dialog
box used
to transfer
cash from a
brokerage
investment
account.

Buying near and selling dear

Buying and selling securities in a brokerage account is very similar to buying and selling shares of a tax-deferred investment. You fill in the same fields in almost the exact same way.

Mutual (fund) acquaintance

I don't want to get into the subject of load mutual funds versus no-load mutual funds — you pay a commission to buy load funds, and you don't pay a commission to buy no-load funds — but if you're interested in how these two types of funds work, flip open the *Wall Street Journal* and look for advertisements from no-load fund managers such as Vanguard, Scudder, and T. Rowe Price. Give them a call, and they'll tell you why they think that you should bypass the middleman — your financial advisor. Next, talk to a financial advisor, who will tell you why you *shouldn't* bypass the middleman. Then you make the decision.

What? You want *my* opinion? With much trepidation, I'll tell you: I always use no-load mutual funds because I'm a big fan of the do-it-yourself approach. You save substantial amounts both in commissions and, typically, in annual maintenance fees. Quite honestly, if you can figure out how to use Quicken and are reading a chapter like this, you have enough smarts to choose your own mutual funds (especially if you're willing to do a bit of research through reading). Try Andrew Tobias's classic, *The Only Investment Guide You'll Ever Need* (Harvest Books) or Burton Malkiel's *A Random Walk Guide to Investing* (W.W. Norton & Company). However, I also think that a good financial advisor — *good* is the operative word here — is well worth the commission fee if he or she helps you avoid expensive mistakes. It is not, however, necessarily easy to find a good financial advisor.

1. **Display the investment account window.**

2. **Click the Enter Transactions button. When Quicken displays the dialog box, choose Buy – Shares Bought in the Enter Transaction drop-down list box.**

   Quicken, ever responsive to your needs, displays the Buy – Shares Bought dialog box (shown in Figure 14-6). When Quicken displays this dialog box, provide the transaction date. Select the security in the Security Name drop-down list box. Use the Number Of Shares, Price Paid, and Commission text boxes to describe your purchase. (You can get this information from your order confirmation slip.)

Figure 14-6:
The Buy –
Shares
Bought
dialog box.

3. **Indicate whether Quicken should adjust a cash account.**

   Use the From This Account's Cash Balance or the From option button to specify which cash account Quicken should adjust for the transaction. You can say the usual cash account (by selecting the From This Account's Cash Balance option button) or specify some different account (by selecting the From option button and then choosing the account in the From drop-down list box).

4. **Click the Enter/New or the Enter/Done button when you're finished.**

   Pretty simple, right?

Selling a security works in the same basic way as buying a security:

1. **Display the investment account window and then click the Enter Transaction button.**

2. **When Quicken displays the dialog box, choose Sell – Shares Sold in the Enter Transaction drop-down list box.**

   Quicken displays the Sell – Shares Sold dialog box (shown in Figure 14-7). Use the Transaction Date box to provide the sales date. Use the Security Name drop-down list box to identify the stock, bond, or mutual fund you're selling. You use the Number Of Shares, Price Received, and Commission text boxes to describe your sale, and you use the To This Account's Cash Balance or the To option button to specify whether Quicken should adjust some bank account balance for this transaction.

Figure 14-7:
The Sell –
Shares Sold
dialog box.

3. **Click the Specify Lots button.**

   If you purchased share lots at different prices or at different times, you can click the Specify Lots button to open the Specify Lots For Investment dialog box. Here, you can pick and choose which lots to sell so that you can minimize the capital gains taxes you'll owe. (Good idea, huh?) A *lot* is simply a batch, or set, of shares that you purchase at one time. If you sell the most expensive lots, you reduce your capital gains and the taxes on those gains.

   - *To pick an entire lot:* Double-click it. (You need to double-click the date field, by the way.)

   - *To pick a portion of a lot:* Select it, then, in the Selected text box, type the number of shares from the lot you want to sell.

   - *To clear your selections and start over:* Click the Reset button.

The Specify Lots For Investment dialog box also provides nifty command buttons for automating the process of selecting lots. If you click the Maximum Gain or the Minimum Gain button, Quicken picks lots for you in a way that produces the largest possible or smallest possible capital gain, respectively. Alternatively, you can click the First Shares In or the Last Shares In button to sell either the oldest shares or newest shares first, respectively. This business about picking the lots you sell is rather arbitrary, of course. By letting Quicken pick lots, you can manipulate the capital gain you'll have and the capital gains taxes you'll pay. But it's all legal (as long as you specifically tell the brokerage company which lots you're selling). And honorable. And it can save you money because you can time your capital gains so that they occur when they'll cost you the least.

If you're someone who has large capital loss carryforwards — as many investors do after the brutal years of the previous decade — your capital loss carryforwards may totally wipe out any gains you have to recognize over the next few years (or decades, gulp). In this case, you may not get much benefit from fooling around with this specific identification business. Consult your tax advisor for details.

4. Click the Enter/New or the Enter/Done button.

Recording dividends, capital gains, and other goodies

Taking care of this stuff is easy. Any time you receive investment income, click the Enter Transactions button and choose Inc – Income (Div, Int, Etc.) in the Enter Transaction drop-down list box. When Quicken displays the dialog box used to record income, use the Security Name drop-down list box to confirm the stock, bond, or mutual fund producing income, and then use the Dividend, Interest, Short-Term Cap Gain Dist, Mid-Term Cap Gain Dist, and Long-Term Cap Gain Dist text boxes to record the amount and type of income, as shown in Figure 14-8.

Figure 14-8:
The dialog box used to record income.

Note: You use the Transfer Account drop-down list box to identify the account into which income amounts are deposited when you don't use the investment account's regular cash account.

To record dividends, capital gains, and other income when you reinvest the money you receive, click the Enter Transaction button and choose Income Reinvested in the Enter Transaction drop-down list box. When Quicken displays the dialog box, describe the amounts received and how you've reinvested.

Recording other not-so-tricky transactions

Quicken lets you record all sorts of transactions in a brokerage account. Not only can you do reminder and stock split actions (which I describe in Chapter 13), but you can also do a bunch of other things.

I briefly describe these other transactions here and explain how to record them because you're more likely to encounter them when you're working with a standard brokerage account.

Bonds . . . James Bonds . . .

If you invest in bonds, you know that a bond's price is actually quoted as a percentage of its face value. A bond that sells for $950 with a face value of $1,000, for example, is quoted as 95 because the $950 price is 95 percent of the $1,000 face value. Quicken, however, doesn't let you describe a bond's price as a percent. You must enter the bond price as its price in dollars and cents.

Going for the gold

You can use Quicken to record precious metal investments. Suppose, for example, that you're hoarding Krugerrands (1-ounce gold coins minted in South Africa). For this investment, the price is the price per Krugerrand, and the shares figure is actually the number of ounces (equal to the number of Krugerrands). Because Quicken doesn't supply price-per-ounce or number-of-ounces fields, you insert the information in the Price and Shares fields on the Investment list.

Recording margin interest expenses

To record margin interest expense, click the Enter Transactions button and select Margin Interest Expense in the Enter Transaction drop-down list box. When you do, Quicken displays the margin interest expense version of the investment transaction entry dialog box, which you use to describe the cost of your financial adventure. Only the most sophisticated investors should be using margin interest expense, anyway. If you're one of these financial cowboys or cowgirls, I assume that you're smart enough to figure out this stuff on your own.

Paying a miscellaneous expense

Sometimes you need to pay an expense. One rarely sees these occur for stock or bond investments. Expenses sometimes do arise with real estate partnership interests (which can be treated like common stock shares) or precious metal investments (which can also be treated like common stock shares).

If you need to pay a fee for account handling or for storing your stash of South African Krugerrands, for example, you can record such an expense by clicking the Enter Transaction button and then choosing Miscellaneous Expense in the Enter Transaction drop-down list box. When Quicken displays the dialog box, fill out the boxes in the miscellaneous expense version of the investment transaction entry dialog box.

Recording a return of capital

The old *return of capital* trick. Sometimes, the money you receive because you own a security isn't really income. Rather, it's a refund of part of the purchase price.

Consider this example: You buy a mortgage-backed security — such as a Ginnie Mae bond — for which the *mortgagee* (the person who borrowed the mortgage money) pays not only periodic interest but also a portion of the mortgage principal.

Obviously, you shouldn't record the principal portion of the payment you receive as income. You must record this payment as a mortgage principal reduction or — in the parlance of investment record keeping — as a *return of capital*.

As another example, suppose that you invest in a limited partnership or real estate investment trust that begins liquidating. Some of the money that the investors receive in this case is really a return of their original investment, or a return of capital.

To record a return of capital action, click the Enter Transaction button. When Quicken displays the return of capital version of the investment transaction entry dialog box, choose Return Of Capital in the Enter Transaction drop-down list box and describe the security that's returning capital.

Special investment transactions

Quicken also supplies some other investment transaction types. Quicken provides special investment transactions to record the receipt of stock options, exercise of stock options, and repricing of stock options. Quicken also supplies investment transaction types for short selling and investment transactions for dealing with corporate mergers, spinoffs, and reorganizations. To use these other special investment transactions, you follow the same general approach described in the preceding sections.

More Quick Stuff about Brokerage Accounts

Let me tell you a couple of other quick things. You'll almost certainly find these tidbits helpful.

Monitoring and updating securities values

Regardless of whether you're working with a mutual fund account or with securities in a brokerage account, you can collect current market prices and store them with the Quicken account information.

To manually record the current market price for a security, click on the Investing tab (so your investments show up) and then use the up-arrow and down-arrow keys to select the security (or click the security with the mouse). Then move the cursor to the Quote/Price field and enter the current price.

To automatically (electronically) grab current market prices, click on the Investing tab's Update button and choose the One Step Update command.

Adjusting errors

You can adjust the cash balance in a brokerage account and the shares balance in brokerage accounts if for some reason the figures are incorrect.

Oops, my brokerage cash balance is wrong

How you adjust the cash balance in a brokerage account depends on how you set up the account.

To adjust an investment account's cash balance, when the cash balance information isn't tracked in a separate linked cash account, click the investment account's name on the Accounts bar, click the Account Actions button, and choose Update Cash Balance. When Quicken displays the Update Cash Balance dialog box, shown in Figure 14-9, specify the correct cash balance and the date as of when the figure you enter is correct.

Figure 14-9:
The Update
Cash
Balance
dialog box.

To adjust an investment account's cash balance (or *cash management account,* as some brokerage houses call them), click the account name on the Accounts bar, click the Account Actions button, and choose Reconcile An Account. You reconcile a brokerage cash account the same way you reconcile a regular old checking account. For information about how to reconcile a checking account, refer to Chapter 8. Chapter 8 describes how to reconcile a bank account, but reconciling a brokerage cash account works the same way.

Oops, my brokerage account shares balance is wrong

To adjust the shares balance for a security in a brokerage account, click the brokerage account on the Accounts bar, click the Account Actions button, and choose Update Share Balance.

Quicken next displays the Adjust Share Balance dialog box, shown in Figure 14-10, where you specify the security, the correct number of shares, and the date for which you're entering the balance. Fill in the text boxes and then click either Enter/New or Enter/Done. Quicken adjusts the shares balance for the security you specified.

Figure 14-10:
The Adjust
Share
Balance
dialog box.

A few words on the Investing tab's other tools

If you've read this whole chapter, you know that I mostly describe how you get information into the windows and dialog boxes of the Investing tab. But before I stop talking about the Investing tab, I want to give you a little more information on how you work with the tab's commands and buttons to monitor your investments.

The first thing to notice is that the Investing tab provides different views (available when you click Portfolio, Performance, or Allocations), each of which provides its own information:

- ✔ **The Portfolio view** (see Figure 14-11) lists the investment accounts you've set up within Quicken, the securities on your watch list, and the major stock market indexes. In addition, the view provides a bit of high-level information about each of these items.

- ✔ **The Performance view** (see Figure 14-12) graphs your investment account values and cost bases over a selected time period and lets you compare these values to some external benchmark, such as the S&P 500.

Figure 14-11:
The Portfolio view of the Investing tab.

Figure 14-12:
The
Performance
view of the
Investing
tab.

✓ **The Allocations view** (see Figure 14-13) provides charts and tables of information that let you see how your overall investments are allocated and how you've said they *should be* allocated. (You need to have identified which asset category your individual investment securities fall into in order to see your portfolio allocation, and you need to have used the first Options button's Change Target Allocations command to set your allocations.)

The other thing I want to just mention in passing are the asset allocation and portfolio analysis tools available when you click the Investing tab's Tools button. Through the Tools button, Quicken provides several useful commands:

✓ **The Asset Allocation Guide** command displays a web page that provides lots of solid information you can use to think smartly about how you allocate your investments between stocks and bonds and other choices. (This command is definitely worth a few minutes of exploration on your part.)

✓ **The Buy/Sell Preview** command lets you estimate the financial effect on your portfolio of buying and/or selling specific investments.

✓ **The Capital Gains Estimator** command calculates the unrealized capital gains and losses in your investment portfolio using the most current prices available to Quicken.

Figure 14-13:
The
Allocations
view of the
Investing
tab.

Part IV
Very Serious Business

The 5th Wave   By Rich Tennant

"I think if you subtract the figure in the 'Days I Go Home Early' column from the figure in the 'Snippy Attitude' column, you'll reach a zero-sum figure."

In this part . . .

*I*f you use Quicken Home & Business for your small business or you use Quicken Rental Property Manager for real estate investments, you'll benefit from some extra information and hand-holding about how to use your flavor of the Quicken program. Sure, you can learn these things by sitting down with your certified public accountant (CPA), having a cup of coffee, and paying about $200 per hour.

Or you can read on, pretend that we're chitchatting over coffee, and save the $200.

Chapter 15

Mind Your Business

. . . .

In This Chapter

▶ Setting up a business using Quicken

▶ Working with your customers

▶ Bookkeeping whistles and bells in Quicken Home & Business

▶ Doing payroll using Quicken

. . . .

*T*he preceding chapters of this little book talk about using Quicken for your personal bookkeeping. But you may be interested to know that Quicken also does just a truly excellent job at small business accounting, too.

If you want to use Quicken for small business accounting, you need to do just a couple of things: First, you want to make sure you're working with the Home & Business version or the Quicken Rental Property Manager version of Quicken, because both these flavors of Quicken supply an extra menu of seriously useful business bookkeeping commands. Second, and this is only my humble opinion, you want to skim through this chapter's discussions so you get the business bookkeeping stuff set up right.

 If you're not already working with Quicken Home & Business, you can upgrade to Home & Business by choosing the Add Business Tools or Add Rental Property Tools command on the Help menu. If that option isn't available or doesn't make sense, contact Intuit by visiting the www.quicken.com website.

Setting Up a Business the Quicken Way

To use Quicken for small business bookkeeping, you need to describe each business you or your spouse operates. For example, if you work as a one-person consultant, and your spouse runs a landscape design business, you need to tell Quicken a little bit about both businesses. Quicken needs this information so it can separately track each business and can produce invoices for each business.

Describing your business (es)

To describe your business to Quicken, you need to give the business's name and identify the owner. Here's how you do this:

1. **Choose the Manage Business Information command.**

   Display the Business tab, click the Business Tools button, and choose the Manage Business Information command. Quicken displays the Manage Business Information window.

   If you don't have a Business tab, either you need to choose View⟳ Standard Menus or you need to choose Help⟳Add Business Tools.

2. **Click the Add button.**

   Quicken displays the Add Business dialog box (see Figure 15-1).

Figure 15-1:
The Add Business dialog box.

> **Add Business**
>
> ## Add Business
>
> * Required fields
>
> Business name * [   ]
>
> Description [   ]
>
> Owner * ⦿ Self ○ Spouse Why does this matter?
>
> Business tag * [   ] What's a tag?
>
> ☑ Business transactions without a tag belong to this business Tell me more
>
> ⓘ   [OK] [Cancel]

3. **Enter your firm's name in the Business Name text box.**

   Optionally, you can also enter a brief description in the Description box, which appears just below the Business Name text box.

4. **Identify the business owner.**

   Use the Owner option buttons, Self and Spouse, to indicate who owns the business — you or your better half.

5. **Create a tag for the business.**

   You want the tag to be a memorable yet short acronym or abbreviation you can use to mark transactions as connected to a particular business. For example, say your family does operate two businesses: a consulting business and a landscape design business. You might use the tags "Cons" (for consulting) and "Land" (for landscape design).

6. **(Optional) Specify this business is the default business.**

   You can tell Quicken that a particular business is the *default* business —
   in other words, that Quicken should assume a business transaction relates
   to this business unless you tell Quicken otherwise. To do this, check the
   Business Transactions Without A Tag Belong To This Business box.

7. **Save your business description.**

   Quicken returns you to the Manage Business Information window,
   which now lists your newly described business venture. If you need to
   add more businesses, repeat Steps 2–7. Click Done to close the Manage
   Business Information window.

The Manage Business Information window provides two useful buttons I
should briefly mention: Delete and Edit. You can click the Delete button
to remove the selected business description. And you can click the Edit
button to display the Edit Business dialog box, which allows you to
change the selected business's description.

Designing business invoices

You need to add your business's name and address to the business
invoice template that Quicken produces. To do this, display the Business
tab, click the Business Actions button, and then choose the Invoices And
Estimates⇨Design Forms command. When Quicken displays the Forms
Designer window, click the Company Address Properties button (the button
next to a double-chevron) so that Quicken displays the Company Address
dialog box (see Figure 15-2). Then enter your business and address. Note that
you may need to click the Let's Get Started button the first time you want to
access this dialog box.

Figure 15-2:
The
Company
Address
dialog box
on top of
the Forms
Designer
window.

Company Address

☑ Print Company Address:

OK   Cancel

I'm not going to discuss the Forms Designer window in more detail, but you may want to poke around the window a bit. You can use the window's buttons and boxes to customize with abandon the invoice form that Quicken produces. Note, too, that you may need or want to create and customize multiple invoice templates — such as if you are using Quicken for more than one business or such as when you want to use distinctly different invoices for different customers, products, or services. You can create a new invoice template by clicking the Forms Designer window's Layout button and then choosing New on the menu that Quicken displays.

Identifying invoice items

The stuff that appears on invoices — product or service descriptions, standard prices, and so forth — needs to be provided up-front to Quicken by setting up invoice items.

Suppose, for example, that you're using Quicken to keep the books for a one-person consulting business, and that you bill your consulting services by the hour, charging people $125 an hour. To describe this standard invoice information, you would set up a "consulting" item, using the following steps:

1. **Choose the View All Invoice Items command.**

   Display the Business tab, click the Business Actions button, and then choose the Invoices And Estimates➪View All Invoice Items command. Quicken displays the Customize Invoice Items window.

2. **Click the New button.**

   Quicken displays the New Item dialog box (see Figure 15-3).

3. **Name the item you're creating.**

   For example, you might name an item for consulting services "consult." You just need to use an item name that's descriptive enough that you remember the item details when you see the item name.

4. **Categorize and tag.**

   Use the Category/Tag box to specify which income category should be used to account for the item and, when you're running multiple businesses, which tag should be used to identify the business. For example, you might want a "consult" item (which bills for professional services) to get categorized using a "Service Revenue" income category while you might want a "client costs" item (which bills for costs you've incurred on behalf of a client) to get categorized using a "Reimbursed Expenses" income category.

   If you've set up two different businesses, consulting and landscape design, and use the tags "cons" and "land" to differentiate, you would enter the "cons" tag into the Tag field for consulting business items. And you would enter the "land" tag into the Tag field to specify for landscape design business invoice items.

5. **Describe the item in more detail, please.**

Use the Description text box to provide the text you want to automatically appear on the invoice for the item. You can (and probably should) be quite descriptive here. Of course, you can add more text to the invoice and edit the invoice item descriptions later on when you actually create the invoice. But Quicken automatically enters the item description for you. You therefore want to make Quicken type up any long, detailed descriptions.

6. **Flag any subtotal items.**

Okay, here's a weird thing about items that appear on an invoice. Anything that you want to put in the body of your invoice is an item. Obviously, the services and products you sell need to be set up as items. But other stuff that you want to put on the invoice — shipping charges, discounts, markups, and so on — also need to be set up as items.

After you understand this weirdness, things become more clear (hopefully) about subtotal items. The Subtotal Of The Preceding Items check box, if marked, tells Quicken that the item simply adds up the preceding items shown on the invoice. Probably, by the way, the right item name and description for a subtotal item is subtotal (for the item name) and Subtotal or Total (for the item description).

If you indicate an item is a subtotal, by the way, you don't provide a category or tag. But that makes sense: Quicken grabs the category and tag information from the individual "real" items getting subtotaled — not the subtotal item.

7. **(Optional) Add a blank line after the item.**

To tell Quicken to add a blank line on invoices after an item, check the Print Extra Blank Line box.

8. **Set the item price.**

   Use the Per Item Rate to specify a default price for the item. In the case where you're setting up an item for a service, for example, you might enter the hourly billing rate into the Per Item Rate box.

9. **Identify items subject to sales tax.**

   If an item is subject to sales tax — in other words, if you're supposed to charge sales tax on the item — check the Taxable box.

10. **Give the percentage for any percentage-based items.**

    You may not need percentage items for your invoices. But if you regularly bill people for items that get calculated as a percentage of some other item on the invoice, you use a percentage item.

    Percentage items calculate an amount for your invoice by multiplying a percentage against the preceding item. For example, if the preceding item shown on an invoice equals $1,000, a 10 percent "percentage" item adds another $100 to the invoice.

    Note that when you check the Percentage box, the value you enter into the Per Item Rate is not a dollar amount but a percentage value. You enter 10 percent, for example, as **10**.

    When you finish describing an item, click the New Item dialog box's OK button. Quicken returns you to the Customize Invoice Items window. To add more items, repeat the preceding steps. Or click the Customize Invoice Item window's Done button.

Working with Customers

You can invoice customers, record their payments, and monitor unpaid amounts after you've described your business, finalized your invoice form(s), and created an item list.

Setting up a Customer Invoices account

Quicken needs you to set up a Customer Invoices account to track the invoices you create. But this isn't difficult to do. Simply display the Business tab, click the Business Actions button, and choose the Invoices And Estimates⇨Customer Invoices command. When you do, Quicken checks to see whether you've already set up an account to track amounts your customers owe you. If you haven't, Quicken asks if it can set up such an account. If you answer "yes," Quicken asks if it's okay to use a name like "Customer

Invoices." When you click the "Sure, I don't care what you name the account" button, Quicken then sets up the account for you. When Quicken sets up the Customer Invoices account, it also sets up a sales tax payable account to track any sales taxes you collect from customers.

I'm not going to talk a bunch more about the Customer Invoices account, but let me make just three quick points:

✔ The Customer Invoices account is a regular Quicken account — sort of like a bank account. You will see the Customer Invoices account listed, for example, in the Accounts bar and on the Accounts List window.

✔ You can enter or edit transactions directly by viewing the account in a register window (the same sort of register window I describe in detail in Chapter 4). Typically, you won't work directly with the register, however, because Quicken provides easy-to-use tools for recording customer invoices and payments (as described a bit later in this chapter).

✔ The Unpaid Invoices List is an easy way to see which customer invoices are open (often these are the only invoices you truly care about). To display this list, display the Business tab, click the Business Tools button, and then choose the Unpaid Invoices List command.

Invoicing your customers

To invoice a customer, follow these steps:

1. **Choose Create Invoice command.**

   Display the Business tab, click the Business Actions button, and choose the Invoices And Estimates⇨Create Invoice command. Quicken displays the Invoice window (see Figure 15-4). The Invoice window in Figure 15-4 shows a bit of information in its boxes, but don't get confused about that. In the steps that follow, I describe how to enter this information.

2. **Identify the customer and provide the address, if necessary.**

   If you're invoicing a customer for the first time, type his or her name into the Customer box in the upper-left corner of the Invoice window. Quicken will copy the company name to the Bill To box. You can then complete the address by adding the street information, city, state, and ZIP code.

   If you're invoicing a customer for the second or subsequent time, open the Customer box and select the customer from the list that Quicken displays.

Figure 15-4:
The Invoice
window.

You can add customers on the fly — which is what I describe in the preceding step — and which means you only briefly describe your customers with sketchy vagueness. Alternatively, you can also go hog wild and describe each and every customer in painstaking detail. To go the painstaking detail route, choose the Business⇨Customers⇨Add Customer command. When Quicken displays the Edit Address Book Record dialog box, use its boxes to describe your customer. Note that you can use the Add Customer command at any time. You don't need to wait until you're ready to record an invoice.

3. **Tag the transaction.**

   If you're using Quicken to track more than one business and you've (very rightly) created a tag for each business, enter the appropriate tag into the Business Tag box.

4. **Provide the Date, Invoice Number, and Purchase Order Number information.**

   Use the Date box to indicate the invoicing date (typically the invoice date is the actual date you create the invoice). Use the Due Date box to specify when you expect payment. Use the Invoice # box to give the invoice a unique number. Finally, if you're billing on purchase order numbers, use the P.O. Number box to provide the customer his or her purchase order number.

5. Describe the individual items you're invoicing the customer for.

To enter an invoice item, click the Item column for the line you want to add and then select an item from the list Quicken displays. Quicken adds the category and description information you provided for the item — but you can edit these if you want. Next, specify the item quantity and verify the rate.

You can initially fit ten items onto an invoice, but if you need more room, click the Add Lines button.

6. Add sales tax if applicable.

If items on the invoice are subject to sales tax, enter the sales tax rate into the Tax box. Quicken then calculates the sales tax for you by multiplying the sales tax percentage against each of the taxable items on the invoice.

Note: Quicken tracks the sales tax you've collected using a liability account. Quicken shows the liability account in the Tax Account drop-down list box at the bottom of the window.

7. (Optional) Add customer messages or memo descriptions to the invoice.

If you want to add a message to the invoice, enter the message in the Customer Message box.

If you want to record a bit of extra information about the invoice — information that won't appear on the invoice — enter that into the Memo box.

8. Save the invoice.

You can save the invoice and close the Invoice window by clicking Save And Done. Or, you can save the invoice and redisplay an empty Invoice window so you can create another invoice by clicking Save And New.

Printing invoices

You can print invoices as you create them. Simply click the Print button on the Invoice window. The Print button looks like a printer and appears in the lower-left corner of the window. When you click the Print button, Quicken displays the Print Invoice dialog box. Click its OK button to print the invoice.

You can also print invoices in batches. To use batch printing, first create your batch of invoices (obviously). Next, display the Business tab, click the Business Tools button, and then choose the Print Invoices/Invoices List command. When Quicken displays the Invoices List, verify that the invoices you want to print are marked with a check, click the Print button so that

Quicken displays a menu of print commands, and then choose the List command. Quicken displays the Print dialog box. Click its OK button to print the selected invoices.

The Print Invoice and Print dialog boxes provide a bunch of buttons and boxes you can use to control how Quicken prints your invoices. If you have questions about how these printing options work, refer to Chapter 5. Chapter 5 describes how to print checks and check registers, but the process for printing those items closely resembles the process for printing invoices.

Recording customer payments

To record a customer payment, follow these steps:

1. **Choose the Receive Customer Payment command.**

   Display the Business tab, click the Business Actions button, and choose the Invoices And Estimates⇨Receive Customer Payment command. Quicken displays the Payment window (see Figure 15-5).

Figure 15-5: The Payment window.

2. **Select the customer.**

   Open the Customer box and select the customer for whom you want to record a payment. After you select the customer and move to the next box, Quicken displays a list of any unpaid invoices the customer owes.

3. **Describe the payment.**

   You should enter the payment amount into the Amount box. That, I'm sure, represents a big surprise.

   You should probably also record the payment date using the Date box and the customer's check number using the Check Number box.

4. **Select the bank account into which you'll deposit the check.**

   This is easy. Open the Deposit To drop-down list box and select the bank account.

5. **Identify the open invoices the customer is paying.**

   Quicken attempts to guess at which unpaid invoices the customer is paying, marking the invoices with a check. Often Quicken guesses correctly, but verify that the correct invoice shows a check mark. You can mark and unmark invoices by clicking the check mark.

   If a payment pays partial amounts of unpaid invoices, you can click the Payment column in the Outstanding Invoices list and then edit the amount.

6. **Record the payment.**

   After you describe the payment and apply it to the correct open invoices, click the Enter button. Quicken records the payment and updates the invoice open balance(s).

Issuing credits and making refunds

Quicken provides commands and windows for issuing credits and for making refunds to customers.

To record a credit — a *credit* is essentially a backwards invoice that says you owe your customer money rather than the other way around — display the Business tab, click the Business Actions button, and choose the Invoices And Estimates⇨Issue Credit command. When Quicken displays the Credit window (which is a mirror image of the Invoice window), record your credit memo. You won't have any trouble using the Credit window if you've previously used the Invoice window. But if you have questions, refer to the steps provided earlier for invoicing your customers.

To refund money to a customer because of an earlier credit memo, display the Business tab, click the Business Actions button, and choose the Invoices And Estimates⇨Issue a Refund command. When Quicken displays the Refund dialog box, identify the account you'll write the refund check on, specify to which customer you want to issue a refund by using the Customer box, and then click Enter. Quicken records a check for you in the appropriate bank account register.

Business Bookkeeping Whistles and Bells

Quicken Home & Business (which is what I've spent the earlier paragraphs of this chapter talking about) provides a handful of additional business book-keeping tools. I'm not going to describe these tools in any detail in this book because I don't think you'll use the tools. Nevertheless, I do want to give you a quick overview.

Jobs and projects

If you're really alert and have good eyes, you'll have noticed a Project/Job box in some of the figures of this chapter and on some of the Quicken Home & Business windows. Just a quick note to explain: Most small businesses probably bill customers. But you can find yourself, in some industries, bill-ing jobs or projects that are in turn owned or managed by a customer. If this sounds like your situation, you'll want to use the Customers⇨Create Project/ Job command (available when you click the Business Actions button avail-able on the Business tab) to set up jobs or projects underneath your custom-ers. When you invoice, you'll want to include not only the customer name on the invoice but also the project or job.

Using finance charges, estimates, and statements

Three customer-invoicing commands (available on the Business tab when you click the Business Actions button and choose the Invoices And Estimates command) deserve a quick description: Create Estimates, Create Finance Charge, and Print Statements.

The Create Estimates command allows you to create a dummy invoice you can give to a customer as a preliminary cost estimate of a job or service. The Estimate window, not surprisingly, mirrors the Invoice window. In fact, if you ultimately need to invoice the customer for something you've previously estimated, you display the Business tab, click the Business Tools button, and choose the Estimates List command. When Quicken displays the Estimates List window, select the estimate from the window that Quicken displays, and click the Convert button.

The Create Finance Charge command allows you to assess a finance charge on a past due invoice. In essence, when you use the command, Quicken creates an invoice for the customer with a single item on it for the finance charge.

The Print Statements command lets you print customer statements, which show the open invoices for a customer at a specific point in time. If you have customers for whom you need a statement, you'll obviously need to use this command.

Managing vendor bills

If you display the Business tab, click the Business Actions button, and choose the Bills And Vendors command, Quicken displays a menu of commands that let you create a simple accounts payable system for tracking your unpaid bills from vendors.

I'm not going to describe these commands here. You really shouldn't need to set up an accounts payable system for a small business except in the special case where someone has foolishly decided your business should use accrual-based accounting rather than cash-basis accounting. (If that is your situation — my apologies, but you need to get help from the nabob who sent you down the accrual-based accounting path.)

 If you just record expenses by writing checks — this is the way that Chapters 4 and 5 describe — you essentially keep your books using cash-basis accounting. Cash-basis accounting usually works best for small businesses. It delays your income tax expenses, and it keeps your bookkeeping simpler.

Vehicle Mileage Tracker

Quicken Home & Business provides a handy utility you can use to keep a log of your business auto or truck usage. As you're probably tired of hearing your accountant say, you need to keep such a log in order to prove your business vehicle usage.

I'm not going to describe the Vehicle Mileage Tracker here, though. You'll find the tool very straightforward to use. Simply display the Business tab, click the Business Tools button, choose the Mileage Tracker command, and poke around a bit.

Quicken Dirty Payroll

A lot of people who own small businesses or who have a household employee (nannies, for example) need to deal with payroll. Although Quicken Home & Business doesn't provide you payroll tools, I still want to provide you with some quick-and-dirty instructions about how to handle simple payroll situations with Quicken. Oh, sure. It won't be fancy. But I promise you it'll be fast and cheap.

Getting ready for payroll

To do payroll in Quicken, you need to set up a couple of payroll expense categories. Fortunately, doing so is not particularly difficult.

I'm going to describe how you do this task for purposes of U.S. federal income and payroll taxes. If you employ people in a state that has a state income tax — California, say — you may also have to deal with state payroll taxes. But you can track and process these the same way you process the federal taxes. (Some counties and cities even have income taxes, but these should also work the same way.)

Setting up the wages expense category

You need to set up a payroll expense category for tracking the wages you pay employees. Here's all you do:

1. **Choose Tools⇨Category List.**

   Quicken, with no hesitation, displays the Category List window.

2. **Click the New button.**

   Quicken displays the Set Up Category dialog box (see Figure 15-6).

Figure 15-6:
The Set Up Category dialog box.

3. **Enter Wages as the category name by moving the cursor to the Category Name text box and typing Wages.**

   If you told Quicken during the setup that you'll use Quicken to track a business, Quicken may have automatically set up the Wages category.

4. **(Optional) Enter a description of the category.**

   If you want, you can type a description in the Description text box.

5. **Select the Expense option button.**

   This choice tells Quicken that you're setting up an expense category.

6. **(Optional) Describe the tax characteristics of this category.**

   To further describe taxable income and tax deduction categories, click the Tax Reporting tab and then select the Tax-Related check box.

   Optionally, if you want to be super-nit-picky and don't care about wasting your time, select the Standard List Item List or Extended Line Item List option button from the Tax Reporting tab and then choose the exact tax form and form line number the category gets reported on when you prepare your federal tax return. One caution: You won't actually know for an absolute certainty which forms and line numbers are used until the end of the year.

7. **Click OK.**

   Quicken adds the category to the category list and redisplays the Category List window.

Setting up the payroll tax expense category

You also need to set up a payroll tax category to track payroll taxes that the employer pays, including the company's share of Social Security taxes, the company's share of Medicare taxes, and any other employer payroll taxes (such as federal unemployment tax or the equivalent state employer taxes).

To set up a payroll tax expense category, follow the same steps I give you for setting up a wages expense category (in the preceding section). You can name the category *payroll taxes,* or *taxes-payroll,* or something else that's even more clever.

Getting the taxes stuff right

You also need to do a couple of other things if you want to do payroll the right way in the U.S. of A.

Requesting (or demanding) an employer ID number

First, you need to file an SS-4, or Request for Employer Identification Number form, with the Internal Revenue Service (IRS) so that you can get an Employer

Identification Number. You can get this form by calling the IRS or by visiting the IRS website (www.irs.gov).

In one of its cooler moves, the IRS allows you to apply for and receive an Employer Identification Number right online. Visit the www.irs.gov website, and then click the Apply For An Employer Identification Number (EIN) Online link located on the left side of the page.

So what about Social Security, Medicare, and withholding taxes?

You need to do two things before you can figure out how to handle all those taxes. First, you need your employees to fill out W-4 forms to let you know what filing status they'll use and how many withholding allowances, or personal exemptions, they'll claim. You can get blank W-4 forms from the www.irs.gov website, too.

While you're visiting the IRS website, you also need to get a *Circular E Employer's Tax Guide* publication. The *Circular E* publication is the pamphlet that tells you how much you should withhold in federal income taxes, Social Security, and Medicare from employees' salaries based on what they say about their filing statuses and the number of withholding allowances they claim on the W-4 forms mentioned in the preceding paragraph.

Paying someone for a job well done

After you set up the two needed expense categories within Quicken and after you collect the necessary tax information, you're ready to pay someone.

Figuring out the gross wages figure

Determining how much to pay your employees should be pretty easy. Does Raoul make $15 per hour? Did he work 40 hours? Then you owe him $600 because $15 times 40 equals $600. Is Betty's salary $400 per week? Then you owe her $400 for the week.

Calculating that deductions stuff

Your next step — after you know how much you're supposed to pay Raoul and Betty — is to figure out what Uncle Sam says you must withhold.

To determine this amount, you need both Raoul's and Betty's W-4s to find out their filing statuses and personal exemptions. Then just flip to the page in the *Circular E* that describes withholding for persons claiming those filing statuses and weekly pay.

If Raoul is single and claims just one personal exemption, for example, you need to flip to the page that shows appropriate withholding amounts for single people receiving weekly payroll checks. That page shows a table that will clearly indicate what you're supposed to withhold from Raoul's check for federal income taxes. For example, the table might say that a single person making $600 a week who claims one withholding allowance should have $79 withheld for federal taxes.

And Betty? Remember that fictional Betty's pay is $400 per week. If Betty's filing status is married, she is filing jointly, and has three personal exemptions, you'd need to need to flip to the page in the *Circular E* that shows withholding amounts for a married person filing a joint return when the person claims three withholding allowances. Pretend just for the sake of illustration that the *Circular E* says you're supposed to withhold $18 each week from Betty's check.

You determine Social Security and Medicare amounts by multiplying the gross wage figure by a set percentage. Social Security is probably 6.2 percent of the gross wages up to roughly $110,000. The Medicare tax is 1.45 percent of the gross wages with no wage limit. Be sure to check your faithful *Circular E* if you think limits come into play for a particular employee. Note, too, that as I'm writing this, Congress is tinkering with the tax laws again. But, of course, Congress is *always* tinkering with the tax laws. (In 2011, the employee part of Social Security equaled 4.2%, not 6.2%. It's possible that Congress will extend this payroll tax reduction into 2012 to help struggling taxpayers.)

Figuring out someone's net wages

Table 15-1 summarizes the payroll calculations based on the examples developed in the preceding paragraphs.

Table 15-1	Payroll for Raoul and Betty		
Item	*Raoul*	*Betty*	*Explanation*
Gross Wages	$600	$400	Their pay
Withholding	$79	$18	From *Circular E*
Social Security	$37.20	$24.80	6.2% of gross wages
Medicare	$8.70	$5.80	1.45% of gross wages
Net Wages	$475.10	$351.40	What's left over

Does Table 15-1 make sense? If it doesn't, quickly skim through the preceding four or five paragraphs. All I've really done in the table is reorganize some information, calculate the Social Security and Medicare taxes, and show how Raoul's and Betty's gross pay gets nickeled and dimed by the various taxes they owe.

Working with other taxes and deductions

If you have other taxes and deductions to make and you know how the federal income taxes, Social Security taxes, and Medicare taxes work, you won't have any problem working with other taxes — whatever they are.

State income tax withholding, for example, works like the federal income tax withholding. (Of course, you need to get the state's equivalent to the *Circular E* guide.)

In general, you treat other taxes and the amounts the employee pays similarly.

In fact, the only thing that you need to be careful about is what affects your employees' gross pay for income taxes but not their Social Security taxes — things such as 401(k) deductions and certain fringe benefits. If you have these kinds of things to deal with and you need help, just ask your accountant. (Providing general answers that will work for everyone who reads this paragraph is just too difficult — and actually kind of dangerous, too. Sorry.)

Recording a payroll check

After you make the tax deduction and net wages calculation, you're ready to record the check. Suppose that you're going to record the check by using the Write Checks window. After you display the window, follow these steps:

1. **Enter the date of the payroll check in the Date field.**

2. **Enter the payroll check number in the Num field.**

3. **Enter the employee name in the Payee field.**

4. **Enter the net wages amount in the Payment field.**

5. **Categorize the payroll tax as wages (see Figure 15-7).**

    Specify the expense category as **Wages**.

6. **To record the payroll check, click Record Check.**

You did it! You recorded a payroll check. Maybe it wasn't all that much fun, but at least it wasn't very difficult. (Chapter 5 describes how to print checks, just in case you're interested.)

Figure 15-7: The Write Checks window recording Betty's $351.40 paycheck.

Depositing taxes

Make no mistake. Uncle Sam wants the money you withhold from an employee's payroll check for federal income taxes, Social Security, and Medicare. Uncle Sam also wants the payroll taxes you owe — such as matching Social Security and Medicare taxes and federal unemployment taxes.

Every so often, then, you need to pay Uncle Sam the amounts you owe.

Making the payments for these taxes is easy.

Depositing the employee withholding

To remit the payroll taxes you withhold from an employee's check, follow these steps:

1. **Sign up for the U.S. Treasury's electronic funds tax payment system, also known as EFTPS.**

   You should visit the www.eftps.gov website a few weeks (at least a couple of weeks and preferably more) before you want to process payroll. Find the link that lets you sign up for the service. And then carefully follow the on-screen instructions to create your EFTPS account. Note that you only need to take this step once.

2. **Log into the eftps.gov website.**

   This is easy. Click the link that indicates you want to log on to the website. Then provide three bits of information: your employer identification number, the PIN (personal identification number) and your password. Both the PIN and your password come in the letter that welcomes you to the EFTPS system.

3. **Indicate you want to make a payment equal to the payroll taxes that you withheld from the employee's check.**

   In the example case of Betty, where the withholding includes $18 of income taxes, $24.80 of Social Security taxes, and $5.80 of Medicare taxes, you would initiate an EFTPS payment for $48.60. Again — and sorry to be so anal about this — but within Quicken you need to categorize the check in the Wages expense category.

   Do not categorize the check that remits the employee's portion of his or her taxes as falling into the payroll tax category. That would be a mistake. And, yes, I know: It seems like payroll tax expense would be the right category. The withheld taxes are tax expenses of the employee, however — not tax expenses of the employer. The money represents a wage expense to the employer.

   Betty's true earnings were $400: the $351.40 net payroll check plus the $48.60 of payroll-related and income taxes that she owed but that you, the employer, withheld.

Paying employer payroll taxes

You have to match any Social Security and Medicare taxes paid by the employee. To record the payment of these payroll taxes, you follow a similar set of steps as in the preceding section. Indicate you want to make another EFTPS payment equal to the payroll taxes you owe as the employer. (In the example case of Betty, where the withholding included $24.80 of Social Security taxes and $5.80 of Medicare taxes, you would make a payment for $30.60 payable to the local bank.).

When you pay the employer's payroll taxes — such as the matching Social Security and Medicare taxes — you want to categorize the check as a payroll tax category. This money absolutely does represent a payroll tax expense to the employer.

Tax deposit tips

Let me make a handful of suggestions about making tax deposits easier and less painful. On the subject of tax deposits, let me also tell you that my fast-but-fancy payroll method has a weakness you should know about.

Tax deposit tip #1: Combine payments

Here's my first tip. In the preceding discussion, I suggest you use one payment to pay the employee's taxes and another payment to pay the employer's taxes.

Specifically, I describe how to initiate a $48.60 EFTPS payment categorized as a wage expense and then how to initiate a second EFTPS payment for $30.60 which gets categorized as a payroll tax expense. But you could, in fact, save yourself a bit of fiddle-faddling by initiating one check for $79.20 that combines both payments. If you do this, just be sure to split the transaction with $48.60 categorized as a wage expense and $30.60 categorized as a payroll tax expense when you go to record the tax deposit within Quicken.

Tax deposit tip #2: Combine employees

In the running example in this chapter, I describe how to deal with payroll taxes for a single employee.

I feel sort of dumb saying this, but you would (of course) often have more than one employee. And in that case, you would probably combine the payroll tax deposits for all the employees.

If you do have multiple employees, you probably want to consider using either a small business accounting system, such as QuickBooks, or an outside payroll service bureau. Most of the payroll calculations and bookkeeping will be pretty easy, but figuring out what you owe in terms of payroll tax deposits can be a bit messy if you have more than one employee to pay at a time.

Tax deposit tip #3: Don't delay your deposit

The system I describe in the preceding paragraphs doesn't keep track of what you owe in *payroll tax liabilities* (the withheld taxes, the company's matching of Social Security tax, and so on). And that's bad, obviously. You shouldn't just foolishly ignore any of your business or personal debts, of course. If you just quickly deposit your payroll taxes (immediately after every payroll), you should be fine.

Tax deposit tip #4: Know the De Minimis rule

While I'm talking about federal payroll tax deposits, I should cover another general — but very useful — rule related to when you need to make the deposit: If your accumulated federal payroll taxes are less than $2,500 for the quarter, you can pay the taxes with your quarterly 941 payroll tax return. (This is called the *De Minimis* rule — named after the Congresswoman Dee Minimis, I think.) Don't rely on this rule, however, without first checking with the IRS or your tax advisor.

Filing quarterly payroll tax returns

At the end of every quarter, you need to file a quarterly payroll tax return. (Specifically, you must file a Form 941 — which is a form you fill out to say how much you paid in gross wages, how much you withheld in federal taxes, and how much you owe for employer payroll taxes.)

If you don't own a business but have household employees — such as a nanny — you file a Form 942. You fill out this form to say how much you paid in gross wages, withheld in federal taxes, and owe in payroll taxes.

To get the gross wages totals and the balances in each of the payroll tax liability accounts, print a Cash Flow report for the quarter you need to report. You can do this by choosing Reports⇨Banking⇨Cash Flow. Quicken displays the Cash Flow report, but the dates will probably be wrong, so click the Customize button. Quicken displays the Customize Cash Flow dialog box.

Specify the range of dates as the start and end of the quarter for which you're preparing a quarterly report. Then click OK. Quicken produces a Cash Flow report, which you can easily use to fill out the quarterly payroll tax return.

You'll also need to report on the 941 tax form how much money you withheld from the employee's checks for federal withholding. You can do this manually (by looking through their payroll records) or algebraically (by comparing whatever the 941 or 942 shows as the total Social Security and Medicare taxes amount with the total payments made to the IRS).

However, you know what? If your accountant fills out the 941 or 942 for you, you don't even need to read the stuff in the preceding three sections. Your accountant won't have any problem completing the quarterly payroll tax return by using the Quicken report, and, in fact — I kid you not — will probably even enjoy it.

Even if you want to do payroll returns yourself in the future, have your tax accountant prepare the first return. You can then use that as a template for correctly preparing any future returns.

Computing annual returns and wage statements

At year end, you need to file some annual returns — like the 940 federal unemployment tax return and the W-2 and W-3 wage statements. (You'll need to prepare these by hand. Perhaps to protest all the work that small businesses have to do in order to comply with tax laws, you could prepare these forms by hand, using a cheap ballpoint pen. Just an idea.)

As a practical matter, as long as you're doing payroll for a single employee, the only thing that's different about filling out these reports is that you need to use a Cash Flow report that covers the entire year — not just a single quarter. So you need to enter the range of dates in the Cash Flow report dialog box as January 1 and December 31.

The 940 annual return is darn easy if you've been wrestling with the 941 or 942 quarterly returns. The 940 annual return works the same basic way as those more difficult quarterly tax returns. You print the old payroll report, enter a few numbers, and then write a check for the amount you owe.

You need to prepare annual state unemployment summaries before preparing the 940. The 940 requires information from the state returns.

For the W-2 statements and the summary W-3 (which summarizes your W-2s), you just print the old Cash Flow report. Then, carefully following directions, enter the gross wages, the Social Security and Medicare taxes withheld, and the federal income taxes withheld into the appropriate blanks.

If you have a little trouble, call the IRS. If you have a lot of trouble, splurge and hire someone to do it. Again, any experienced bookkeeper can do the job for you.

Doing the state payroll taxes thing

Yeah. I haven't talked about state payroll taxes — at least not in any great detail. I wish I could provide this sort of detailed, state-specific help to you. Unfortunately, doing so would make this chapter about 150 pages long. It would also cause me to go stark-raving mad.

However, you still need to deal with the state payroll taxes. State payroll taxes follow the same basic mechanics you apply to federal payroll taxes. For example, state income tax works the same way federal income tax works, employer-paid state unemployment taxes work the same way employer-paid federal unemployment taxes work, and employee-paid state taxes work the same way employee-paid Social Security and Medicare taxes work.

If you're tuned in to how federal payroll taxes work in Quicken, you really shouldn't have a problem with the mechanics of the state payroll taxes.

Chapter 16

Managing Rentals

. . . .

In This Chapter

▶ Describing a rental property

▶ Describing tenants

▶ Recording tenant rent payments

▶ Recording rental expenses

▶ Tracking rental property profits

. . . .

*T*he Quicken Rental Property Manager version of Quicken — the focus of this short chapter — provides everything available in the other versions of Quicken. The Rental Property Manager version also includes tools for tracking both your rental properties and your rental income and expense.

If you own rental properties — and I say this as a CPA who breaks down and cries several times each year when I see the messy financial records that most real estate investors keep — you definitely want to make the investment and buy Quicken Rental Property Manager. You'll have a much better handle on your rental property investments, the rental income the properties earn, and the rental deductions the properties produce.

Describing a Rental Property

In order to track rental properties with Quicken, you need to describe each property. To describe a property, follow these steps:

1. **Display the Rental Property tab.**

    If you purchased the Rental Manager version of Quicken, you should also have a Rental Property tab available in the Quicken window. If you want to manage rental properties but didn't buy the Rental Manager version of Quicken, you may be able to buy and immediately turn on the Rental Manager functionality by choosing Help⇨Add Rental Property Tools.

2. **Click the Properties button and choose Add Property.**

   Quicken displays the Add Rental Property dialog box.

   The Properties button also displays another command, Show Property List, which displays a window that lists the previously added rental properties. You can edit a rental property that appears in this property list by selecting the property and then clicking the Edit button. You can remove a rental property that appears in this property list by selecting the property and then clicking the Delete button.

3. **Describe the property.**

   Describe the rental property you're going to track in Quicken. You'll want to name the property using the Property Name text box. You can then create a tag for the property's income and expense transactions using the Tag text box. Optionally, you can enter the street, city, state, and ZIP code information in the appropriately labeled text boxes.

   Note: You use the tag to mark, or *tag,* each income or expense transaction for a specific property. By tagging the transactions in this way, Quicken easily produces a profit and loss statement by rental property. You want a profit and loss statement by property to manage your real estate investments, of course. But you also need a profit and loss statement by property for your year-end income tax returns.

4. **Indicate whether the property is a single or multiple unit.**

   Use the Property Type Information option buttons — Single Unit Property and Multiunit Property — to specify whether the property is a single unit property (like a single family rental house) or a multiunit property (like a four-plex or a strip mall).

5. **(Optional) Identify the multiple units.**

   If you indicate in Step 4 that a rental property is multiunit, Quicken adds the Unit Information text boxes to the Add Rental Property dialog box. Use these boxes to name each of the rental units using, for example, apartment letters, suite numbers, or some similar identifying label.

6. **(Optional) Track the net worth of the property.**

   If you want to track the fair market value or your estimate of the fair market value of the rental property, mark the Yes I Want To Track The Value Of This Rental Property button. Then, without laughing, enter the fair market value of the property in the Approximate Value text box.

   Note: If you decide to track the net worth of the property, Quicken adds an asset account to the Quicken account list.

7. **Click OK.**

   Quicken displays the Rental Property tab, or window, with the rental property you just created.

Describing Tenants

After you describe your rental property or properties, you need to describe the tenants that occupy the property or properties. To describe the tenants, follow these steps:

1. **Display the Rental Property tab.**

2. **Click the Properties & Tenants button and choose Add Tenant.**

   Quicken displays the Add Rental Property Tenant dialog box.

   The Tenants button also displays another command, Show Tenants List. Choose the Show Tenants List command to display a window that lists the previously added tenants. You can edit and delete tenants that appear in the list by clicking the tenant and clicking either the Edit or Delete button.

3. **Describe the tenant.**

   Describe the tenant by clicking the Rent Details tab and then entering the renter's name in the Tenant Name text box and the monthly rent in the Rent Amount text box.

   Select the bank account name into which you'll deposit rent in the Account Name drop-down list box and the property (or property and unit) the tenant occupies in the Property drop-down list box.

   You can specify the rent due date — and I'm sure this is a big surprise — using the Rent Due On drop-down list box.

   Optionally, you can use the Contact tab of the Add Rental Property Tenant window to collect and store contact information for the tenant, including work phone number, home phone number, e-mail, and so on.

4. **(Optional) Document the lease agreement.**

   You can use the Terms And Agreement tab to document the rental agreement, recording items such as the lease term, lease start date, late fee, and so forth.

   You can use the Security Deposit tab to record the security deposit you collect at the start of the lease and any security deposit you return at the end of the lease.

5. **Click OK.**

   Quicken displays the Rental Property tab, or window. The tenant or tenants you've added appear indented below the rental property they occupy.

292 Part IV: Very Serious Business

Recording Tenant Rent Payments

After you describe your properties and your tenants, you can begin recording tenant rent payments as tenants pay you, the lord of manor. Simply follow these steps:

1. **Display the Rental Property tab.**

   No problem here, right? You just click on the tab.

2. **Select the tenant.**

   Select the tenant for whom you want to record rent. Quicken highlights the tenant information and adds two, tiny, rather cute buttons labeled Enter and Skip to the tenant information.

3. **Click the tenant's Enter button.**

   Quicken displays the Enter Rent dialog box. Quicken knows most of what it needs to know in order to record the rent payment: the property, the tenant name, the rent amount, and so on. But confirm that this information is correct. You might want to edit the contents of the Memo text box, for example. Or you may need to assess a late fee if the tenant has paid late.

4. **Click Add to record the transaction.**

   Quicken adds the rent payment to your records, recording the rent check as a deposit into the specified bank account. Behind the scenes, Quicken tags the transaction as income related to a specific property — just as you want it to do.

Recording Rental Expenses

I'm not going to provide you with a blow-by-blow recipe for recording rental expenses. The reason? You actually already know how to record rental property expenses if you've used Quicken for recording checks and other payments from a bank account.

All you need to do to record a rental property expense is tag the transaction with the property's tag. That's it. Seriously. Take a peek at Figure 16-1. See the last highlighted transaction — written to Joe's Plumbing for $75? That Repairs expense shows as a rental property expense for the specific rental property "Wetmore" because the Tag text box shows the rental property tag, Wetmore.

If you have questions about how to record checks into a Quicken bank account, refer to Chapter 4.

Figure 16-1:
Use tags
to record
rental
property
expenses.

Tracking Rental Property Profits

I don't want to talk too long about the Rental Property Manager features. If I do that, you'll think the tools are complicated to learn and use. The tools aren't complicated. They're really, really easy.

Before I quit, however, I do want to share one quick reminder: In Chapter 7, I talk about how to produce reports in Quicken, including how to produce reports specifically designed to track your rental properties. Peek back there.

Another thing to point out — and this is sort of redundant, but it's so darn important — is that the Rental Property Manager features let you track rental income and rental expenses *by properties* using those tags you create for each property. This tagging means you can produce reports that show profit by property. This "profit by property" measurement is really important. You use the segmented profit data to manage your properties — and to report what's happening with your rental properties on your tax return.

Working with tags

The Quicken tags aren't just for rental properties. In fact, tags (which used to be called *classes* in a previous version of Quicken) provide you with a second method for organizing the data. Categories, of course, are the first data organization method, but tags are the second. And they deserve your respect and admiration.

Because tags can get used for other purposes, Quicken's Tools menu provides a Tag List command.

Choose this command, and Quicken displays the Tag List window. This window lists all the tags you've set up — and all the tags that the Quicken Rental Property Manager has set up for you. You can add still more tags by choosing the Add button. You can edit and delete existing tags by selecting a tag and then choosing the Edit or Delete button.

Part V
The Part of Tens

The 5th Wave   By Rich Tennant

"Oh, that's Jack's area for his paper crafts.
He's made some wonderful U.S. Treasury
Bonds, certificates of deposit, $20's, $50's,
$100's that sort of thing."

In this part . . .

As a writing tool, laundry lists aren't something that high school English teachers encourage. But you know what? The old laundry-list format is pretty handy for certain sorts of information.

With this idea in mind (and, of course, with deepest apologies to my high school English teacher, Mrs. O'Rourke), this part simply provides you with lists of information about Quicken. It includes answers to (slightly more than) ten commonly asked questions about Quicken, (almost) ten things you should definitely not do unless you want to turn your financial life into a mess, and (nearly) ten trouble-shooting tips you can try if you get into a messy situation.

Chapter 17

(Slightly More Than) Ten Questions I'm Frequently Asked about Quicken

*W*hen people find out that I've written a book about Quicken, they always ask a question or two. In this chapter, I list the most common questions and their answers.

What Are Quicken's Best Features?

Quicken has become more and more complicated over the years, so I think it may be fair to include a few sentences that review its most valuable and least valuable features. As far as what's best or most valuable, I would say that its checkbook feature is still clearly the most valuable. If you should use one feature in Quicken, it's the checkbook stuff. (To do so, set up a bank account for your checking account as described in Chapter 1, and then use Quicken to keep track of your balances, income, and expenditures as described in Chapter 4.)

I also have to say that I think that Intuit, the maker of Quicken, provides pretty neat stuff at its Quicken website, so I'd give that feature my vote as the second best. I don't talk about the Quicken.com website a whole lot in this book. That's because you can have more fun and more success with Quicken. com by exploring the site on your own.

Just because I'm super-compulsive not only about my personal finances but also about yours, let me say that I think that the Quicken financial calculators (I describe them in Chapter 10) are also really valuable. If you're willing and able to do just a bit of planning right now, you'll be truly amazed by the positive impact that planning has on your financial affairs a few years down the road.

So this leads rather nicely to another question: What are Quicken's least valuable features? I think the answer really depends on the person. I used to pooh-pooh the online banking because my bank caused me headaches, and my at-home, dialup Internet connection was unreliable. (With a fast cable modem connection now, however, I really do like online banking.) The credit card stuff and cash account stuff don't do much for me. But you know what? Those tools may do wonderful things for you. It depends on the way you've organized your finances.

I guess the bottom line, to me, is that the least useful features depend on what you don't need to do. But what you don't need to do will probably differ from what I don't need to do. I'm sorry that I don't have more helpful criticism.

Does Quicken Work for a Corporation?

Sure. But let me talk for a minute about what's unique — at least from an accountant's perspective — about a corporation.

In addition to recording assets (such as bank accounts and receivables) and liabilities (such as mortgages and trade payables), a corporation often needs to *track*, or keep records for, stockholder equity.

Stockholder equity includes the amount people originally paid for their stock, any earnings the corporation has retained, cumulative income for the current year, and sometimes other stuff, too.

"Ugh," you're probably saying to yourself. "Ugh" is right. Accounting for stockholder equity of a corporation is mighty complicated at times. It's so complicated, in fact, that Quicken can't track a corporation's stockholder equity.

I'm not saying that you can't use Quicken if you're a corporation, and I'm not saying that you shouldn't. (I do business as a corporation, and I used to use Quicken just for laughs.) Just remember that someone — probably your poor accountant — periodically needs to calculate your stockholders' equity.

Fortunately, the financial information you collect with Quicken provides, in rough form, much of the information that your poor accountant needs in order to do things manually.

But, er, this all makes me remember something else. If your corporation enjoys revenue of $250,000 per year or more or owns assets that total $250,000 or more, you must include a balance sheet with your corporate tax return. (This isn't something I just made up. It's actually the law.) Quicken isn't very good about creating business balance sheets — or at least the sort of balance sheet that needs to get included with your tax return. Accordingly, if your corporation grows so that its revenues or assets equal or exceed $250,000, consider retiring Quicken and upgrading to QuickBooks.

What Happens to Stockholders' Equity in Quicken?

Quicken doesn't exactly ignore a corporation's stockholder equity. In an Account Balances report, the difference between the total assets and the total liabilities actually represents the total stockholder equity. (Quicken labels this total Net Worth.) So, to the extent that your total assets and total liabilities figures are correct, you know your total stockholder equity.

Does Quicken Work for a Partnership?

Yep, it does. But a partnership that uses Quicken faces the same basic problem as a corporation that uses Quicken. In a partnership, the partners want to track their partnership capital accounts (or at least they should). A partnership capital account simply shows what a partner has put into and taken out of a business.

As noted in the preceding section, Quicken calculates a net worth figure for you by subtracting total liabilities from total assets. So, to the extent that your total assets and total liabilities are accurately accounted for in Quicken, you know roughly the total partnership capital.

To solve this problem, you (or someone else) need to track what each partner puts into the business, earns as a partner in the business, and then takes out of the business. You can also (and I've helped clients do this) just use the Quicken loan accounts for partnership equity accounts. You just need to not get freaked out when your net worth shows as zero, and you need to remember that the partnership equity accounts aren't really loans — they're capital.

One other thing to think about here concerns your partnership tax return. If your partnership books revenue of $250,000 per year or more or owns assets that total $650,000 or more, you will need to include a balance sheet with your partnership tax return. As mentioned in my earlier discussion about using Quicken for a corporation's accounting, Quicken isn't very good about creating the sort of balance sheet that needs to get included with a tax return. Accordingly, if your partnership grows so that its revenues equal or exceed $250,000 or so that its assets equal or exceed $650,000, consider upgrading to QuickBooks.

Can I Use Quicken for More Than One Business?

Yeah, but be very careful. *Very* careful. You must be especially diligent in keeping the two businesses' financial records separate.

Quicken provides a handy tool for keeping them straight: You can work with more than one file. Each file, in effect, is like a separate set of financial records. You can't record automatic transfers between accounts in different files; instead, you must record each side of the transaction separately. You can, however, keep truly separate business records.

To create a separate file, choose File⇨New.

If you've been using Quicken for a while, you can probably figure out for yourself how the File⇨New command works.

Keeping separate bank accounts is a must. If you keep separate records for two distinct businesses in Quicken, you need to set up separate bank accounts for them. In fact, my attorney tells me that in the case of a corporation, you must set up a separate corporate bank account for the corporation to be truly considered as an independent legal entity. Talk to your attorney if you have questions; attorneys can tell you the specifics that apply to a particular state and situation.

What Kinds of Businesses Shouldn't Use Quicken?

You're probably saying to yourself, "Quicken works for corporations (sort of), and it works for partnerships (sort of). Does that mean that it works for just about any kind of business?"

The answer is no. Quicken is a darn good product. In fact, for many small businesses, it's a great product. But it doesn't work in every situation.

The following is a three-part test that you can use to determine whether your business should use Quicken. If you answer yes to two or three of the questions, you should seriously consider moving up to a full-featured, small-business accounting system (like QuickBooks).

✔ **Do you regularly need to produce business forms other than checks?**

- If you answer no to this question, you're in good shape with Quicken, which produces checks easily. And if all you need is an occasional invoice, you can create it easily enough on your computer. To produce a handful of invoices per month, for example, you can use your word processor. If you want to, you can also use one of the super-sized versions of Quicken: Quicken Home & Business or Quicken Rental Property Manager. Both of these versions of Quicken not only do invoices but also monthly customer statements. (I talk about these features in Chapter 15.)

- If you do produce a lot of forms besides checks and invoices — for example, purchase orders — you should probably consider moving to a small business accounting system that produces the forms you want. If you've been using Quicken, for example, take a look at QuickBooks, another Intuit product. Another more powerful but wonderfully designed product you might try is Peachtree Accounting for Windows from Sage Software. You can probably buy any of these programs at the local office supplies store. You can certainly buy the QuickBooks and Peachtree Accounting programs by visiting www.quickbooks.com or www.peachtree.com. For reference, I can recommend these two books, both published by John Wiley & Sons, Inc.: *QuickBooks 2012 For Dummies,* by yours truly (earlier versions of QuickBooks have their own editions), and *Peachtree For Dummies,* 3rd Edition, by Elaine Marmel and Diane Koers.

✔ **Do you need to track assets other than cash, accounts receivable, or investments?**

For example, do you buy and resell inventory? Do you have a bunch of fixed assets (furniture, equipment, and stuff like that) that you need to track? An accounting system is usually helpful in tracking these items. Quicken doesn't do a very good job of tracking these other assets, so you may want to look at one of the other small business accounting products — QuickBooks, for example.

✔ **Are you having problems measuring your profits with cash-basis accounting?**

I'm not going to get into a big, tangled discussion of cash-basis versus accrual-basis accounting. It wouldn't be any fun for you. It wouldn't be any fun for me, either. Nevertheless, you should know that if you can't accurately measure your business profits by using cash-basis accounting (which is what Quicken uses), you may be able to more accurately measure your business profits by using accrual-basis accounting. To do so, use an accounting system that supports accrual-basis accounting. I should be totally honest with you and tell you that to measure your profits the right way, you (or your accountant) need to use — horror of horrors — double-entry bookkeeping.

If you're a Quicken user but realize that you're outgrowing the checkbook-on-a-computer scene, check out QuickBooks. (No, I don't get a kickback from Intuit.) Here's the deal: QuickBooks looks and feels a lot like Quicken. Plus, it uses the data that you've already collected with Quicken, so you'll find that moving from Quicken to QuickBooks is only slightly more complicated than rolling off a log.

Can I Use Quicken for Real Estate Investing?

Yeah. Absolutely.

In a nutshell, all you need to do is set up an income category to track your rental income and then some expense categories to track your rental expenses. (In Chapter 2, in the section about changing a category list, I describe how to set up income and expense categories.)

To see which rental expense categories you need, either look at the Schedule E tax form that went with last year's tax return (if you've already been investing in real estate) or grab a Schedule E tax form from www.irs.gov (if you're new to real estate investing).

Now, before you stop reading and rush off to do the bookkeeping for your growing real estate empire, let me tell you one other critical thing: The Schedule E tax form on which you report your real estate income and deductions requires you to segregate your income and deductions by property.

For example, if you have two rental properties — a duplex on Winston Street and a single-family cottage on Roosevelt Avenue — you'll need to break down your income and expenses by property.

To break down income and expenses by property, you use a Quicken feature called *tags.* Oh, yes, it all sounds complicated. But all you need to do is enter the tag name in the Tag field. For example, rather than just enter **rent** in the Category field when recording a rent payment from your tenants living in the Winston Street duplex, you enter **rent** (as the Category) and then also enter **Winston** (as the Tag).

By appending the tag **Winston** to the transaction, you can later easily produce a cash flow that shows income and expenses for the Winston duplex.

Just to make sure that you understand this, let me give you another example. Rather than record a check to pay the utilities expenses for the house on Roosevelt as **utilities,** enter **utilities** as the category and **Roosevelt** as the tag.

By appending the tag **Roosevelt** to the transaction, you can easily produce a cash flow later that shows income and expenses for the Roosevelt cottage.

A couple of other notes about this: The first time you enter a tag name into the Tag field, Quicken asks whether you want to set up a new tag. When you click "Heck yeah," Quicken prompts you for a bit of information about the tag. After that, though, you just enter the tag without fanfare or embarrassment.

To produce a report that summarizes income and deduction information by tag, choose Reports⇨Banking⇨Cash Flow By Tag.

I talk a bit about the rental property management features in Quicken in Chapter 16.

Can I Use Quicken Retroactively?

Yeah. And the idea is better than it may seem at first.

Entering one year's worth of transactions doesn't take long in Quicken (as long as you have decent records to work with). If you're a millionaire, the task may take you a couple of days. (Of course, in this case, you can hire someone to do it for you.) If you're a regular, ordinary person, I bet you can get it done on a rainy Saturday afternoon.

After you enter all the information into a Quicken register, you can easily monitor your spending in various categories, track your income and outgo, and reconcile your bank accounts. I know one professional who uses Quicken records to do these things every year. Hey, it's not the most efficient way to do things. And it's not a very good way to manage business or personal financial affairs. But it works. Sort of.

Can I Do Payroll with Quicken?

Yes. See Chapter 15 for more details.

By the way, if you have only one or two salaried employees who always earn the same amount — a nanny, for example — you can rather easily use Quicken for payroll. But if you have a bunch of employees or even a single hourly employee, you'll probably want to either purchase a full-featured, real-live, small business accounting program (such as QuickBooks) or use a payroll service (such as Paychex or ADP) to take care of the whole thing for you.

Intuit makes and sells QuickBooks, as you may guess by its name. You can get QuickBooks from the local software store, from one of the mail-order places, or by downloading it from the Intuit website.

You can look up either payroll service — Paychex or ADP — in the telephone book. You can also look up either payroll service — Paychex or ADP — at www.paychex.com or www.adp.com, respectively.

Can I Prepare Invoices?

Not with Quicken Premier or Quicken Deluxe, but you can (very nicely, thank you) with Quicken Home & Business and with Quicken Rental Property Manager. If you want invoices, at least step up to Quicken Home & Business. This requirement may also be a symptom indicating that you should consider moving up to a full-featured, small business accounting system, such as QuickBooks.

Can I Import Data from an Old Accounting System?

Someone had to ask this question, I guess. (Imagine me taking a deep breath here.) Yes, you can import data from your old accounting system. To do so, export the old system's data into a file that matches the Quicken Interchange

Format, or QIF, specification. (A QIF file just neatly organizes financial information in a well-documented structure so that other programs — and even people — can read and understand the data.) Then import this file into an empty Quicken file. Keep in mind, however, that this process isn't for the timid or fainthearted. I would also say that it isn't for people who have better things to do with their time.

My advice to you? Go to a movie. Mow your lawn. Read a trashy novel. Forget all about this importing business. Or, if you're really determined, look for a QIF conversion tool on the Internet. They do, er, exist.

What Do You Think about Quicken?

I think it's great. But I bet your question isn't really whether Quicken is good or not. Heck, the package has something like 10 million happy users, so we both know that the package is pretty good, right? My guess is that what you really want is my opinion about using Quicken in particular business or personal situations.

It's tough to answer this question in a one-way conversation. Even so, let me give you some of the best reasons for using Quicken:

- ✔ You always know your bank account balances, so you won't ever have to wonder whether you have enough money to pay a bill or charge a purchase.
- ✔ Reconciling your account takes about two minutes. (I'm not joking.)
- ✔ You get a firm handle on what you're really making and spending.
- ✔ You can budget your spending and then track your spending against your budget.
- ✔ If you're a business, you can measure your profits as often as you want by using cash-basis accounting.
- ✔ If you're an investor, you can monitor your investments and measure their actual returns.

I hope these answers help. My guess is that if you think that a program such as Quicken will help you better manage your financial affairs, it probably will.

Chapter 18

(Almost) Ten Tips on How Not to Become a Millionaire

In This Chapter

▶ Ignore the fact that one can build surprising wealth by investing in ownership investments and earning just average returns

▶ Ignore that one can get much, and maybe most, of the money from tax savings and employer matching

▶ Don't tap your computer's and the Quicken program's power to develop powerful, wealth-building insights

▶ Give up, because it's too late to start anyway

▶ Get entangled in at least one get-rich-quick scheme

▶ Fake it with false affluence

▶ Give in to the first big temptation of wealth building

▶ Give in to the second big temptation of wealth building

*Y*ou read the chapter title right. But let me explain a couple of things. First, about ten years ago, I wrote a book about how to save a million dollars for one's retirement. That sounds a little money-grubbing, I'll agree, but my argument then (and now) is that most people need to accumulate a nice-sized nest egg for retirement because most of us can't or shouldn't really count on things like pensions and Social Security for all our retirement needs.

If Congress does nothing — absolutely nothing — to save Social Security in the United States, the best studies show that, about 25–30 years from now, the government will need to reduce benefits to around 76 percent of the amount it pays today. For example, someone who may receive $1,000 per month today may instead receive $760 in the future. Likewise, someone who receives $400 today may instead receive $300 in the future. Although that difference isn't quite the financial meltdown some people think, it does mean that you and I really must prepare to augment our retirement income by having our own savings.

So, anyway, as part of promoting this book, I spent several weeks on the road doing radio call-in shows, bookstore appearances, and television talk shows. I learned several things from that experience. First, I learned that after one appears on some television show, it is, apparently, customary to remove the strange makeup that's applied for the cameras. This step is especially important if you plan to appear later in public.

I also learned something else in my travels and talking with people. Although everyone is interested in becoming a millionaire or in preparing financially for retirement, it turns out that most people are really more interested in how *not* to become a millionaire. In other words, they wanted me to explain in financial terms why people *don't* accumulate wealth.

At first, I thought that this was a little strange. But then finally somebody explained, "We all know you need to save and invest to build wealth. What we *don't* know are those things that prevent or sabotage our attempts to do this." People in the audience didn't want to make the same mistakes.

And so that is what I want to cover here. I want to share with you my observations and research results about why people who know they should save at least some money for retirement don't end up building wealth. I've observed that eight really common problems or traps foul up most people.

Before I begin, note that one thing that happens when you start talking about compound interest and future values is that inflation makes comparing apples to apples difficult. In other words, I can say something like, " . . . and then you'll have $3,000,000." But you then have to wonder what that amount will be worth factoring in inflation. To deal with this annoying complexity, I adjust for inflation all the numbers I use in the following paragraphs. I subtract the inflation amount and give you only the adjusted-for-inflation numbers in current-day dollars. Note that the Quicken financial planners also let you adjust for inflation by checking the Adjust For Inflation check box, which appears in most of the calculator dialog boxes.

Ignore the Fact That You Can Build Wealth by Investing in Ownership Investments and Earning Average Returns

You can build surprising wealth just by investing in ownership investments that produce average returns. By *ownership investments,* I mean basically stocks and maybe real estate. Here are three examples:

✔ Just by earning the stock market's average inflated adjusted return of around 6 percent, a 25-year-old saving $150 per month can build as much as $300,000 by age 65.

✔ Just by earning the stock market's average inflated adjusted return of around 6 percent, a 35-year-old saving $300 per month can build as much as $300,000 by age 65.

✔ Just by earning the stock market's average inflated adjusted return of around 6 percent, a 50-year-old saving $850 per month can build as much as $300,000 by age 65.

I want to stop here. An important truth here is that, sadly, most people miss this information. Consider what this means: You don't have to get fancy. You don't have to spend a bunch of time worrying. You don't need to spend a bunch of money on advisors, newsletters, or commissions — or even on books about using Quicken.

Compound interest is a powerful engine, and it creates wealth. And that means that you can build surprising wealth by investing in ownership investments and earning just average returns.

Note, too, that you can lock in average returns by choosing a low-cost index fund, such as The Vanguard Group's Index 500 or Total Stock Market Portfolio mutual fund.

If you choose an actively managed mutual fund or a mutual fund that charges average fees for managing your money, you basically don't have a snowball's chance in you-know-where of actually earning an average return over time. Over the long investment horizon required to prepare for retirement, if you go this route, chances are you'll actually earn a return that's equal to the market's return *less the expense ratio that the mutual fund manager charges and the trading costs the manager incurs.* Expense ratios for actively managed funds run about 2 percent annually. So, rather than a 6 percent annual adjusted-for-inflation return, you'll actually earn a 4 percent annual adjusted-for-inflation return on actively managed mutual funds. That's brutal.

One final point: People see way more risk in this investing than really exists — particularly after the last few years. But over decades, which is how long you'll invest, the risk drops. If you had begun investing in the stock market in the mid-1920s and then continued systematically investing for 25 years through the crash of 1929, the global depression of the '30s, World War II, and the start of the Cold War, you would have earned about an 8 percent return on your money. Given that the inflation rate was just 2 to 3 percent over this same period of time, you still could have built wealth by investing in ownership investments producing average 5 to 6 percent returns. I honestly expect similar real returns over the remaining decades (I hope) of my life.

Ignore the Fact That You Can Get Much, and Maybe Most, of the Money from Tax Savings and Employer Matching

Okay. I'm moving on to another really important point. It's fine to say that you need to invest just $300 per month, and that produces the wealth you need. The big question is this: *Where do you get that money?*

You've got bills to pay and a rent or mortgage check to write. You want to enjoy at least a few of the material pleasures — like food and drink — that life offers up. Where in the world does someone come up with this kind of money?

Well, the answer is mostly from the tax man and your employer. No kidding. Because of the way that employer-matching provisions work in things like 401(k) and Simple-IRA plans and because of the way our progressive income tax system works, you can get a lot of money from your employer and from the government in the form of tax-deduction savings. You may even be able to get most of the money you need for your retirement savings from these sources.

Table 18-1 shows how someone who wants to save $300 a month might come up with the money. And, in fact, the first line of Table 18-1 shows how much you want to save: $300.

The second line of the table shows how much you might get from your employer in a 401(k) or Simple-IRA plan. Note that an IRA obviously doesn't include employer matching. (This line shows up, therefore, as zero in Table 18-1.) But 401(k) plans commonly provide a 50 percent match on at least the first portion of your contribution. (This shows up as $100 in the table.) And basically by law, Simple-IRAs provide a 100 percent match on the first portion of your contribution (which shows up as $150 in the table).

Table 18-1	Ways to Come Up with $300 Monthly		
	IRA	*401(k)*	*Simple-IRA*
What you want to save	$300	$300	$300
What you can get from employer	$0	$100	$150
What you can get from tax man	$90	$60	$45
What you come up with yourself	$210	$140	$105

The third line of the table shows how much you might get in the way of tax savings. For example, if you're contributing $300 per month to an IRA, you might actually enjoy $90 per month in federal and state income tax savings if the tax rate you pay on your last dollars of income equals 30 percent. (This rate would be the case for many readers.)

The fourth line of the table shows what you need to come up with yourself. The IRA is the worst case shown in the table. With an IRA and $300 per month of savings, you would need to come up with $210 yourself. The 401(k) plan looks better; with it, you need to come up with $140 yourself. The Simple-IRA is the best case in the table. With it, you need to come up with only $105.

I don't want to overload you with data. But please note that this is an incredibly powerful insight. Much, and maybe most, of the money you need to build wealth can come from other people — specifically the tax man and your employer, if you work someplace that offers a 401(k) or Simple-IRA plan.

Don't Tap Your Computer's Power to Develop Wealth-Building Insights

This is hard to describe in general terms because by definition, what the computer lets you do is get very specific. Consider this: Personal financial planning is essentially applied mathematics. What that means is that to make a decision, you often need to tally up the costs and benefits of Option A versus Option B, and then you need to make time/value of money calculations. (Practically speaking, this just means that you also need to figure in things like interest expense and investment income.) These sorts of tasks are the perfect applications for the personal computer.

When you use your computer to make better personal financial decisions, you develop powerful, wealth-building insights that often supply the rest of the money you need for your investing. More specifically, if you need to save $300 per month and you can get $150 of this from your employer and through tax savings, you still need to come up with that last $150 per month. But what I'm saying is that your computer can, and should, help you find this money.

Here's one example: Have you heard about early mortgage repayment? It sounds like a good idea, at least on the surface. If you add an extra $25 per month to the regular mortgage payment on a typical mortgage, you often save about $25,000 in interest. (Maybe more. How much you save depends on the interest rate, the mortgage balance, and the remaining number of payments.)

Based on that bit of financial data, early mortgage repayment sounds like a pretty good idea. Lots of people — encouraged by financial writers — have started doing this. But is it a good idea? It depends.

To determine whether this is truly a good idea, however, you need to weigh your options. If you can instead put an extra $25 a month into a 401(k), you end up with about $100,000.

So there you have it: Option A, which is early mortgage repayment, sounds pretty good because $25,000 of interest savings is a lot of money. But Option B, the 401(k) option, is clearly better because, for no extra pain or hassle, you end up with $100,000.

But other important financial decisions and personal financial planning issues often provide you with similar opportunities for free money or extra wealth because you use your computer:

- ✔ **ARMs:** Sometimes, adjustable-rate mortgages (ARMs) actually make you bear less risk and work better.

- ✔ **Buying a home:** Sometimes this isn't a good investment — even when it seems like it is.

- ✔ **Car leases:** They can be great deals or terrible deals. It all depends on the implicit interest rate that the lease charges.

In Chapter 10, I talk about how you use the Quicken financial planners to make better financial decisions. The Internet also provides a ton of tools, many helpful, for doing personal financial planning. I don't want to sound like your mother or some cranky uncle, but I urge you to use these sorts of computer-based financial tools to make wiser decisions. A little extra money here, a little there — and pretty soon, you've found that last bit of money you need to save for a comfortable retirement. No kidding.

Give Up, Because It's Too Late to Start Anyway

Another common trap that prevents people from saving money for retirement is they give up, thinking that it's too late to start. I have to tell you that, mathematically speaking, that's just dead wrong.

You may think that wealth-building schemes that rely on compound interest work only for young people. It's true that wealth building can be very easy for someone who's young. Often, young people need to make only a single, clever decision in order to build wealth. For example, if a 25-year-old, pack-per-day smoker quits smoking and puts the money he saves into savings, he can rather easily build $1,000,000 by retirement. All he needs to do is save his money in an IRA and select a small-company, stock mutual index fund. (Remember, I adjust for inflation; so really, this person will probably have between $3,000,000 and $4,000,000 of inflated dollars.)

You can't do that if you're 50 years old. I mean, you can't make one decision and expect that single good decision to grow to $1,000,000.

But there's another angle in all this: You aren't limited to making a single good decision. Oh, sure. That's easiest. But I really believe that if you make five or six or seven — maybe even ten — good decisions, you can still build substantial wealth by the time you stop working.

I don't think that surprises you if you're a mature investor. And I don't think it should discourage you. You possess more life experience and, I daresay, more wisdom, than someone who's 25. You can use your experience and wisdom to make a greater number of good decisions, and that can produce the wealth you need.

Get Entangled in at Least One "Get-Rich-Quick" Scheme

Get-rich-quick schemes don't work except for the person selling the scheme. And, in fact, they drain off energy and money you really should be using to build your investments. You know all this, of course. We all do. But I think that all of us have a tendency to assume that this one particular great investment or business we're presented with is different. Oh, sure, we know that other dummies get suckered, but "fill in the blank" is different.

I actually don't think trying the occasional flier is a bad idea. If you have some small percentage of your investment money chasing speculative returns, that's okay, but only as long as this iffy investing doesn't foul up your other, more important, boring-but-predictable wealth building for retirement. That's fair, right? If you or I want to try chasing down the hottest new mutual fund or try online day-trading or invest in some friend's start-up business, that seems okay. But you can't allow these get-rich-quick schemes to foul up your meat-and-potatoes investing.

Unfortunately, I see that most of the people who get involved in get-rich-quick schemes try to use this speculation as a replacement for true, disciplined investing. And I have never seen a get-rich-quick scheme that consistently works.

I offer one other comment: Many, and perhaps even most, of the best-selling books about money and investment techniques amount to just new get-rich-quick schemes. I'm not going to name names here. Neither my attorney nor the publisher will let me. But any book that promises you some way to magically and consistently double or triple the returns that other investors earn is a get-rich-quick scheme.

However, some wonderful books out there show you how to better manage your money. For example, Eric Tyson's book, *Personal Finance For Dummies,* 5th Edition, is a really good book about the basics. And I'm not just saying this to schmooze the publisher. (Both Eric's book and this book are published by John Wiley & Sons, Inc.) I also love basically everything that Andrew Tobias writes, plus John Bogle's books about mutual fund investing — *Bogle on Mutual Funds* (Irwin) and *Common Sense on Mutual Funds* (John Wiley & Sons, Inc.) — and Burton Malkiel's *The Random Walk Guide to Investing* (Norton). All these books provide good, fact-based advice that leads you in the right direction.

Fake It with False Affluence

I talk about this a bit in Chapter 3, but it's an important point and worth repeating. When people spend all their money trying to look rich, they don't have any money left over to save and invest. That means that most people have to decide — either explicitly or implicitly — whether they want to be rich or look rich. Weird, right?

Yet, most millionaires live average lives. They live in average houses located in middle-class neighborhoods. They drive average cars.

Ironically, most of the people who live in big houses or drive expensive cars aren't rich. They may have high incomes, but they aren't rich. And yet that makes sense. You can't become rich if you're spending all your money trying to look rich.

Faking affluence is a trap that goofs up more people than you'd guess.

Give In to the First Big Temptation of Wealth Building

I think that when you boil everything down to its very essence, the big problem is that most people lack the commitment. We all must be culturally programmed this way or something. But most of us — I'm the same way — stumble over a couple of big temptations. So I mention these temptations here and in the next section.

Temptation #1: I can tell you, and so can any good financial planner, how to come up with an extra $100 or even $500 per month. Also, if you really do use Quicken in a disciplined way to manage your financial affairs, you'll find yourself freeing up money. You'll save a little bit of money here, waste a little less over there; pretty soon, you'll find yourself with a bit of extra cash. But you must have the commitment to save and invest that money. You and I have to decide to dedicate the next $100 or $500 to investments. If we do, we don't have to worry about financial security in retirement. And if we don't, we should worry. But anyway, that's the first temptation. When you find some extra money, you need to have the discipline to save and invest those funds. And if you do start to do this, you'll rather quickly amass thousands of dollars.

Give In to the Second Big Temptation of Wealth Building

Ironically, resisting Temptation #1 leads rather quickly to . . .

Temptation #2: After you collect an extra $5,000 or $25,000 or $50,000 in your portfolio, you need to have the commitment necessary to let that money grow. That seems obvious, of course. But I've also noticed that a lot of people don't do this. A lot of people, after they amass a nice little pot of money, decide it's time to abandon a strategy that has worked wonderfully. They decide to buy a bigger house or a boat. Or they change investment strategies, maybe by investing in some friend's or family member's new business. Or they turn their money into a hobby — perhaps deciding that they're going to use their retirement money to try out this online investing thing or leveraged real estate investing.

It's your money, of course. You get to do with it whatever you want. But I am going to be honest with you and say that if you really want to build up a nice nest egg for retirement, you need to be committed enough to resist these two big temptations.

Chapter 19

(Almost) Ten Troubleshooting Tips

After writing about Quicken for almost 20 years, I've had a revelation of sorts. People not only want specific, step-by-step information about how to use the program, but they also want troubleshooting advice. They want techniques and tactics that they can use to solve the inevitable problems they encounter while using Quicken in real-life settings. What follows is my list of the best troubleshooting techniques that I can offer you.

Tactics #1 and #2: Use the Quicken Help File and This Book

I know what you may be thinking: You have some problem that you can't solve by using Help, and it's either a bug or some glaring error in the Quicken documentation. And, of course, you've looked through this book, and it says nothing — absolutely nothing — about your question. In fact, upon further reflection, you may be thinking that you've encountered some problem that you can't possibly solve by consulting the Quicken Help file or this book.

Maybe you're right.

But in my experience (when I talk with people who have problems), about half the time, the problem is that people don't know enough about Quicken to know what to do. People simply experience a mechanical problem, and they can't make the program work because they haven't used Quicken enough to figure out how it works. Therefore, the right way to solve this sort of problem is to find out more about Quicken and try again. For example, if you're having problems printing a report, just finding out more about printing and reports often solves your problem.

In most cases, though not all, you should be able to find the information in this book by using either its Index or Table of Contents.

Usually, you should be able to find the information (perhaps in a slightly less friendly form) in the Quicken Help file. To find information in the Quicken Help file, choose Help⇨Quicken Help to display the Help window, click on the Search Quicken Help tab, and then enter the word or phrase that you want to look up.

Tactic #3: Visit the Quicken Product Support Website

Another really good resource for troubleshooting is the Intuit product support website for Quicken. This website, available at `http://quicken.intuit.com/support/`, supplies a rich database of troubleshooting information.

To use the website, you select the version of Quicken you're using. After you click your version, you see a web page that lists common categories of problems or questions. You select a category, and you're on your way. The product support website then displays a list of troubleshooting articles that may help you solve your problem.

Tactics #4 and #5: Check the Microsoft or the Hardware Vendor Product Support Website

Keep in mind the possibility that your problem may not be a problem with Quicken at all, but rather a problem with your computer and its hardware or with Microsoft Windows. If your problem stems from the hardware or the operating system, you can consult the hardware or software maker's product support website for troubleshooting information. The Microsoft product support website, which is phenomenally rich in information, is available at `http://support.microsoft.com`. You can usually find the hardware maker product support website easily by using a good Internet search engine. For example, to locate Dell Computer's product support website, type something like **Dell Computer product support** into a search engine such as `www.google.com`.

You can find troubleshooting information about Intuit products at the Microsoft product support website. If the solutions that the site offers aren't very reassuring, at least you can find out whether others have experienced the same problem. Microsoft may suggest that you contact the vendor (which is Intuit) or that you upgrade to a newer version of the Quicken software. But knowing that the problem you've encountered is a real problem that Microsoft has logged into its product support knowledge base (that's what Microsoft calls it) and described in some technical detail is often useful.

Tactic #6: Contact Intuit Directly

In addition to the option of using the Intuit product support website, you can also contact Intuit directly. The URL for Intuit support is `http://quicken.intuit.com/support/`.

If you're willing to wait for your help, you should also know that free support is available by e-mail (consult the Intuit support website for current details). Finally, the Intuit site also offers a free chat service, 24 hours a day, 7 days a week.

Tactic #7: Try a Quicken Newsgroup

If your problem with Quicken isn't really a program bug or can't be easily solved by getting more information, you can sometimes find an answer by consulting other Quicken users. One of the easiest ways to do this is by browsing the Quicken newsgroup at `http://groups.google.com/group/alt.comp.software.financial.quicken/topics`.

You can also visit the Quicken community site at `https://qlc.intuit.com/app/full_page`.

You may not need this background information, but I'm going to point out a few important things about newsgroups. A specific organization doesn't typically support or police newsgroups. For example, Intuit doesn't maintain or support the Quicken newsgroup. Newsgroups, including the Quicken newsgroup, really amount to freeform — and, sometimes, unruly — discussions among users. You can't expect to have your question answered. And good newsgroup etiquette suggests that, if you're going to ask questions, you should also try to answer questions.

Tactic #8: Install and Use Antivirus Software

Okay, this shouldn't really be tactic #8. This tactic deserves a higher ranking than that. But that's beside the point. The point is this: If you can't solve a problem and you have Internet access and you've been downloading files or accepting e-mail messages with attachments from strangers, your computer may have a virus. And it may be that your Quicken problems (particularly Quicken problems that you can't solve in other ways) stem from the virus.

In this case, I'd buy, install, and use antivirus software such as Norton AntiVirus or McAfee VirusScan. Consider one of these software programs just another part of the price of Internet connectivity. To locate online stores where you can download antivirus software, use www.google.com to search for *Norton AntiVirus* or *McAfee VirusScan*.

Tactic #9: When All Else Fails . . .

If you use a CPA to prepare your federal and state income taxes, you can probably get a quick (and perhaps free) answer from him or her. CPAs, as you may guess, have spent years learning about and working with accounting systems. Commonly, the problems people have with Quicken aren't technical software problems but accounting or bookkeeping conundrums. So what you think is a Quicken bug may, er, really be an operator error.

Let me also mention that even if you don't have a CPA prepare your tax return, you may want to find one whom you can ask for help and then pay him or her. Even if you're using Quicken for a small business or for real estate investing — something a wee bit complicated — an hour or so of personalized training is often all you need to get all your questions answered.

Part VI
Appendixes

In this part . . .

*I*f you're new to Windows 7, this part contains a lot of useful information, such as how to get the system up and running, find things you need, and get your computer to respond when you want it to do something.

I also include a glossary of the business, financial, and computer terms you see throughout the book. Throw around some of these terms in casual conversation, and everybody will think you're an expert.

Appendix A

Quick-and-Dirty Windows 7

If you're new to Microsoft Windows 7, you need to know a few things about the Windows 7 user interface. Although this appendix doesn't reveal anything earthshaking, it does provide a quick-and-dirty overview of what you need to know to get around.

If you've used other Windows applications, you probably don't need to read this appendix because you already know the material it covers.

I won't bore you with technical details. The information here, though, will enable you not only to operate Quicken, but also to converse easily about the newest versions of Windows at cocktail parties, over lunch, or with the guy at the computer store.

If you want more information, you may want to read a book such as *Windows 7 For Dummies,* by Andy Rathbone (John Wiley & Sons, Inc.).

If you're working with Windows XP or Windows Vista, much of what this appendix talks about will also apply to your use of Quicken 2012.

What Is Windows 7?

Windows 7 — and when I use the term *Windows 7* here, again, I mean any version of Microsoft Windows 7 — is an operating environment that manages your *system resources* (things like memory, your monitor, your printer, and so on).

Applications (programs such as Quicken) run on top of Windows 7. In other words, you first start Windows 7 by turning on your personal computer (PC). Then, after Windows 7 is running, you can start applications, such as Quicken.

Windows 7 provides a standard graphical interface. In English, Windows 7 provides a common approach for using *visual elements* — icons, buttons, check boxes, and so on. (This appendix describes how the major pieces of this graphical interface work.)

Windows 7 enables you to run more than one application at a time. You may, for example, run Quicken, a tax preparation package, and even a Windows accessory program, such as the Calculator.

Starting Windows 7

Starting Windows 7 is easy. You just turn on your personal computer (PC). If you can find the on-off switch, you're set.

If you can't find the on-off switch or it doesn't seem to work, don't feel silly. Ask someone who has used that computer. Sometimes the on-off switch is on the front of the computer and is labeled On-Off (which makes good sense, of course). Sometimes, I'm afraid, manufacturers stick the on-off switch on the back of the computer or label the switch something really stupid, such as 0 and 1. Sometimes, too, people plug a computer and all its peripherals (printers, modems, and all that junk) into a power strip that needs to be turned on to turn on the computer. So just ask someone. (If you bought the computer, of course, you can just telephone the place you bought it from.)

Just so you don't feel like a complete imbecile, I have to tell you something. I once had to call someone to learn how to click the stupid mouse that I got with my laptop computer.

Figure A-1 shows a typical Windows 7 desktop. The *desktop* is what you see after Windows 7 starts. Other Windows desktops look similar.

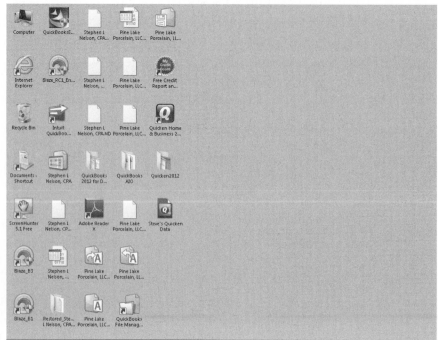

Figure A-1:
The
Windows 7
desktop.

Starting Programs

To start a program like Quicken, you click the Start button (the round Windows button in the lower-left corner of the screen) so that Windows 7 displays the Start menu. Then you choose the All Programs menu option so that Windows 7 lists all the programs that you, Windows 7, or someone else has installed. And then you click one of the listed programs to start that program.

Sometimes programs — such as Quicken — don't appear as options on the All Programs menu. They appear on submenus. If you click Start and don't see the Quicken 2012 item, then choose the All Programs menu and you should then see a Quicken item. (Pointing to some object like the Start button and then pressing the mouse's left button is called *clicking* the object.)

To practice this starting business, try starting the WordPad application that comes with Windows 7 by following these steps:

1. **Click the Start button.**

2. **Choose All Programs⇨Accessories⇨WordPad.**

    Windows 7 opens the WordPad program. Figure A-2 shows the WordPad program window. (A *program window* is just the window that a program like WordPad or Quicken displays.)

Figure A-2:
The WordPad window.

A tidbit about the taskbar

At the bottom of your screen, Windows 7 displays a *taskbar*. It provides the Start button, which I talk about earlier in this chapter, so that you can start another program. (With Windows 7, you can run several programs at the same time.) The taskbar also provides buttons that you can click to move among the programs you're running. If you look closely at it while you're running WordPad, for example, you see a taskbar button for the WordPad program. You also see a taskbar button for any other program you're running at the same time. You probably will be glad to know that *multitasking,* which is what running multiple programs is called, is this easy to do — just click the buttons on the taskbar to switch from one running program to another. By the way, in this book, I hide the taskbar so it doesn't obscure any of the Quicken program windows.

Choosing Commands from Menus

To set something in motion in Windows 7, you usually need to choose *commands* from menus.

I don't know why they're called commands. Perhaps because you often (but not always) use them to command Windows 7 and applications to do things. "Hello, Windows 7? I command thee to start this application," or "Quicken, I command thee to print this report."

Most application windows have a *menu bar* — a row of menus across the top of the window. Predictably, not every menu bar contains the same menus, but they're often darn similar. Some of the commands on the Quicken menus, for example, mirror commands on the WordPad menus.

This menu similarity isn't some nefarious conspiracy. The common command sets make things easier for users.

If you choose to read the next section, don't worry about what particular commands or menus do. Just focus on the mechanics of choosing commands.

Choosing commands with the furry little rodent

I think that the easiest way to choose a command is to use the mouse.

To select one of the menus by using a mouse, move the _mouse pointer_ — the small arrow that moves across your screen as you physically roll the mouse across your desk — so that it points to the name of the menu that you want to select. Then click the mouse's left button: Windows 7 or the application program displays the menu. Now click the command that you want to choose.

If you inadvertently display a menu, you can _deselect_ it (that is, make it go away) by clicking anywhere outside the menu box.

Choosing commands by using the Alt+key combinations

Another way to choose a command is to use an _Alt_ key (cleverly labeled Alt, these keys are usually at either end of the spacebar):

1. **Press the Alt key.**

   Doing so tells Windows 7 or the application that you want to choose a command.

2. **Press the letter representing the menu that you want to choose.**

   Doing so tells Windows 7 or the application program which menu contains the command you want.

3. **Press the underlined letter of the command you want to choose.**

   Each command on a menu is usually underlined, too, so that you can tell the program which command you want to choose by pressing the underlined letter of that command. For example, if you've chosen the File menu, you can choose the last option, Exit, by pressing the letter _X_. (You can try choosing Exit if you want, but then restart WordPad so that you can continue to follow along, okay?)

   For example, press Alt to activate the menus bar and the letter F to select the File menu (see Figure A-3). Then the letter P to select the Print command.

 Some Windows 7 programs, Quicken and WordPad included, don't show you the underlined letter that chooses menus and menu commands until you press the Alt key. And then when you do press the Alt key, the programs display pictures of the keyboard keys. Weird, huh?

Figure A-3:
The
WordPad
File menu.

Windows 7 and Windows 7 applications often offer yet another way to choose menu commands. After you press the Alt key, use the left- and right-arrow keys to highlight the menu that you want. Then press Enter. Windows 7 or the Windows 7 application displays the menu. Use the up- and down-arrow keys to highlight the command that you want to choose. Then press Enter.

If you want to deselect a menu but still leave the menu bar activated, press the Esc key once. To deselect the displayed menu and, at the same time, deactivate the menu bar, press the Esc key twice.

Using shortcut-key combinations

For many menu commands, Windows 7 and Windows 7 applications offer shortcut-key combinations. When you press a shortcut-key combination, Windows 7 or the Windows 7 application program simultaneously activates the menu bar, chooses a menu, and chooses a command.

Windows 7 (and application programs, such as WordPad and Quicken) displays the shortcut-key combination that you can use for a command on the menu beside the command.

If you start Quicken and then use one of the menu selection techniques that I describe earlier to display the Quicken Tools menu, you'll see that many of the commands listed on the menu are followed by cryptic codes. Following the Tools⇨Account List command, for example, you can just barely make out the code Ctrl+A. And following the Category List command, you can see the code Shift+Ctrl+C. These are the shortcut-key combinations. If you simultaneously press the two or three keys listed — the Ctrl key and the A key, for example — you choose the command. (Shortcut-key combinations often use funny keys — such as Ctrl, Alt, and Shift — in combination with letters or numbers. If you're not familiar with some of these keys' locations, check your keyboard.)

Disabled commands

Oh, jeepers. I almost forgot to tell you something. Not every menu command makes sense in every situation. So Windows 7 and Windows 7 applications disable commands that would be just plain kooky to choose. To show you when a command has been disabled, the program displays disabled commands in gray letters. In comparison, commands you can choose show up in black letters. Figure A-3 does not show any disabled commands. But commonly, Windows 7 or the Windows 7 application will disable commands that make no sense.

Using command icons

Let me make one other point about choosing commands in the Windows 7 environment. Windows 7, as the screen shots in this book show, makes your computing experience as visual and graphical as possible. Accordingly, if Windows 7 or a program designed for Windows 7 can replace a boring old menu command with a clickable picture or icon, that's how it appears.

The WordPad program shown in Figures A-2 and A-3 does this visualization a bit. While past versions of WordPad use old-style menus and commands, the newest, Windows 7 version of WordPad, has created collections of buttons and boxes (grouped under the Home and View ribbons). Quicken 2012 doesn't yet make fetishlike use of command icons. If you poke around Windows 7 much or if you work with other Microsoft programs, such as Office 2010, you'll see what I mean. Oh, baby, will you see what I mean.

Working with Dialog Boxes

Windows 7 (and application programs like Quicken) uses a special type of window, called a *dialog box,* to communicate with you. In fact, after you choose a command, Windows 7 and application programs often display a dialog box to get the information they need to carry out the command.

Dialog boxes have these unique design elements: text boxes, check boxes, tabs, option buttons (also called *radio buttons*), command buttons, and list boxes.

Text boxes

Text boxes provide a space into which you can enter text. To see what a text box looks like, start WordPad (if you haven't already), type **Semper fidelis**, and then click the Home tab's Find button. WordPad, responding nicely to your deft touch, displays the Find dialog box (shown in Figure A-4). The text box is the box to the right of the words Find What.

Figure A-4:
The Find
dialog box.

If the *selection cursor* — the flashing line or outline that selects the active element of a dialog box — isn't already in the text box, you need to move it there by clicking in the text box. Then type in the text. If this "active element" mumbo-jumbo seems too technical, just press Tab a bunch of times and watch the dialog box. See that thing that moves around from box to button to box? It selects the active element.

You can move the selection cursor several ways:

- Click in the text box.
- Press Tab or Shift+Tab until the selection cursor is in the text box. (Pressing Tab moves the selection cursor to the next element; pressing Shift+Tab moves the selection cursor to the preceding element.)
- Press the Alt+*key* combination. For example, press Alt+N to move the selection cursor to the Find What text box.

If you make a typing mistake in the text box, use the Backspace key to erase incorrect characters. Other editing tricks are available, but I don't describe them here. (After all, this chapter is just a quick-and-dirty overview of Windows 7.)

You also can move the *insertion bar* — the vertical line that shows where what your type gets placed — by using the left- and right-arrow keys. The left-arrow key moves the insertion bar one character to the left without deleting any characters. The right-arrow key moves the insertion bar one character to the right without deleting any characters.

Check boxes

Check boxes work like on-off switches. A check box is "on" if the box is selected with a check mark. A check box is "off" if the box is empty. Figure A-4 shows the Match Case check box turned off and Figure A-5 shows the Insert Object dialog box with the Display As Icon check box turned off, as well. (WordPad displays the Insert Object dialog box when you click the Home tab's Insert Object button.)

Figure A-5:
A dialog box with a list box and a check box.

To turn a check box on or off with the mouse, click the check box. If the check box is on, your click turns off the check box. If the check box is off, your click turns on the check box.

You also can use the spacebar to select and deselect a check box. After you move the selection cursor to the check box, press the spacebar to alternatively select and deselect the check box. Toggle, toggle, toggle.

Tabs

Figures A-4 and A-5 don't use them, but sometimes *tabs* appear in dialog boxes. Click a tab to see it.

Option buttons

Option buttons (or *radio buttons*) are sets of buttons representing mutually exclusive choices. The Insert Object dialog box, which appears when you click WordPad's Insert Object, uses the Create New and Create From File option buttons (refer to Figure A-5).

You can select only one option button in a set. Windows 7 or the Windows 7 application identifies the selected button by putting a *bullet,* or darkened circle, inside the button. In Figure A-5, for example, the Create New option button is selected. The easiest way to select an option button is to click the option button you want.

Command buttons

Every dialog box has command buttons. *Command buttons* tell Windows 7 or an application program what you want to do after you finish with a dialog box.

Figure A-5, for example, shows command buttons labeled OK and Cancel. If you use the Insert Object dialog box to make some changes, you click OK after completing the rest of the dialog box. If you don't want to use the Insert Object dialog box after all, you click Cancel.

To choose a command button, either click it or move the selection cursor to a command button, and then press Enter.

List boxes

List boxes list a series of possible choices. And you see list boxes all over the place. For example, in Figure A-5, WordPad uses the Object Type list box to show the different types of objects you can plop into a WordPad document.

Windows 7 and Windows 7 applications use two types of list boxes: a regular list box like the one shown in Figure A-5 (which is always displayed) and a *drop-down* list box, shown in Figure A-6 (which Windows 7 won't display until you tell it to).

Drop-down list boxes look like text boxes with a down-arrow key at the right end of the box, and the Home tab of the WordPad program window supplies several drop-down list boxes.

After it's opened, a drop-down list box works the same as a regular list box. After you select an item from the list box (by using the mouse or the arrow keys), press Enter.

Figure A-6:
The
WordPad
window
with the font
drop-down
list box
"dropped."

Unfortunately, a list is sometimes too long for the list box to completely display. When this minor tragedy occurs, you can use the PgUp and PgDn keys to page through the list.

You also can use the *scroll bar* — the vertical bar with arrows at either end. Just drag the square scroll bar selector up or down. You also can click the arrows at either end of the scroll bar, or you can click the scroll bar itself. (This last trick moves the scroll bar selector toward the place where you clicked.)

Stopping Quicken in Windows 7

To stop an application program like Quicken, either click the application's Close box — the button with the X in it that appears in the top-right corner of the application window — or choose File⇨Exit.

A Yelp for Help

Help, a separate application within Windows 7, has powerful tools to help you learn about Windows 7 and application programs, such as WordPad and Quicken. To access Help, select the Help menu or click the ? icon.

The Quicken 2012 Help menu (see Figure A-7) lists as many as 12 commands: Getting Started Guide, Quicken Help, Quicken Live Community, Quicken Support, Submit Feedback On Quicken, Join The Quicken Inner Circle,

Privacy Preferences, Log Files, About Quicken, Unlock Again, Add Business Tools, and Add Rental Property Tools. Different versions of Quicken have different Help menus and supply different commands. For the most part, they all work pretty much in the same way. So in the following paragraphs, I briefly describe how each command shown in Figure A-7 works.

The Getting Started Guide command

The Getting Started Guide command displays windows that list Quicken Help topics related to getting the Quicken program set up and getting started using Quicken.

The Quicken Help command

If you choose Help⇨Quicken Help, the Help program displays a window (shown in Figure A-8) that has two tabs: Contents and Search Quicken Help.

Figure A-7:
The Quicken
Help menu.

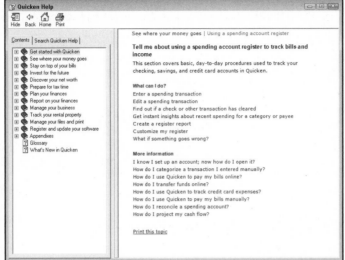

Figure A-8:
The
Contents tab
lists major
Help topics.

The Contents tab lists some of the major Help topic categories. To display the topics within a particular category, double-click the Help topic category. Help expands the list shown so that it shows the topics within each category. Double-click the topic to display the Help information on that topic.

You can click on the Search Quicken Help tab (shown in Figure A-9) to search through the Help topics. To use the Search tab, enter your search words, or keywords, into the first text box, and then select the Help topic from the last list box.

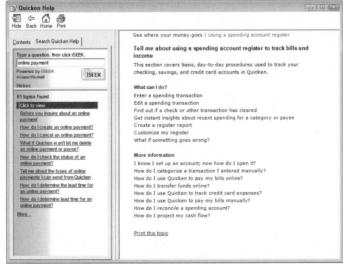

Figure A-9:
The Search
Quicken
Help tab lets
you search
for Help
topics by
keywords.

The Quicken Live Community command

The Quicken Live Community command connects you to an Intuit-sponsored Quicken support forums website (https://qlc.intuit.com) so that you can discuss Quicken problems and solutions with other Quicken users.

The Quicken Support command

The Quicken Support command opens a web page at Intuit's product support website for Quicken. There's lots of good information here.

The Submit Feedback On Quicken command

The Submit Feedback On Quicken command opens a web page that you can use to submit suggestions, share comments, or report bugs. If you have something you need to say, this is the way you do it.

The Join The Quicken Inner Circle command

The Join The Quicken Inner Circle command lets you sign up with Intuit, Inc., to participate in customer feedback programs where you can share comments with the Quicken product managers, marketers, and developers. I understand there may also be a secret handshake.

The Privacy Preferences command

This command displays information about the ways Intuit attempts to keep your financial data secure and about the business practices that Intuit employs. The command also provides a couple of check boxes you can use to tell Intuit whether you're cool with them collecting usage statistics. If you're not, you uncheck some boxes and your copy of Quicken won't share information with Intuit about how easily Quicken connects to your online banking vendor and so on.

The Log Files command

The Log Files command displays a web page with links you can click to easily access the log files that Quicken maintains in case some part of the Quicken program goes haywire, you need to call Intuit's technical support, and then need to know what in the world happened.

The About Quicken command

The About Quicken command displays a dialog box that gives the application's complete name (for example, Quicken Premier 2012). To remove this dialog box from the screen, click OK.

The Unlock Again command

The Unlock Again command (which is also called *Enter Unlock Code* in some versions of Quicken) isn't really a Help command. What this command does is walk you through the steps for accessing a more powerful version of Quicken, such as Quicken Home & Business. (Essentially, you pay an unlock fee, and Intuit supplies an unlock code.)

The Add Business Tools and Rental Property Tools commands

Figure A-7 shows a Help menu that includes an Add Rental Property Tools command. These commands on the Help menu, available in the Premier version of Quicken 2012, let the user upgrade automatically to the Business or Rental Manager versions of Quicken. Note that in other versions of Quicken, you might not see these commands on the Help menu — though you might have another command in its place that lets you upgrade to some other version of Quicken.

Quitting Windows 7

To quit Windows 7, click the Start button and then the button in the lower-right corner of the Start menu that shows an arrowhead pointing to the right. When Windows 7 displays the menu of commands related to shutting down, choose the Shut Down command.

If you exit Quicken the wrong way

If you exit Quicken by turning off (or resetting) your computer, the file that Quicken uses to organize your financial records gets, well, wasted. Quicken rebuilds the file when you restart, but this process takes a few seconds.

Don't exit Quicken (or Windows 7) by turning off your computer. Doing so may not cause serious problems (let me say, though, that Windows 7 isn't always as forgiving as Quicken), but it is bad form — akin to eating the last potato chip or leaving the gas tank empty in your spouse's car.

Appendix B

Glossary of Business, Financial, and Computer Terms

• •

940 Payroll Tax Form: The annual federal unemployment tax return. A 940EZ version is supposed to be EZ-er to fill out.

941 Payroll Tax Form: The quarterly federal payroll tax form that tells the IRS what federal employee payroll taxes (Social Security, Medicare, and Federal withholding tax) you've collected and remitted.

942 Payroll Tax Form: The quarterly payroll tax form that tells the IRS what domestic employee payroll taxes an employer has collected and remitted.

account: In Quicken, a list of the increases and decreases in an asset's value or in a liability's balance.

account balance: The value of an asset or the outstanding principal owed for a liability. For example, the value of a checking account is the cash value of the account. The balance of a mortgage liability is the principal you still owe.

account transfer: An amount you move from one account (such as a checking account) to another (such as a savings account).

account type: Different Quicken versions, or types, of accounts. There are accounts both for keeping records of the things you own (checking, saving, money market, cash, brokerage, IRA or Keogh, 401(k), dividend reinvestment plan, other investments, house, and vehicle), and for keeping records of the amounts you owe (credit card and liability).

Accounts bar: The list of accounts and hyperlinks that appears in a vertical list along the left edge of the Quicken program window. If you click an account hyperlink, Quicken displays the account in a register.

accounts payable: In a business, the amounts you owe your trade creditors — your landlord, the office supplies store, the distributor from whom you purchase your inventory, and so on. People who prefer monosyllabic speech often refer to accounts payable as *A/P*.

accounts receivable: In a business, the amounts your customers or clients owe you. People who prefer monosyllabic speech often refer to accounts receivable as *A/R*.

amortization: The itsy-bitsy principal payments you make over the course of repaying a loan. Eventually, these principal reductions pay off the loan.

ASCII: An acronym for the American Standard Code for Information Interchange. People usually use the term to refer to files — in other words, ASCII files — that contain just regular old text: letters, numbers, symbols from the keyboard, and so on.

backing up: Making a copy. If something terrible happens — fire, hard drive failure, thermonuclear exchange — you still have a copy on removable media, such as CDs, DVDs, or flash drives, safely stored away from your computer, preferably offsite.

balancing an account: The steps you take to explain the difference between what your records show as a balance and what the bank's records (statements) show as a balance. Also referred to as *reconciling an account*.

bookkeeper: Someone who keeps the "books," or financial records.

brokerage account: A Quicken account specifically set up to track a brokerage account that you use to invest in securities. Unlike a mutual fund account, a brokerage account includes a cash element. See also *account type*.

budget: A plan that says how you will make and spend money.

capital account: The money a sole proprietor leaves in or contributes to the sole proprietorship. Also, the money a partner leaves in or contributes to a partnership.

capital gain: What you earn by selling an investment for more than you paid. Capital gains (and losses) receive special treatment on your income tax return.

capital loss: What you lose by selling an investment for less than you paid.

category: In Quicken, how you summarize income and outgo. For example, you may use a category, such as Wages, to summarize your payroll check deposits. You may use categories (such as Housing, Food, and Fun) to summarize your checks.

category group: A group of categories that you monitor as a group. You create category groups so that you can monitor them. See also *supercategories*.

category list: The list of categories you can use. Quicken suggests category lists for home users and for business users as part of the setup.

certified public accountant (CPA): Someone who's taken a bunch of undergraduate and graduate accounting courses, passed a rather challenging test, and worked for at least a few years under a CPA doing things like auditing, tax planning and preparation, and consulting. Real exciting stuff, in other words.

chart: A picture that shows numbers. In Quicken, you can produce pie charts, bar charts, line charts, and so on.

check date: The date you write your payment instructions, or check. Technically, the check date is the date on which your payment instructions to the bank become valid.

check form: The preprinted form that you use to provide payment instructions to your bank: "Okay, Mammoth National, pay Joe Shmoe $32 from my account, 00704-844." Theoretically, you could use just about anything as a check form — a scrap of paper, a block of wood, and so on. In fact, rumor has it that someone once used a cowhide. It's easier for your poor bank, though, if you use check forms that follow the usual style and provide OCR (optical character recognition) characters along the form's bottom edge.

Circular E: Instructions from the IRS to employers. This publication tells stuff like how much federal income tax to withhold. Call the IRS and request a copy if you need one. Or visit the IRS website (`http://www.irs.gov`).

class: The old name for what Quicken now calls tags.

cleared: When a check or deposit has been received by the bank. An *uncleared* transaction hasn't been received by the bank.

commands: What you use to tell Quicken what it should do. For example, "Quicken, I command thee to print a report." Note that in addition to using menu commands to navigate within Quicken, you can also use the buttons, QuickTabs, and the hyperlinks that appear within the Quicken windows. Just thought I'd mention this.

controller: A business's chief accountant — and usually the brunt of most accountant jokes. Also known as a *comptroller*.

corporation: A legal business entity created by state law, owned by shareholders, and managed by directors and officers. As a business entity, a corporation has unique advantages and some disadvantages. Ask your attorney for more information. But know that for small businesses, a limited liability company (LLC) is usually better. See also *LLC*.

credit card account: A Quicken account specifically set up to track credit card charges, payments, and balances. See also *account type*.

deleted transaction: A transaction that Quicken has removed from the register.

disc/disk: The thingamajig in your computer on which Windows stores your programs (such as Quicken) and your data files (such as the Quicken file for your financial records). A hard drive inside your computer can store a great deal of information; removable storage devices (such as CDs, DVDs, and flash drives) typically store a lot less data than a hard drive.

exit: To shut down, terminate, or stop a program. By the way, you want to always do this the right way, which means by using the File menu's Exit command or by clicking the program window's Close button. Don't just turn off your computer.

file: Where data is stored. Your Quicken financial records, for example, are stored in a set of files.

filename: The name of a file in which Quicken stores data. Actually, what Quicken calls a filename is actually the name used for several files. You don't need to worry about this unless you create multiple files.

financial wizards: People who believe that they know so much about the world of finance that it is actually their God-given duty to share their expertise with you. See also *wizard*.

Find: A tremendous bargain, as in: "At $22,000, the five-bedroom house was a real find." In Quicken, also an Edit menu command that you can use to locate transactions. See also *search criteria*.

fiscal year: An accounting year. Most of the time, a fiscal year is the same as the calendar year, starting on January 1 and ending on December 31. Some businesses and foreign taxpayers use a different fiscal year, though. (Why they do that is way, way beyond the scope of this book.)

folder: What Windows uses to organize your hard drive. Some people call folders *directories*.

formatting: Hey, this word is too complicated for a book like this, isn't it? Let me just say that formatting means doing some things to a disc so that you can write files to that disc. It can also mean setting up some nice typesetting "looks" in your printed documents.

Help: A program's online documentation — which can almost always be accessed by pressing F1. Also, a verbalized cry for assistance.

hyperlink: A bit of clickable text (and sometimes a clickable picture) that you can use (by clicking, of course) to move to some other Quicken feature or some other web page. Quicken 2012, as you may have noticed, scatters hyperlinks everywhere. And I mean everywhere.

index fund: What almost everybody should use for retirement investments but almost nobody does. . . . Alas.

internal rate of return: An investment's profit expressed as a percentage of the investment. If you go to the bank and buy a certificate of deposit earning 3 percent interest, for example, 3 percent is the CD's internal rate of return. I don't want to give you the heebie-jeebies, but internal rates of return can get really complicated really fast.

liability account: A Quicken account specifically set up for tracking loans, payments, the principal and interest portions of these payments, and the outstanding balance. See also *account type.*

limited liability company: See *LLC.*

LLC: An abbreviation for *limited liability company.* LLCs are popular with tax accountants and tax attorneys because they sort of give you the best of both the corporation and partnership worlds. For small businesses and real estate investments, LLCs are nice because (compared with corporations) they offer both simplicity and less paperwork.

memo: A brief description of a transaction. Because you also give the payee and category for a transaction, it usually makes sense to use the Memo field to record some other bit of information about a check or deposit.

menu: In Quicken, a list of commands. In a restaurant, a list of things you can order from the kitchen.

menu bar: A horizontally arranged row, or bar, of menus. Yes, it does sound like a place where menus go for a drink after work.

missing check: A gap in the check numbers. For example, if your register shows a check 101 and a check 103, check 102 is a missing check.

mutual fund account: A Quicken account specifically set up to track a mutual fund investment.

online banking: An extra service you can buy from your bank. With online banking, you record a payment in your Quicken register and then transmit the payment information to your bank so that it can make the actual payment. Online banking also lets you electronically transfer money between your accounts and grab your statement electronically.

Online Bill Payment: An extra service you can buy from Intuit, the folks who bring you Quicken. With Online Bill Payment, you record a payment in your Quicken register and then transmit the payment information to Intuit's computer or your bank. Intuit or your bank then uses this information to make the actual payment.

online investing: Downloading transactions from many (and maybe even most) of the online brokerage services right into your investment accounts. If you're buying and selling securities, downloading these transactions (rather than entering them by hand) saves you time. This is a particularly valuable feature for people who want to see how quickly they can lose everything they own through day trading.

partnership: A business entity that combines two or more soon-to-be-former friends. In general, each partner is liable for the entire debts of the partnership.

password: A word you have to give Quicken before Quicken gives you access to a file. The first password, "Open sesame," was used by Ali Baba.

payee: The person to whom a check is made payable. (If you write a check to me, Steve Nelson, I'm the payee.) In Quicken, however, you can fill in a Payee field for deposits and for account transfers.

power user: Someone who's spent far more time than is healthy fooling around with a computer. Power users are good people to have as friends because they can often solve your worst technical nightmares. However, note that most people who describe themselves as power users aren't.

QIF: An abbreviation for *Quicken Interchange Format.* Basically, QIF is a set of rules that prescribes how an ASCII file must look if you want Quicken to read it. If you're a clever sort, you can import category lists and even transactions from ASCII files that follow the QIF rules.

Quicken: The name of the checkbook-on-a-computer program that this book is about. You didn't really need to look this up, did you?

Quicken.com: The Intuit Corporation website especially for Quicken users. Visit this website, my friend. It's really good.

Quicken Premier: A supercharged version of Quicken that includes a bunch of extra whistles and bells, including a really neat program for locating great mutual funds (called, cleverly enough, Mutual Fund Finder) and a Home Inventory System program. This book is about Quicken Premier, but Quicken Basic, Quicken Deluxe, Quicken Home & Business, and Quicken Rental Property Manager users can apply this book to their products. (All the products are similar in their core functionality.)

Quicken Quotes: An online service that you can use to grab up-to-date price information on stocks and bonds. This book doesn't talk much about Quicken Quotes.

QuickFill: A clever little feature. If Quicken can guess what you'll type next in a field, it types, or *QuickFills,* the field for you. QuickFill types in transactions, payee names, and category names.

register: Another name for the transaction list, a register shows the increases and decreases in an account balance.

report: An on-screen or printed summary of financial information from one or more registers.

restore: Replace the current version of a file with the backup version. You may need to do this after a fire, hard drive failure, or thermonuclear exchange. See also *backing up*.

savings goal accounts: A Quicken pseudo-account. In effect, a savings goal account is a compartment in a banking account where you can "hide" or set aside money that you're saving for a special purpose. A new car. A boat. A trip to Montana. Whatever.

scroll bars: The vertical bars along the window's right edge and the horizontal bars along the window's bottom edge. Use them to scroll or page through your view of something that's too big to fit on one page.

search criteria: A description of the transaction that you want to locate. See also *Find*.

sole proprietorship: A business that's owned by just one person and that doesn't have a separate legal identity. In general, businesses are sole proprietorships, partnerships, corporations, or limited liability companies.

split transactions: A transaction assigned to more than one category or transferred to more than one account. A split-check transaction, for example, might show a $50 check to the convenience store paying for both groceries and automobile expenses. (Now that's what I call one-stop shopping!)

stockholder equity: The money that shareholders have contributed to a corporation or allowed to be retained in the corporation. You can't track stockholders' equity with Quicken.

subcategory: A category within a category. For example, the suggested Quicken home categories list breaks down utilities spending into Cable TV, Gas and Electric, Telephone, and Water subcategories.

supercategory: A group of categories that you monitor as a group. You create supercategories so that you can monitor them. See also *category group*.

tabs: The clickable labels that look like file folder tabs and appear near the top of the Quicken program window underneath the menu bar and icon bar.

tag: Another way (formerly known as a class) to summarize Quicken data when categories just aren't enough. This book doesn't really talk about tags much. Sorry.

tax deduction: For an individual, an amount that can be deducted from total income (such as alimony or IRA contributions) or used as an itemized deduction and deducted from adjusted gross income (such as home mortgage interest or charitable contributions). For a business, any amount that represents an ordinary and necessary business expense. Be sure to consult with your tax advisor if you have any questions about what is or isn't a valid tax deduction.

tax-deferred account: Some accounts aren't taxable — IRAs, for one example, and 401(k) plans for another. To deal with this real-life complexity, Quicken lets you tag any account as being tax-deferred. As a practical matter, however, it'll probably be only investment accounts and the occasional bank account that are tax-deferred.

technogeek: Someone who believes that fooling around with a computer is more fun than anything else in the world.

transaction list: The list of increases and decreases in an account balance. Quicken displays a transaction list in a window that looks remarkably similar to a crummy old paper register — your checkbook. To print a copy of the register that you see on your screen, press Ctrl+P and then press the Enter key.

transposition: Flip-flopped numbers — for example, 23.45 entered as 24.35 (the 3 and 4 are flip-flopped as 4 and 3). These common little mistakes have caused many bookkeepers and accountants to go insane.

Vista: The version of the Microsoft Windows operating system that preceded Windows 7. See also *Windows*.

W-2: The annual wages statement that employers use to tell employees what they made and to tell the IRS what employees made.

W-3: A summary form of W-2s. When employers send a stack of W-2s to the IRS, they also fill out a W-3 form that summarizes all the individual W-2s. W-2s and W-3s aren't much fun, but they're not hard to fill out.

Windows: The Microsoft Windows operating system. Quicken 2012 for Windows relies on Windows to do a bunch of system stuff, such as print. Refer to Appendix A for more information.

Windows 7: The latest edition of Windows; available since mid-2010.

wizard: A little program that walks you through the steps to completing some tasks that some programmer thinks you're too dense to figure out on your own. Although a wizard sounds bad, it actually isn't. Quicken supplies a bunch of cool wizards, including wizards for setting up accounts and setting up how you want to record a paycheck, planning for retirement, planning for your kid's college expenses, reducing your debts, and so on.

Index

Notes

Notes